WHEN THE GAME WAS SIMPLE
AND THE SONG WAS SWEET

WHEN THE GAME WAS SIMPLE
AND THE SONG WAS SWEET

A Newspaperman's
Story Remembered

By Bob Hilliard

Editing and additional writing by
John Tucker

Page design and layout by
Norm Welsh

Peter E. Randall Publisher
Portsmouth, New Hampshire
2002

Printed in the United States of America

ISBN 0-931807-10-8

Most of the stories in this book have been published previously, some in slightly altered form, in the pages of *The Union-Leader* and the *New Hampshire Sunday News* and are reprinted with permission.

Many of the photos in this book are courtesy of The Union Leader Corp. of Manchester, New Hampshire, and are credited to several of its long-time photographers.

Frontispiece: The author works the phones during an earlier time at *The Union Leader.*

Peter E. Randall Publisher
Box 4726. Portsmouth, NH 03802

Additional copies available from the Author at
331 Oak Street, Manchester, NH 03104

Foreword

Was it sitting in the cockpit of Charles Lindbergh's plane, *The Spirit of St. Louis*, that inspired 10-year-old Bob Hilliard to pursue a career as a journalist, writing about people?

Was it this Concord, New Hampshire native son's first assignment covering sports for his high school newspaper that deepened his love of sports—particularly baseball? We can picture the 12-year-old watching Babe Ruth at Fenway Park in the late 1920s.

Was it Guy Lombardo—on a day in December, 1934—inviting Bob to join him and his Royal Canadians in a football game at a field not far from the City Auditorium in Concord, where that evening Guy's band would play "the sweetest music this side of heaven." Guy and his talented brother, Carmen—a composer-arranger-musician—would remain life-long friends of the Hilliards.

We know, for a fact, that it was the love of his life—Barbara Marshall Hilliard—who turned the music-lover-sports writer's eye and ear to the Metropolitan Opera and the Broadway stage.

It wasn't difficult for Bob to sit at his typewriter at his Manchester, New Hampshire, home and begin what has become this book of memoirs.

I came into Bob Hilliard's life as a reporter-writer for the *Manchester Union Leader* in the mid-1950s. When I write my memoirs, they will include thoughts of the evening when I was introduced to this gentle, sports-loving man, a journalist whose curiosity, attitude and love of life were to be found in the words of his newspaper columns... moments of history which have become a legacy of the past century and that will be the subjects for researchers in the new millennium.

Bob, we thank you and Barbara for bringing much happiness into our lives. And I know that her memory has inspired you to the full measure of the sweetest.

Lu Dumont

Remembering Barbara

BARBARA MARSHALL HILLIARD
1919-1976
Salisbury, England

She was sold on hockey, and for that matter, so was I.

When we were at the Bruins camp at Fitchburg, Mass. that day, she had a long talk with the coach, Don Cherry, and she advanced her views. Don told her, "Barbara, you think the way I do...hit 'em hard." They laughed.

Barbara's views were always quite solid, whether in hockey or otherwise. Earlier on, while Bobby Jr. and I were watching TV football, Barbara asked, "How about listening to the Met Opera on TV for a change?"

It was an order, of course, and soon we were listening to the glorious voice of the young Mario Del Monaco singing Radames in Verdi's spellbinding "Aida." It was simply glorious, with Zinka Milanov singing the title role. We were captured that day, thanks to Barbara, and that was to become, for me, the start of an exciting career.

Barbara started things rolling, as in this case—and "Aida" became more compelling to me than most sports. All because of Barbara.

That was a long time ago, sadly, and we miss our beautiful girl so very much. Oh, but had she lived longer and enjoyed all those operas and Broadway plays with me as I reviewed them for *The Union Leader* and *New Hampshire Sunday News.* To my anguish, it was just not to be.

Author's Note

Inasmuch as I have endeavored to present these various interviews from years past, dating to the late Twenties on, some of the individuals may be portrayed as still living, though they may have passed on. To me, they've never died. They live on as before, as fresh and alive as yesteryear.

And so, some are still portrayed as when I first interviewed them. One of them, indeed, songwriter Irving Caesar, lived to 105, still brimming over with fantastic stories, and bars from great song hits, many of his own. He wrote the words to the immortal "Tea For Two," among hundreds of others. I hummed this number one day on the tour bus in China, and the female guide heard it and told me: "I love that song, Meester Hilliard, could you please teach it to me." I did just that after lunch, and she went away humming it. She later learned it by heart, and we heard it every day on the visit to the tea gardens and elsewhere.

Life is a song, so they say, and it brought the whole gang together. It brought us together, and that is why I must keep them all as they were then.

Acknowledgments

This book would not have been possible without the friendship and assistance of John Tucker, day sports editor, and Norm Welsh, a graphics editor, both of the *Union-Leader,* who helped to gather the articles and photographs and designed the book. And special thanks to Terrie Tucker who, working from old clippings, retyped all the articles into computer format. And to my friend Dennis Paiste of *The Union-Leader,* for his support and encouragement.

Contents

A simpler time

The author, center, with boyhood friend
Frank Morono, left, and Bob's brother John
getting ready for some sandlot baseball
around 1828 or 1929.

Today's big league ballplayers would probably balk at the idea of playing a game with those ridiculously small, pocketless and webless gloves from that bygone era when America's favorite pastime was still, for the most part, unadulterated. Black Sox scandal notwithstanding, yes, the game was still pure back in the Twenties, at least in the sense that it hadn't yet been compromised by those ever so familiar primadonna ballplayers of today and by the perverse pay they command to play a game so many of us loved to play as kids.

Those Roaring Twenties were a simpler time, for sure, so a simple glove made sense. A pocket? Who needs a pocket? The ball's just going from one hand to the other anyway. Those simple gloves just lessened the time of the exchange.

I had one of those gloves when I was a lanky 12-year-old growing up in Concord, N.H. And like many kids of my time, I dreamed of the day when I'd get a chance to play in the bigs. As I made my way to the mound, I'd hear the thousands cheering as Bob Hilliard was announced as the starting pitcher for the St. Louis Cardinals.

I had to be a Cardinal; that much I knew for sure. I worshipped the great Lefty O'Doul, Tommy Thevenow, Taylor Douthit, Sunny Jim Bottomley and Charlie Gelbert because they were Cardinals and because, even back in the late Twenties, they wore the most beautiful uniform of them all: bright red birds on a golden bat.

These are the luckiest of men, I thought. They get to wear the Cardinal uniform, and they travel in easy chair Pullman cars around America to its great Eastern and Midwest cities, and all for free. They stay at America's grand hotels, eat their meals in the finest restaurants, ordering steaks everyday...

It all sounded so sweet; sounds even sweeter today...fly within hours to any destination in the continental U.S., enjoy the umpteen luxuries of the day, spare no expense, have a few mansions at your locations of choice and maybe even a private jet, thank you very much, and retire to wherever at whatever age you wish and enjoy your vacation for the rest of your life.

When I was entertaining those Big League dreams in the mid to late Twenties, I never imagined what it would be like to be respected and admired, let alone befriended, by the very sports figures I worshipped...

Like I said, it was a bygone era...There's no love lost between the media and many professional athletes of today. Wonder why?

Maybe, just maybe, it has something to do with the complex nature of today's baseball gloves, the massive webbing and deep, deep pockets...and the distorted view of some simple-minded millionaires.

But that's today. Remember. We're talking about when I was a youngster. That was the Twenties. Those Roaring Twenties. Hell, in 1927, I was just 10. I was just starting to dream about playing Big League baseball, not writing about it. That seed wouldn't be planted for at least another couple of years.

When I was about 13, I got to see a professional hockey game for the first time, a Stanley Cup showdown between the Boston Bruins and Montreal Canadiens at the then brand spanking new Boston Garden, the sports event showplace of New England. The Garden was torn down just a few years ago and replaced by a beautiful new sports arena that bears the name of a huge banking conglomerate. Boston Garden was not a corporate sponsor. But, as I said before, that was a simpler time, a bygone era.

I felt like the biggest teenager in the Garden that night. I was there to watch and enjoy the game, for sure, but I was on a special mission as well.

Ruel Newton Colby, a Dartmouth scholar who was sports editor of the *Concord* (N.H.) *Monitor* and who was a friend of my brother, had asked me to write a student's account of what turned out to be a classic Bruins-Canadiens hockey clash, decided in sudden-death overtime when the Bruins scored the winning goal.

It was an incredible game beyond imagination, with a combination of intricate skating and smashing bodychecks and many dazzling forays on the two goalies. When the Bruins triumphed in overtime, 14,000 Boston fans went berserk, tossing everything they could onto the ice, except for the seats, which were bolted down.

I can't remember who scored the winning goal for the Bruins, although it may have been off the stick of Ralph "Cooney" Weiland, who later became a very successful coach at Harvard University. Cooney was a fast and brilliant stickhandler, and it seems he was the one who provided the red light that sent the Garden into Pandemonium that night.

For me, the thrill was extraordinary. I was still just a boy, and here I was covering a major sports event for my hometown newspaper. I wish I'd saved that article and didn't have to rely on my 85-year-old memory to recall who scored the winning goal. But trust that somewhere in the archives of the Concord Monitor is an article by a young Bob Hilliard and trust that the article says that Cooney scored that winning goal. Trust that, because I grew up in a simpler time and wore a simpler glove. And I trusted that glove.

Baseball to me was a part of the glory of the soul, a driving force and a reason for wanting to be a part of this incredible artistry that plays itself out, indeed, on these fields where dreams are realized. And yet never, in my wildest of dreams, could I have foreseen the grandest of operas that was to become my life.

Ruel Colby opened the door, and I stepped in without hesitation, never looking back and never once doubting that I'd chosen the right path, one that would cross those of such famous artists as Charles Lindberg, Ty Cobb, Ted Williams, Robert "Red" Rolfe, Bobby Orr, Luciano Pavarotti, Placido Domingo, Mario Del Monaco and Irving Berlin, just to name a few.

And why do I call them all artists? The answer takes me back to an interview I once had while in Detroit for a Bruins-Red Wings game. Johnny Peirson of the TV team coupled with veteran Fred Cusick asked if I'd like to be interviewed between periods, and I was more than happy to oblige.

During the interview, I remember Peirson asking, "Bob, isn't it difficult to cover the Bruins and the Red Sox and the Celtics, and still write about all those New York plays and the Metroplitan Opera?"

My answer went something like this: "It isn't difficult at all when you consider Shakespeare's depiction of the world as a stage, and realize that the Bruins, Red Sox and Celtics are simply actors upon it, as with Rex

Harrison, Richard Burton and so many others, and Luciano Pavarotti, Placido Domingo, Renata Tebaldi and Zinka Milanov at the Met. And the Met boos as well in its own gracious way, when it sits on its hands if the artist isn't too enthralling. So you see, there is an affinity of the two worlds after all."

What I forgot to add was that many athletes drift to the opera world later, such as Bob Feller and the late Hank Greenberg, just as many of the male opera stars find a kind of solace in sports, which they, too, enjoy with a passion. Pavarotti, for instance, likes tennis, which brings to mind a funny story involving Luciano and *Boston Globe* sportswriter Bud Collins, both of whom are friends of mine.

Bud was an exceptional sportswriter whose area of expertise was tennis and for years he was a fixture at the most prestigious tennis tournament in the world, Wimbledon. Back in the Sixties, Bud and I were among the honored guests at the National Sportswriters and Sportscasters event in Salisbury, N.C. At dinner one night after Bud and I had been out on the golf course, my wife, Barbara, asked Bud, "Why don't you learn opera as Bob did?"

Bud, looking a bit astonished, answered, "Barbara, are you kidding? That's the last thing in the world I'd want to learn."

Several years later, during a visit to Boston, the great opera tenor himself, Luciano, expressed a wish to learn some tennis. His host suggested Bud Collins as an instructor, saying that what Bud knew about tennis exceeded everything that could be found in any textbook on the subject.

So, the two got together, and guess who taught who. Luciano picked up the tennis game, for sure, and Bud picked up the Grand Opera, just as Barbara had suggested a few years earlier.

I guess maybe I, perhaps even more so than Bud, was destined to fall in love with the opera and with the stage. And it was an introduction to Guy Lombardo back on Dec. 3, 1934 that probably should have provided an early sign of what fate lie ahead.

It was an unseasonably warm day for December, as a sound truck made its way around Concord, playing Lombaro's recordings while announcing that Lombardo and his world famous "Royal Canadians" would be appearing that night at the City Auditorium. I could hardly believe that Guy Lombardo and his orchestra would be playing a concert in my hometown.

Early that afternoon, I ventured downtown to see if I could get a personal story from the touring Lombardos. They were in the midst of an extended tour for Esso, and they were playing all the state capitals along the eastern seaboard, from Maine to Florida. And what made these concerts even more special was that they were free of charge, which appealed tremendously to many thousands of fans in this time of the Great Depression. It was a simpler time, and it was just what the people needed to take their minds off the drab times...to be treated to the magnificent music that the whole world loved.

I arrived at the Eagle Hotel, which is still standing directly across from the State House, and I met Guy and his brothers, Carmen, Lebert and Victor. Guy was preparing to meet the press, and he looked quite dapper.

Guy was affable as we met, and he began telling a few stories about life aboard their sumptuous Esso Cruiser and the problems they encountered, such as preparing for an afternoon football game before the evening concert.

"I sent some of the boys out to pick up a football for a game this afternoon," said Guy. "They came back with seven footballs. I'm glad I didn't send them out for grand pianos."

I should have realized it then, when I was playing a pickup game of touch football on a nearby field in Concord, N.H. with one of the most famous musicians of his time. I should have seen that inseparable connection and how one is drawn to the other...music and sports. Of course, it was a simpler time.

Guy liked his music unhurried and styled especially for dancers young and old, and romantic, music that tells a story — a ballad like "Annie Doesn't Live Here Anymore" or "You're Gonna Lose Your Gal" or a love song like "Stars Fell on Alabama."

As I listened to the glorious music that night, "Thirty Days Has September," "Love Is Just Around the Corner," a swingy "Footloose and

Fancy Free," "I Saw Stars," the haunting "Lost in a Fog" and so many more, I wondered how all of this could be possible from a group of kids picked for the task because they were playmates back home in London, Ontario, not far from Toronto and Detroit. They were playing such a disciplined game, with such class and style, and it seemed amazing that they could accomplish such musical feats while still just in their 20s.

I figured it had to be the leadership, and Guy (Gaetano) was a superb leader. He led his little group of stalwarts out of a small community in Ontario right smack into the bright lights of Broadway where they remained forever after.

O.O. McIntyre, the celebrated columnist of several decades ago, called Lombardo one of the five greatest band leaders of all time.

Guy employed a core of about 13 musicians. He himself played the violin, but seldom with the orchestra. Guy knew the tone he wanted and he stuck to it...four saxes, a bass, two pianos (because there were two fellows in the neighborhood who played that instrument), a guitar, a brass section and a drum. His vocalists, for the most part, were selected from the orchestra. However, Kenny Gardner, who joined the band about the time of the outbreak of World War II, was principally a vocalist in his many years with the Royal Canadians.

Guy was atop the heap of America's dance music from the early days in Cleveland and Chicago to 1929 when New York City beckoned. He bowed at The Roosevelt, where he remained for more than 30 years. The night after he opened at The Roosevelt, the stock market crashed, but Guy weathered the storm, weighing in with a new song of the times, "Brother, Can You Spare a Dime?"

On his first night at The Roosevelt, Guy once told me, celebrities abounded, including the famous songwriter, Irving Berlin. "I was worried," Guy said, "that it would be like previous openings for us in Cleveland and Chicago, where it took the installation of a radio wire to bring the crowds out."

To some, it might seem an awkward bond, sportswriter and musician. Sportswriters, after all, aren't generally the type who look forward to the halftime show; that's usually when they skip out for a cigarette or to make a call to their editors. There's supposed to be an understood cultural barrier between the two.

But Ruel Colby, the scholar/sports editor who was once recruited by the New York Times to write his "Old Leather Stocking" column for the Big Apple audience, broke that barrier for me at an early age. I thank God he turned down that job at the Times.

After giving me an opportunity for which I've been forever grateful and while taking me under his wing, the Old Scout gave me a piece of advice which opened a whole new world of journalistic opportunities for me, and fate, as you will see, guided the rest.

Ruel suggested I take a long hard look at the world around me, and that I not lose sight of the cultural side of life. And so, in the period of five or six years, I tackled stories ranging from musicals in Boston's Back Bay, a concert by world renowned violinist Ruth Posselt (at Governor Fuller's mansion on Beacon Street), to plays and interviews of stars of the day, including movie star Elissa Landi.

In the meantime, I was interviewing such heavyweight celebrities as boxer Max Baer as he waited on customers at Jack Sharkey's Bar in Boston. What a day of story gathering that was!

The year was about 1935. I remember venturing into Buckley's Gym, where Baer, the world champion, was the feature attraction, and Sharkey, the former champ, was the host.

Baer was serving drinks at the bar, when somebody mentioned Max Schmeling, hinting that the German slugger might pose an interesting challenge for the heavyweight champ. The ebullient Baer snarled, "Schmeling, who's he? He can't lick his own lips!" It brought the house down.

Baer went through his routine upstairs in the gym, pulverizing the sandbag with punches so powerful, the bag bounced around like it was stuffed with feathers. The champ was notorious for his brutal punching power and is said to have killed two men in the ring. Ernie Schaff of Boston, himself a heavy hitter and once a challenger to the throne, died of injuries several claimed were suffered in a bout with Baer. The brother of Chicago Cubs star Dolph Camilli also died after suffering a terrible beating delivered by the hands of Baer.

After watching Baer pummel that sandbag like a stuffed animal with his thundering blows and then trying to lift the bag myself, there was no doubt in my mind that Baer was a harder puncher than even Jack Dempsey.

Baer continued his workout that day at Buckley's Gym, skip-rope-jumping and trading wisecracks with several fans before disappearing into a dressing room behind a locked door, with a peephole. I tried the door and couldn't get in, so I began banging on it. Suddenly, a fat nose appeared in the peephole.

"Whadda ya want, kid?" a gruff voice asked.

"I want in, I'm a writer," I asserted.

I could hear the guy say to somebody in the room, "A kid wants in, says he's a writer...Whadda I do?"

Somebody I assumed was another reporter, sounding a bit agitated, said, "Well, let him in!"

Suddenly, the door was flung open, and I found myself facing a room full of husky men. It was a bit intimidating for a young fellow of my stature, but I wasn't about to clue them in on it.

Sharkey was sitting on a rubbing table to my left, while Baer was being worked on by a trainer on another. Next to Baer stood his towering brother, Buddy.

I asked a few questions of Baer, but it was clear he had a mind to ignore me. So I decided to deliver a jab of my own.

"Max, when are you going to give Sharkey a shot at the title?" That got Baer's attention, as he quickly sat up, looked me directly in the eye and asked, "Do you know what Sharkey told me when I asked him for a shot at the title when he was champ? ... He suggested that I go out and get a reputation first, then he would think it over."

Sharkey grimaced and Baer laughed. "So," Baer said, "I'm giving Jack right now the same treatment he accorded me a year or so ago." By now, Sharkey was squirming, clearly agitated and possibly somewhat embarrassed by the champ's jabs. And more than 50 years later, while sitting in his Epping, N.H. home, Sharkey still remembered the encounter, admitting to me that he was "a little annoyed" by the low blows Baer delivered in the dressing room above Sharkey's Boston bar that day.

It was the kind of chance encounter, nonetheless, that made for good copy, especially from a newspaperman's perspective.

Looking back to one such story from my boyhood years, I realized later that I was somehow just destined to happen upon stories involving famous people.

On a dreary, rainy day in July of 1927, I and some of my baseball buddies were having a mid-afternoon bunting practice on my back lawn in Concord, N.H. when we heard the roar of a low-flying airplane.

In those days, any airplane was an object of curiosity, and this one quickly grabbed our attention. It was approaching from the east and heading due west. When we saw its number, NX-211, on the underside of the wings, though we could hardly believe it, we knew almost immediately this was some special aircraft. This was the number of Charles A. Lindbergh's "Spirit of St. Louis," the plane which Lindbergh piloted across the Atlantic, from New York to Paris, just a couple of months before. In May of 1927, Lindbergh became the first aviator to fly non-stop across the Atlantic, a feat believed impossible at the time.

Lindbergh completed the 3,500-mile journey in the single-engine monoplane, a heroic and daring attempt that caused some skeptics to dub Lindy "The Flying Fool." As it turned out, it was Lindbergh's skeptics who were left looking like fools, as he single handedly opened a bold new world of aviation.

As Lindbergh's plane continued to roar overhead, he appeared to be looking for a place to land, so we waved him in the direction of the Concord Airport. He acknowledged our help by flapping his wings to say thank you.

He was flying so low over my home, you could see him quite clearly at the controls. Lindbergh's plane had been reported lost in the inclement weather on a flight from Boston, Mass. to Portland, Maine, and it was feared he had crashed at Old Orchard Beach, Maine. The story had already made headlines in all the major newspapers across Europe and America, as an entire nation worried about its missing hero.

But, like most 10-year-olds, my buddies and I were more worried about whether we could get enough players together for a pickup game of baseball than we were about the day's major news events. So we were unaware of Lindbergh's plight until a few hours later.

We wanted to get over to the airport to make sure Lindy had landed safely, but my sister, Madeline, had taken the family car to go shopping, so we were without transportation for more than an hour. When we got there, police officer Perley Morse was standing duty beside the "Spirit of St. Louis." Morse, in my mind, was the nicest cop on earth, at least on that day. He helped to lift me into the very seat in which Lindbergh made his famous journey across the Atlantic.

It was the thrill of a lifetime, and one I would never forget.

Later, at a big parade New Hampshire's capital city extended in Lindbergh's honor, he waved to my 3-year-old sister, Betty, when she shouted, "Hi, Lindy!" His mere presence had captivated the entire city, and the throng waved wildly while cheering on the famous aviator as he made his way up Main Street. I can't recall a more glorious day for the people of Concord. But then again, that was a simpler time, a bygone era.

Considering Lindbergh's significance to the evolution of aviation and his memorable chance visit that gave all of Concord a reason to celebrate during those hard times, it was a sad twist of fate nearly 60 years later, when the entire capital city had reason to mourn, having lost one of its own heroes, teacher/astronaut Christa McAuliffe.

Unlike the widespread poverty of the late Twenties, the '80s were a time of prosperity, an era of economic expansion and space exploration, when shuttle trips among the stars were much less of an event of their time than was Lindbergh's flight to Paris. Much less of an event, that is, until that fateful flight of the space shuttle Challenger on Jan. 28, 1986.

Because McAuliffe was a schoolteacher and this was the first time a civilian had been chosen to take a shuttle flight, the Challenger expedition was getting far more than the usual amount of publicity, but it was still a far cry from the worldwide acclaim that Lindbergh's landing in Paris created on May 21, 1927.

But, as the nation watched on televisions in homes, workplaces and in schools, just 73 seconds after liftoff, the Challenger exploded in a cloud of smoke, killing all seven aboard, including Concord's beloved schoolteacher, whose dreams are preserved in the Christa McAuliffe Planetarium in the state's capital.

A few years after the Lindy landing in Concord, in the early '30s, I and some other not so heavy sleepers in the area were afforded another unique sighting in the skies.

I was sound asleep about 6 a.m., when I was awakened by what I at first thought was a fleet of tar trucks. I jumped out of bed and looked out the window but saw no sign of any trucks. I was about to turn back in when I just happened to glance up at the sky, and what to my wondering eyes did appear...with the summer morning sun glistening on its silvery side, the U.S. Navy dirigible, "City of Los Angeles," approaching the neighborhood at about 800 feet.

At approximately 600 feet in length, this blimp was monstrous, yet purring smoothly on all of its engines. What a sight! I've never forgotten it, nor how my uncontrolled excitement must have awakened the entire neighborhood to watch this aerial spectacle unfold before our eyes.

In later years, Paul Lacaillade, a fellow newsman at *The Union Leader*, New Hampshire's largest daily, told me that he, too, had seen the "City of Los Angeles" that day in the early '30s when it flew over his home in Laconia, in the state's Lakes Region.

The *City of Los Angeles* was perhaps the most successful of all the dirigibles with which the U.S. Navy had experimented. It was built in Germany and was a real workhorse, perhaps even the most beautiful.

Another incident in my youth that may have helped to shape the way I approached my news coverage in later years was a surprise meeting with the young daughter of Tom Mix, the movie star cowboy.

Some buddies and I were playing a baseball game in Teddy Brooks' backyard about 9 or 10 in the morning, when this little girl walked across the banker neighbor's back lawn, came over and introduced herself.

"I'm Thomasina Mix, and my father is the cowboy star of the movies," she said. Needless to say, we were all a bit stunned. Tom Mix's daughter? What would she be doing in Concord and why in the world would she interrupt a bunch of boys who were playing baseball?

"What are you playing?" she asked. We told her we had a little game of baseball under way and asked if she'd like to join us. She smiled and said quite confidently, "Of course."

After playing for about an hour at the Leavitt home, near Auburn Street, Thomasina asked if we'd like to meet her father. Having just seen him in a movie at the Star Theatre, we told her we'd love to meet her famous dad. In fact, we were thrilled with the idea.

We asked if he'd be wearing his famous white cowboy hat and whether he had Tony, his famous horse, along with him. As to the white Stetson hat, she said yes, but the horse was stalled someplace else in the city and we wouldn't be able to see it. Too bad, cause we had plenty of apples to keep him happy, for sure.

We sneaked up to a window of the banker's house and saw the famous cowboy star, wearing his white Stetson and talking with the banker, Harry L. Alexander. We were ecstatic, having a chance to see in person the very movie star we had seen on the screen so many Saturday afternoons.

Mix looked around and caught us gawking. At first, he laughed, and then he said he'd be right out. All of us, including Thomasina, jumped for joy.

In a few breathtaking moments, Mix joined us and went around shaking all of our hands. He asked if we enjoyed the ballgame and asked how his daughter had done. We said she'd done very well, that she hit the ball real hard. I remember us telling him as well that seeing him in person was the greatest thing that had ever happened to us. He smiled that nice smile, patted a few of us on the head and said goodbye, waving as he and Thomasina went inside the banker's home.

It was a memorable meeting for all of us, but for me in particular, as this was the first of hundreds of meetings and interviews with celebrities over the many years to come.

I've thought a lot over the years about that impromptu meeting with Tom Mix and his little Thomasina that summer day in Concord, wondering how it might have steered my own career. If nothing else, it seemed to provide more reinforcement for what appeared by now to be my calling, that fate had to have something to do with these chance encounters with celebrities.

To my knowledge, Mix's visit to Concord was never reported in the local newspaper, so I promised someday to get the story out. Now it's done.

I can't help think about the unlikelihood of such a story happening today in Concord or in any other city across the United States for that matter. Can you imagine any famous actor or actress today, letting his or her young daughter or son out to play with a bunch of kids in a strange neighborhood? It's not going to happen.

But then again, the Thirties, much like the Twenties, were a simpler time, a bygone era.

On a sad footnote to the Tom Mix story, Teddy Brooks, my playmate and son of Lt. Gen. Edward Brooks, while on duty in the European Theatre of Operations during World War II, was killed in Belgium in the closing days of the war. Brooks was a pilot, and a damned good one. He wasn't shot down, but as I understand it, his plane developed engine trouble and crashed.

A year or so after Teddy's death, I had the task of interviewing his famous father, who was attached to Gen. Patch's Seventh Army and who was a close friend of Gen. Patton. Brooks and Patton loved a robust lifestyle, Patton as "Old Blood and Guts," leading his troops on a foray, and Brooks as a football coach at Norwich, Vermont, leading his gridders on the field of battle.

Gen. Brooks and I spent quite a while talking about his son's happy childhood and of our meeting that day with Tom Mix's daughter. On the same day, I was interviewing Brooks for The *Manchester Union Leader*, Joe Gendron of the *Concord Monitor*, on leave with the Army, interviewed Brooks as well.

Gendron wrote a humorous story that, in part, included a paragraph in which Joe, a private first class, recalled delivering an order to the general while he was mowing his lawn. "General," Joe recalled saying, "I think you missed a few blades of grass here...would you mind?"

Gen. Brooks, having never taken an order from a private, stopped cutting his grass for a moment and, while controlling his laughter, said, "It's been many years, and I wish you might have been a sargeant, at least."

The general had a glorious military career, stretching from Fort Riley, Kansas to the Philippines and to the battlefields of Europe before wrapping up at Fort Meade, Maryland, where he was in command of the troops. His uniform bore the medals of many honors.

I can remember Ted and I ransacking through the general's memorabilia from World War I, parading about and saluting as we tried on a shiny black German dress helmet that must have belonged to a command officer.

Those days in the mid-Twenties were happy times, but it wasn't long before a new war had engulfed the states, the war on the homeland between gangsters and the government, waged by the likes of mob kingpin Al Capone and FBI director J. Edgar Hoover.

Then came the Depression and a period of widespread poverty like never seen before; it was a brutal time for Americans, who had little time to rejoice after just winning the first World War.

Those were my formative years, those Roaring Twenties. It was a far simpler time, which was a darn good thing, at least for me.

When I waded into the field of journalism, I was full of hope and yet minus a college diploma, which I had hoped to attain at Boston University's celebrated School of Journalism. I had BU's catalogue and books, and my thoughtful Aunt Katie had presented me with a Remington typewriter for college life at Boston. I revered writing, and I followed its path, wherever it led.

Soon, the stories were flowing off the Remington, and with Ruel Colby as my tutor, I began my life as a writer and newspaperman. As time went on, and with a Dartmouth-educated mentor to guide me, I ventured into a career that was to become my lifeblood for more than 50 years.

It's been so much fun and so wonderfully rewarding as the stories that follow will attest: meeting Rex Harrison soon after his triumph in "My Fair Lady," romping backstage with Richard Burton, listening to the fabulous voices of Mario Del Monaco of the Metropolitan Opera, Luciano Pavarotti, Placido Domingo, and of Renata Tebaldi and Eileen Farrell. Add to that a veritable tidal wave of Broadway plays on tryout in Boston, hundreds of operas, Stanley Cup action, baseball games and a World Series that featured the famous home run by New Hampshire's own, Hall-of-Famer Carlton Fisk.

I never imagined in my early years that the celebrity traffic along my journalistic path would get so congested, so much so that, at times, I longed for Main Street in Concord for surcease. The excitement never lagged, and at times, it sustained me when the workload grew heavy, and the body asked for a little respite.

I remember attending a party for Liz Taylor and Richard Burton after a performance of "Private Lives" at the Shubert Theatre, where Bea Dowd held sway backstage as America's First Lady of The Stars. Besides Taylor and Burton, two of the most profound artists to ever set foot on Broadway or on the streets of Hollywood, the party upstairs at Pier Four featured several of the Kennedys, the cast of the play, Massachusetts Senate President Billy Bulger and a 7-foot-tall ice statue of an Indian chief.

I attended that fabulous party at the invitation of Dowd. When I pried myself away about 3:30 in the morning, the party was still in progress. My greatest disappointment was missing a chance to swirl around the dance floor with the beautifully captivating Miss Taylor.

When I arrived back in Manchester, N.H., it was 4:30 a.m., and I had to be at work in the newsroom by 8. That gave me an hour to write my review of "Private Lives" and about an hour to catch a little shuteye, all of which preceded a day of sports reporting.

It was an exhausting 24 hours, but I wouldn't have missed the party, cause you never know when you might miss a better show than the one you saw on stage.

Usually the invitations are given by a whisper in the ear, "The party is at the club in the alleyway at 11:30. See you there." I've been to hundreds of them over the years, and they've all been entertaining. I'll mention one, in particular, later that attorney/writer Bob Woolf attended, with four casts and a band blazing away. Bob came away with top honors on the dance floor.

Woolf was one of the nicest most thoughtful people I've ever known. He once offered to accommodate me with his living quarters in The Prudential building, his chauffeur and his elegant home in the suburbs when my dear wife, Barbara, lie dying at Phillips House, Mass General Hospital.

The Lindbergh incident, "The City of Los Angeles," the chance meeting with Tom Mix and that encounter with the intimidating Max Baer when I was but a cub reporter at age 17, such were the stories, the motivation that catapulted me into a career from which I could never part.

Having embraced and been embraced by so many celebrities over so many years, the anecdotes of which follow, I could never, ever forget how fortunate I've been nor how thankful I am.

Lindy's Feat Tops All

We cross into Millennium Three, confident that it will surpass M-2 in major endeavors. Still, Millennium Two opened the door to M-3 in countless ways; flight for one thing, exploration for another, medicine for still another, putting a man on the moon, and many, many inventions, among them airplanes and automobiles. Oh, yes. and music and stage productions that have been little short of sensational.

I must say, however, that Lindbergh's famed non-stop flight, New York to Paris on a gray, drizzly day in May, 1927, stood the world on its head and presaged a fantastic era that is still with us. So we salute "Lucky Lindy" for his phenomenal achievement, witnessed by hundreds of thousands of roaring French fans that evening at Le Bourget. Fortunately, Lindbergh and his trusty monoplane, "Spirit of St. Louis," emerged in good shape after touching down as the French Faithful engulfed the scene. Lindbergh is said to have uttered these words, "We Made It."

Charles Lindbergh planted the idea that awoke the world from its slumber, and it hasn't been the same since. One can fly all over the world these days, and nothing seems impossible. What an extraordinary life he made possible with that one flight, which is undertaken every day of the year nowadays. Now, it's on to Mars, no less.

It is today still the most electrifying moment of my life, and I have encountered many of them in the years that have followed. Less than two months after Paris, he landed at our own Concord Airport after bad weather in Portland, Maine caused him to divert, and I was lucky enough to sit in the "Spirit of St. Louis" a few hours later, thanks to Police Officer Perley Morse. "Make it quick, Bobby," he told me. And for a few seconds I dreamed I was flying to Paris myself. I was the new "Lone Eagle."

I was 10 years old at the time of Lindbergh's incredible feat, and everything seemed to be changing for me, including new long pants.

Two years later, in 1929, a family friend, Ruel Newton Colby, who went to Dartmouth, invited me to compose a few words on a Stanley Cup hockey game I had witnessed the night before at a roaring Boston Garden with my older brother Harry, a classmate of Ruel's.

"Write it, and I will use it," Ruel promised. I did and he did. It appeared the following day in The *Monitor*, with a byline. It was my first, of course, and I was really proud of my short essay. I wish I had saved it because that was the beginning of my writing career, as primitive as it was.

A few years later, my Aunt Addie (on my mother's side) was using various of my stories in her *Franklin*, (N.H.) *Journal Transcript*. Addie was an honors graduate of Mt. Holyoke College, and taught German there for several years. She and Frances Perkins, a classmate at Holyoke, were close friends, and Frances served in Roosevelt's Cabinet for many years.

That's when my career started. Interviews seemed to be popping up everywhere. When I was 17, I did the interview with heavyweight champion Max Baer at Jack Sharkey's Bar in Boston. It was memorable in that I persuaded Max to talk to me in a dressing room full of talented writers from Boston.

I had many interviews after that—concert violinist Ruth Posselt, Met opera star Mario Del Monaco, tap-dancer Bill "Bojangles" Robinson, comedian Joe Penner and many others.

I didn't mention the roadblock to that interview with Max Baer, heavyweight champion of the world at the time. I was met by a test I really wasn't expecting at the dressing room door. I think it was the year 1935. The door had been shut in my face. I pounded on the door for admission. The peep-hole opened, and a fat nose appeared.

"Whadda ya want, Kid?", a gruff voice from within asked. "I want in," I answered. "I'm a reporter." The guy covered the peep-hole with his hand, and asked a reporter standing nearby what he should do—"The kid says he is a reporter and wants in". The reporter snapped "Well, let him in, he's OK." The reporter worked for the *Boston Herald*, and I was grateful for what he did for me. It led to the interview with the world champ. After that, it was really apple pie.

Baer had a murderous punch, and exhibited it in his workout that afternoon, which was interspersed with occasional quips from the champ like "Get me a beer, will you please, before I die," and "How much longer am I supposed to do this thing?" amongst various other sallies. It was all so entertaining. I had a chance to test the big sandbag Baer was pummeling, and it was heavy, heavy. He had it bouncing around like a toy.

I had countless interviews with celebrities, which I have detailed in following chapters, one with spy/ballplayer Moe Berg, a major league catcher with the Red Sox, Senators and White Sox; another with Tammy Grimes, which told the story of why she was by-passed for the title movie role in "Unsinkable Molly Brown" as Hollywood goofed; and one other, Ira Levin's sensational "Death Trap," in which the apparent murder victim stumbles out of the little garden in which he was entombed. It was shuddering, but I tell myself it is just a play. Ira wrote me a nice note a few weeks after its grand opening in Boston thanking me for the review - "It's reviews like yours that have made my Death Trap the big hit that it is."

I have selected at random some of the outstanding interviews over the years, and I may have missed a few. If I did, I'm sorry.

Back to Baer for a few moments.

After having his rubdown, the champ showered and dressed, and looking very natty, descended with his large entourage of boxing officials and reporters to the first floor of Sharkey's Bar, and promptly started serving customers with the well-known Baer flourish - "What will it be, sir?" - and engulfing all with some fabulous stories of his wild career.

One customer proffered a question. "What about Max Schmeling, the German contender?" he asked. "Schmeling?" Baer retorted, "Hell, he couldn't even lick his own lips." The customers all laughed uproariously. Baer was throwing sharp hooks, and the crowd loved every bit of it. It was his show, clearly, and his day in Boston.

As I left Sharkey's that day, I thought what a commanding figure was

Baer, and what a colorful champion. That was so many years ago, and whenever I see a replay of "Beverly Hillbillies" with his son, Max Baer Jr., I think of the moment all over again, of Max Baer whacking that punching bag with wicked lefts and rights, of the champ doing his calisthenics and pleading for a short beer, and waiting on the bar downstairs in a totally irreverent way. He stole the show, and he stole Boston that day.

One heck of a Guy...

Famous big band leader Guy
Lombardo chats over coffee with
author Bob Hilliard during a social
visit to Hilliard's Manchester, N.H.,
home. George Naum/*Union Leader.*

Guy Lombardo's musical talent was something incredibly special, a gift from God that blessed the country for several years with hundreds of fabulous songs that were "The Sweetest This Side of Heaven." Guy's mastery of music had to come from God; there's simply no other way to explain the beauty and the artistry of his famous orchestra, the Royal Canadians.

But despite the Royal Canadians' incredible success and Guy's resulting fame, the orchestra leader was just an ordinary Guy with extraordinary talent.

Guy Lombardo was no stranger to New Hampshire. He visited the Granite State many times during his great career and made several friends here. Fortunately, I was lucky enough to be one of them.

On one occasion, Guy and his song-writing brother, Carmen, paid a visit to my home in Manchester. Guy wanted to spend the rest of the evening at the party and had to be prodded to leave by his brother to attend to band-leading duties at the State Armory.

There were four brothers in the Royal Canadians, the aforementioned Guy and Carmen, who composed all those great songs of another era - "Coquette," "Boo-Hoo," "Sweethearts on Parade," "Seems Like Old Times," "Return To Me," and so many others; plus trumpet-playing Lebert, who grew up to be the last brother on the podium following the deaths of Carmen, in 1970, and Guy, in 1977. Victor, a tenor-sax virtuoso, and Lebert, who died in the mid-90s.

Guy was pretty well formalized when his mother asked that he take in his younger brother Victor. "No room, Mother," Guy replied, to which she retorted, "I think that you could find room for your own brother." And he did. Guy surrendered to maternity and forwarded travel money to his young, precocious brother, who set out for New York, sax in hand, and expectations running high.

When Victor failed to show in New York in a week's time, Mama Lombardo and the rest of the Lombardos grew concerned. They put out tracers for Victor , and finally he showed up, minus his sax and all his money. Guy put him to work at once, and he easily made the grade.

This is somewhat the little-told story of Victor and how he gave his brothers some difficult moments over the many years that followed, at various times bolting from the scene and leaving the Royal Canadians minus a sax player. Make no mistake, either, Victor was adept on the tenor sax, described by experts as one of the best in the business.

At one time after Guy's death in 1977, Lebert, then in charge, put Victor up front to lead the red-jacketed Canadians, and he did well. However, he suddenly bounced out again to "form my own band," which revealed, at least, that Victor certainly had a mind of his own.

The question for Victor should have been, finally, how did the Royal Canadians pile up all those awards over the years; how many times were they nominated top band in the land; how many song hits were they entrusted with introducing? About 600, minimum. And who kept the band going all those years - Carmen, Guy and Lebert and some trusty side men.

This is the story of how Guy Lombardo overcame the toughest obstacle of all to prevail, and to give the music world all those toe-tapping tunes, first-off, of Irving Berlin, Harry Warren, Cole Porter, Irving Caesar, Vincent Youmans and so many others. They cranked them out; Guy introduced them. And why? Because Guy did not corrupt them. He played the music as written, and in his very own smooth style that the world grew to love.

A story of success, even to conquering family twists and turns. And now that all are gone, it can be told what great brothers Victor had. Among the New Hampshire communities that loved "The Sweetest Music This Side of Heaven" were Concord (double performance), Keene, Manchester (Carousel, several), Rockingham and others.

After Guy's death in 1977, the first serious bits of disintegration started falling into place. Some veteran members of the band retired, and a few others, especially the youngest brother-member, Victor Lombardo, departed, as Lebert Lombardo, the last surviving brother of those who formed the Royal Canadians, desperately tried to hold the orchestra together.

It was all to little avail, as a new band was accorded the full rights to perform as the Guy Lombardo Orchestra. The members have done a good job, but they are by no means an exact replica of the original band from London, Ontario.

A sour note was detected as early as February 1978, when Victor quit for good and formed his own group. He had left the band in 1971 with different views on the style that Guy and Carmen and Lebert Lombardo had instituted with unswerving success, and had returned to the fold once again after Guy's death in 1977 to front the Royal Canadians in the New Year's Eve telecast that night. He lacked Guy's aplomb and astuteness, sadly, and he looked the part of a sub filling in for a beloved leader. It just did not work.

Victor cited "little differences," but Lebert said they were not 'little' at all. Lebert wanted to run things like Guy and vowed there would be no changes. Victor wanted to fire four members, and "he had no authority at all," according to Lebert. Lebert told me as the band rehearsed at the Waldorf for the New Year's Eve show the following year, with Lebert's son Bill up front, that he was irate with Victor's action and told him to "get lost," that he was no longer a member of the band, and that things would "not change two inches." Lebert was tough and would not budge. "Our fans are very happy," he said at the time.

It was a sad ending for an orchestra that had conquered the dance world for so many years, and whose members I knew so well.

There are some poignant memories in Guy Lombardo's last few months. I reported on them in two articles, the first in July of 1977, the second and last, sadly, in early November of the same year, both published in The *Manchester Union Leader.*

Then New Hampshire Gov. Meldrim Thomson had issued an official proclamation citing the many lifetime accomplishments of Lombardo in the field of popular music, in show business over a long period at Jones Beach, N.Y., and many triumphs, including the prestigious Gold Cup, in the field of speedboat racing. At one time, Guy was the world champion. In addition, Gov. Thomson also noted the many pleasures Guy had brought to the citizens of New Hampshire with his sweet and incomparable tempos, the "Sweetest This Side of Heaven."

It was a dramatic night as Jones Beach. New York City, just a few short miles west of Jones Beach, lost all its electrical power and lights. People were stuck in elevators between floors, and the skyline had all but disappeared. It was weird. The power breakdown did not affect Jones Beach, and the stage show, "Finian's Rainbow," continued after mild interruptions.

Later in the evening after the show, Guy and his Royal Canadians braved sheets of rain and wind pummeling the Schaefer Tent nearby to bring their delectable dance tunes to the hundreds of dancers. No one seemed to mind their soggy attire, and they danced on to the music. It ended an hour or so later as the storm waned.

As Guy was getting into his car, clutching his maple syrup from the governor and other trophies of the night, he shouted at me, "Well, Bob, I'm gonna have some nice waffles with maple syrup tomorrow morning. Lillibelle is going to make me a big breakfast, and I thank you ever so much for making it possible."

Little did I know that that would be the last time I'd see or talk with Guy. He died three months later. I did tell my sister Betty and her husband, Morton Tuttle, that Guy appeared a bit frail to me when the photos were being taken of the two of us at the pre-show party, but I passed it off as a bit of tiredness and weariness. Ironically, the band was in Manchester the night Guy died, playing a date at the nearby Carousel in Bedford. The bad news was phoned in to brother Leibert and brother-in-law Kenny Gardner from Houston Guy had succombed on the operating table.

Some of the boys in the band were to gather at my son's house for a little party after the dance, but Guy's death threw a pall over everything, and we mourned the loss of a great band leader, perhaps the best ever. He had given the world a whole new style of music, easy to listen to, easy to dance to and loved by millions, especially on New Year's Eve. Guy owned that holiday.

His death was my last personal story on Guy, and, as I wrote it, I thought back to that December day in 1934 when Guy and Carmen invited my brother John and me to play football with the bandsmen on Higgins Field in Concord, and although it was touch football, it was still quite rough, with bruised shins and such. I marveled over their elegant appearance on the stage that evening at the City Auditorium, and the thunderous ovation the red-jacketed Royal Canadians received after each number. There were many: "Love is Just Around the Corner," "Footloose and Fancy-Free," "Thirty Days Has September," and the haunting "Lost in a Fog" (My mind is weary, what can I do?) A memorable night, to be sure.

When I first met guy in Concord, one of my first questions was how did he hit upon his musical style. Guy said he had listened to the bands of the land in his youthful days in London, Ontario, and then developed a style that he and his brothers liked...an unencumbered style, soft and sweet and swingy, "with the right beat."

Guy liked his music unhurried and styled especially for dancers young and old, and romantic, music that "told a story"—a ballad, like "Annie Doesn't Live Here Anymore" or "You're Gonna Lose Your Gal" or a love song like "Stars Fell on Alabama." The Royal Canadians played that number that evening in Concord, with Carmen taking a vocal chorus, and the audience was entranced with its beautiful, soft and sweet tones and its delightful lyrics.

How could any music be this soft and sweet and romantic? The audience's thunderous applause spoke volumes, and Guy, debonair and in his tux, bowed graciously and went into the next number. They fell like sparkling diamonds on the mesmerized listeners, and toes were tapping as the selections pored forth.

Guy's pace was not fast, but was exceedingly pleasant, as the orchestra went through the many selections that night. In the audience, sitting directly in front of me in a roped off section, was Governor H. Styles Bridges, later a prominent United States senator, and he "just loved" the show.

As I listened to the world of glorious sound and richly endowed lyrics, I asked myself, "How could all this be possible from a group of kids picked for the task because they were playmates back home in London, Ontario, not far from Toronto and Detroit? Playing such a disciplined game, and with such class and style. How could they accomplish such deeds on the music stage, and barely in their twenties? I figured then and there, it was leadership that told the story. Guy (Gaetano) was a superb leader, and he led his little group of stalwarts out of a relatively small community in Ontario right smack into the bright lights of Broadway where they remained forever after.

O.O. McIntyre, the celebrated columnist of several decades ago, stamped Lombardo even then as one of the five greatest bandleaders. Fred Waring, who brought a somewhat classical style to popular music, I remember was listed as one of O.O.'s other selections, and wisely. He had unusual symphonic arrangements that were pleasant to the ear. He also featured a fine Glee Club style.

Guy employed a basic core of about 13 musicians. He himself played the violin and seldom with the orchestra. He knew, however, the tone he wanted and he stuck to it. Four saxes, a bass, two pianos (because there were two fellows in the neighborhood who played that instrument), a guitar, and a brass section, and a drum, of course, by George Gowans. His vocalists were picked, largely, from the orchestra, although Kenny Gardner, who joined the band about the time of the outbreak of World War II, was principally a vocalist in his many years with the "Royal Canadians."

I'll make a bit of an exception here: Kenny tried to help all the members about him, playing the bass horn on occasion, and sometimes, en route to the mike, tossing a handful of coins into the instrument for a musical changeup as the audience would roar with laughter.

Brother Carmen was also a prolific songwriter in addition to being about the smoothest sax man in America. He could make his sax sing, and the tone was just throbbing. Together, that sax section became the tone of the orchestra and provided the sweet tones that Guy desired.

When a Chicago music critic, Aston Stevens, first heard the orchestra perform on stage, he knighted the band with the phrase that stuck forever, "The sweetest music this side of Heaven." After that, Guy and his band played to capacity crowds wherever they performed. Listeners flocked by the thousands upon thousands to hear this band perform its musical magic, its nostalgic love songs, its fascinating quick-tempoed selections with chorus by the Lombardo Trio. Intertwined in all this were the melodic breaks and runs on the twinkling twin pianos. It wasn't long before their music became the talk of America, on college campuses and in every major city's nightclubs.

So, as I listened to "The Sweetest Music This Side of Heaven" at the venerable Concord Auditorium that evening in 1934, I told myself this, for sure, is one of the biggest nights in my young life. Never had I heard music so utterly transporting as this, and I became a fan for life. I admired Guy for his able leadership, and I admired this doughty little band for holding together in the face of adversity and proving that some hometowners, after all, could make it big in the new America. All America knew, too, that Canada was proud of this family that had its inception from Momma and Poppa in ancient Sicily and raised their sons and daughters to know and love music. This Guy did with acclaim.

What I admired most about Guy was that he knew what he was doing. When he reached stardom, he once jokingly said, "These fellows know musical notes, I know bank notes," and with that, Guy headed straight to the bank. That may or may not be accurate, but it does sum up the fantastic success story of the "Royal Canadians." Everything they touched seemed to turn to gold. His father had told Guy much earlier, "Give the customer a little bit more than he expects, and you will create a following."

I knew Guy personally for more than 50 years. When I would introduce Guy to friends, he would always add this postscript: "This guy and I played football one day back in the Thirties." And it was quite a game. Carmen was first to pick, being the captain of the other side. He chose my younger brother, John. Guy selected next: "I'll pick Bob." That was ever so many years ago, but even then Guy was directing well. He knew the gang needed exercise, and he made sure the bandsmen received it.

I don't even remember how that game turned out, whether Guys' side or Carmen's prevailed. All I remember is that it was somewhat rough, for these guys were more accustomed to ice hockey and the severe body checking that is part and parcel of that game. There were no taped noses, no arms in cast, but there were plenty of aching bones. They all looked magnificent for the concert, just like the clean-cut kids next door, which actually they were, in London, Ontario.

Guy was always Mr. Debonair on stage, seldom unruffled when something went wrong, but one night at Bedford Grove in Manchester, I saw him briefly lose his aplomb. Vocalist Don Rodney had just finished a number and was returning to his chair to pick up the last strains of the song on his guitar, when a bat dived out of the night air. Someone shouted "air attack, dive for cover," and Don picked up his guitar and went after the dive bomber, swinging wildly. Guy and the others ducked for cover, and the bat flew off.

Guy wasn't happy, and his face showed it. He liked his shows to be perfect. One of Don's wild swings with the guitar almost decked Guy, who ducked just in time. He was not pleased with this kind of a circus, and for a few minutes, he was a stern maestro, totally displeased with the fiasco of bat-swinging. Guy was a perfectionist.

Earlier in the year 1934, Guy and his team were invited to Hollywood to make a picture called "Many Happy Returns of the Day," and in addition to the featured Lombardo brothers, it featured George Burns and Gracie Allen. It was doubtless their first film, as well, and it contained a lot of humor and many good musical numbers by the "Royal Canadians."

When Guy first became world famous, he gave George and Gracie their first real break in big time show business and coast-to-coast treatment. They were always close friends, and the friendship extended back over many years. I think Guy picked up some of his one-liners from that team, like "I'm glad I didn't send the boys out for grand pianos" when they were asked to pick up a football for the team's daily practice that day in Concord and came back with seven.

George Burns might have proffered his own one-liner that night.

There were several good musical numbers in "Many Happy Returns," including "The Sweetest Music This Side of Heaven" and "Fare-Thee-Well." I think Lebert Lombardo, with his soft, velvety voice, had the vocal chorus for the latter number, Carmen for the former. These two numbers were typical of the smooth music of the day, with appropriate lyrics, and were examples of what Tin Pan Alley could accomplish for the music world. That work ethic is gone for good now, and music lovers are left with a definite void. Guy despised the new order, and he made no bones about it. A writer one day asked him about it. "You call that music," he asked, "three or four guys banging the hell out of their drums and electric guitar?" He answered himself. "Well, I don't."

Guy's music always featured romantic lines and singable music, with an enticing beat. It was a combination hard to beat, and when I heard the band for the first time that evening in 1934, I knew that this band was the one for me. Their waltzes were dreamy, their fox trots exciting and with a good beat. I overheard one woman saying on the dance floor at the Roosevelt: "Guy's songs just make you want to get up and dance." And shortly, she and her husband did just that as they moved their way toward the bandstand and the smiling maestro, keeping in time with his baton, and doing it ever so gracefully as the evening advanced toward the early morning hours, and the dancers whispered their bon mots. That, by the way, is a picture that has vanished.

One person who helped create the sweet tones and the compelling beat and did many of the orchestrations that the world knew so well from all those broadcasts late in the evening, was Larry Owen, a master musician and an arranger unsurpassed. His wife, Marie, told us one day on a visit to their home in Manhatten: "You know Larry, he just goes into his study, locks the door and says, 'I'll be out in a few hours.' And I can hear all those beautiful breaks and melodies as Larry plays them on the piano. They're so gorgeous."

Larry, who died not long after Guy, turned them out endlessly, and all were a work of art. He was helped in the orchestrations by Carmen, principally, and by other members of the band who were also adept at the chore. To write good music, to create the right effect, one has to be able to hear it in his mind, and with the Lombardos it was a very professional undertaking. They could hear it in their minds before it even reached the song sheet.

Lebert told me about one such song after Guy had died and Lebert was at the helm. I remember it so clearly. The band was in The Empire Room, I believe, at the Waldorf Astoria preparing for the New Year's Eve concert heard around the world. It was during a break, and the band, under the direction of Bill Lombardo, Lebert's son and Guy's nephew, had just completed a swingy arrangement of "Baby Face," and Lebert beckoned me across the ballroom.

"Bob," Lebert said, "these composers are really something. The music I know sounds grand, but you should see how we get it. One night, Walter Donaldson, the composer, called Guy, Larry and me over to his table at the Roosevelt. We traipsed over, and he said, "Look, you guys, I've just had an inspiration for a song." "Well, where is it, Walter?" Guy asked. He replied, "Right there in front of your eyes, Guy, right there on the table cloth."

"Guy was startled, and took a closer look. Sure enough, there it was. 'I thought you guys might like to see it,' Walter said, 'and make an orchestration from the table cloth.' Carmen and Larry and I leaned over and started scribbling, as Guy looked on rather amused. In a short time, we had completed the work, and Guy asked Walter, 'Well, where are the lyrics, and what is the title?' 'Well,' Walter answered, looking down at the ink-stained tablecloth, 'You can call it 'You're Driving Me Crazy' or something,' and so, without the lyrics, we told Walter we would play it in the next set, and we did. The crowd went wild. We told them it was so new, the lyrics hadn't even been written. I think Walter was cagy. I think he had the lyrics even then but was holding them back so he could command a greater fee. I think he produced them the very next night, and the song became an instant hit. I really think Walter planned it that way, but I wanted you to know, Bob, that it really isn't that easy all the time, especially with a guy like Walter Donaldson. Sometimes you have to work at it."

Lebert broke into a shy grin as he thought of Walter. "This guy was something," he recalled. "One day he was at Hialeah in Miami. He loved to gamble on the horses, you know, and because of his talent at song writing, he always had plenty of cash. This day, after he had played three or four races and dropped about five grand, he went scouting for friends so he could borrow more. He finally spied a guy from Tin Pan Alley he knew, and went up and asked him for a loan of ten grand. 'Gee, Walter,' said his friend. 'I don't have that kind of dough on me, but I got $800 with me if that will help.' 'No,' said Walter, 'I need ten grand because I got sure bets in all the races remaining.' He was disconsolate, and so was his friend, until the latter looked up and saw a bank in the distance. 'Hey, Walter,' he said, 'that bank stays open until 7 or 8 o'clock. Maybe you can hit 'em up there. By the way, have you written anything lately, Walt?' 'Yeah, sure,' Walter replied. 'Well,' answered his friend, 'I'll write out a chit for you on one of our vouchers, and you can take it over to the bank and cash it. Ten grand, did you say? Well, what is the title of your new song?' 'The title of my new song?' Walter asked, puzzled. 'Yeah,' the friend answered, 'I'll need it for our records.'

Walter looked away as sunset approached and answered promptly: 'Oh, the title? At Sundown,' he replied. "The friend wrote it down, and Walter collected his $10,000. Walter hadn't written anything, but he saw it getting darker and figured that title was as good as anything, so he named his song, which he had not yet written, and he collected his money. It didn't stay with him long," Lebert lamented, "he lost it all before evening."

That song, Lebert said, became a major hit, and earned him a lot more money. "Walter was a crazy guy," Lebert revealed, "but a lovable one, who knew little about horses."

Lebert arose and went over to the bandstand with his son. There was still work to be done and music to be played, maybe "You're Driving Me Crazy," or "At Sundown," with remembrances of the composer.

I was there at the Waldorf that New Year's Eve, and it was a joyous occasion, with the Lombardos trundling out all the old hits and many of the new ones as well. They had a beat that was enticing, one that drew you to the dance floor. There would come a time when Guy's team would no longer be at the music stands on stage, and the world would be empty for it. As one of my dear friends once remarked, "The music ended when Guy died," and in so many ways it did, although a band that plays the Lombardo style still functions, though hardly with the same finesse heard in the Twenties through the early Seventies. That style, though simple and melodious, was hard to duplicate; the moaning saxes, the pin-point trumpeting, the artistry of all the instruments and vocalizing. It was a sound that will remain forever, and I just hope the orechestrations are still intact, for as we enter a new century, some new band leader may come in contact with them and put them to work as "that new tone of the new age" and start the cycle going again.

Of Lombardo through the years, I would have to say that the original tones of the late Twenties and through the Thirties and Forties were hard to beat, but it seems that Guy was always improving. He put the winning touch on anything he tried, and that included a long list of vacalists, among them his two brothers and a brother-in-law. Guy knew talent when he heard it. Carmen perhaps was his first featured vocalist, together with brother Lebert. Neither cared especially for the billing, but each had an individual style that was notable. Carmen's was precise and comforting, and one could hear every word, a legacy that Momma Lombardo left. She would insist that lyrics be understood and words pronounced most properly, and Carmen did just that. He had many imitators, it is true, including Tony Randall, the movie star, who did sound a lot like Carmen, but there was only one original. Lebert's voice was soft and sweet and totally different from his brother's. It had a soothing effect. It portrayed intimacy, and the girls just fell in love with Lebert's renditions, although he was more concerned with his trumpet solos than his vocalizing.

So Guy, like Old Man River, rolled on through the years, making slight changes from time to time in the style, adding an instrument when he thought it wise, or a new vocalist, and at the same time always working on the tones that America and the world had grown to love. He was very definitely a perfectionist, and when he added Kenny Gardner to his band at the start of World War II, he hit the jackpot. There are still those who claim Kenny was better than Bing Crosby himself, and I for one feel that he was. I think Kenny had a bit more sophistication than Crosby, but certainly the two were in a class by themselves and portrayed vocal artistry, Kenny especially doing the honors on "Harbor Lights" or "Red Sails in the Sunset."

Guy always strove for the perfect tone, of course, and he experimented at times with various of the instruments. Once he added a tone that seemed to embrace a piano and a guitar. It had been created by pianist Frank Vigneau. I think it was called a spinetino, and it was pleasing to the ear. That was like composer Richard Wagner doing his celebrated music dramas and noting that the instrument for the sound he desired had not been invented at that time. Wagner promised that it would. Guy, with the same ear for betterment, did the same thing, and then along came Vigneau's invention. I would call it a cross between a guitar and a piano, and its tone was something like that of a hurdy-girdy of Italian street song days... It was very appealing. I believe that it was featured, among many other songs, in "The Old Apple Tree."

Through the years, Guy introduced song after song, and most of them became musical standards. He had an ear for the melodious ones, and they became the hits for all time. He also introduced some that did not make it to the top, but should have in my estimation, including "Sing an Old Fashioned Song To a Young Sophisticated Lady." It had melody, and it told a story like most of Guy's selections. Guy oftentimes referred to them as ballads, which in truth they were, and many may yet be rediscovered with a closer, more discernable look at the music. A couple of others were "There's a Little Picture Playhouse in My Heart" ("And the four-star feature is a wonderful creature called you"), "My Heart Sings" (a simple play on the sales but wonderfully effective), and Carmen's own composition, "A Sailboat in the Moonlight, and You," among many others. These stand out, and they will continue to stand out in any era where there is a boy-girl relationship and matters pertaining to the heart. Just a little research on the matter would certainly be a step in the right direction in promoting these luscious works of the past when Tin Pan Alley was producing them on almost an assembly line scale. I oftentimes wondered where Guy had stored his immaculate charts, or orechestrations, where they might be dragged out again for restoration like the old masters. The rock and hard rock syndrome will not last forever.

If inspiration were needed for a U.S.A. success story, it would be that of the Lombardos. They started out with the three brothers, Guy, Carmen and Lebert, selected neighborhood kids for a nucleus, with not that much musical ability, taught them as best they and other friends could and saw the project develop into a small orchestra that made nice music even then in the youthful years. I was addicted early to this romantic beginning.

There were, in addition to the Lombardos, the originals:

With Carmen in the sax section, an integral part of the orchestra, were Fred Higman and Larry Owen, who later became an arranger and business manager. Larry was with a big successful band in Cleveland when he first met and heard the "Royal Canadians." He was so carried away with their tones that he quit his job and went to work for Guy, and many of the orchestrations that we hear today via tapes are Larry's own arrangements, and they are delectable and ear catching. Incidentally, that was the original vocal trio as well: Carmen, Fred Higman and Larry, and they were always poised and professional. Victor Lombardo joined the section shortly after, playing the soprano sax.

Ben Davies played the bass horn, Jim Dillon the trombone, and Lebert Lombardo the trumpet. Francis Henry, who composed the all-time favorite, "Little Girl," played the guitar, and he was one of the best. Guy even then had a musical concept, and it featured the guitar, and the twin pianos when the three interplayed on a break, and it was innovative and delightful. Fred Kreitzer and Hugh D'Ippolito were the wizards of the keyboard, and their piano solos were a thing of musical beauty and perfection that would attract dancers by the hundreds to their side. They made it look so easy, and that perhaps is the most heard compliment in the hundreds of times I attended their concerts and dances.

"Look at those fellows," they would say, "they make it look so easy that even I could play like that." Maybe, but with a lot of lessons and an inborn talent for the keyboard. Finally, the last man on the team, though one of the most important ones, was George Gowans, the drummer who fell asleep on a lounge at Radio City one afternoon just before Guy's coast-to-coast network appearance, and he missed the show and also a few cymbal smashes in the concert hit, "Song of India." Guy was amazed to see his chair empty when the big moment came, but he forgave him. George was afraid to face him that afternoon and sent Guy a telegram in the very same building. George, a fine drummer, never forgot it, but Guy always looked on it as past history. He was so articulate that it must have spoiled his Sunday that somebody missed the Big Bang.

Guy had the soft and sweet touch, a delicate presentation, and he is said to have told Gowans at one time, "I barely want to hear your beat, George, I want to hear the music." One drummer once told me that George Gowans was an artist in his own right. "I go to hear him only. He picks up Guy's tempo instantly with a nice soft beat." And that is why, possibly, the "Royal Canadians" were so famous, their uncanny timing. They could slide from one song to another, and George's soft beat led the way.

I remember now the many evenings I heard Guy, from the Hotel Roosevelt Grill Room, to the Waldorf, to Jones Beach (his summer date) to various ballrooms around the country, and what I most admired were his opening strains of "Auld Lang Syne," I would tell friends to listen to the first seconds of that great throbbing theme introduction that would send the dancers on their way, and I knew they were captives from that moment on.

To this day, one of the first songs I ever heard Guy play remains my overwhelming favorite to this day, "Stars Fell on Alabama." It was so gorgeous that evening at the auditorium in Concord, the guys with whom I had just been playing football, playing such heavenly music and looking so resplendent in their red jackets on stage, that I had trouble believing that I had played even a part of this very stunning day. Guy made it happen, as he did through his life as the suave maestro. His selections were unmatchable, and he must have had his finger on the public pulse, for the applause that followed each score was literally explosive.

I think one of his most dramatic appearances came at the old Metropolitan Theatre in Boston, now the beautifully restored Wang Center for the Performing Arts. The film ended, the house lights went out, the audience went still, and suddenly there was that silky, majestic tone that engulfed the house, the rich tones of "Auld Lang Syne" as the entire band emerged on an elevated stage from the deep recesses, and the spotlights directed their glaring beams to Guy and his Band. What an introduction; ever the master showman, Guy Lombardo! I remember they opened suddenly with the trio singing "My Little Grass Shack," and the audience was positively transfixed. They went on with "I'm In the Mood for Love," to roars from the audience, and to other great hits of the day, "You Are My Lucky Star" (I believe from the Eleanor Powell hit film of that day), to "Love in Bloom" to "Million Dollar Baby" and others of the calibre that have not been duplicated to this day.

Lombardo-Style music went out with his death in November, 1977. I knew I had lost a good friend, and that America, and yes, the world, had lost a bandleader who had carved out a niche for himself in the presentation of popular music. His music was such that when first heard, it was remembered. No wonder that Berlin and Jerome Kern and Walter Donaldson wanted their songs to be played by the Lombardos. His very acceptance was their assurance that a song would make it big in the music industry. His delicate treatment, the seductive saxes, the crisp trumpet tones, the trombones, the twinkling twin pianos, the dulcet vocals. Guy put them all together, and critic Aston Stevens hit it right on the nose in Chicago when he termed it "the Sweetest Music This Side of Heaven." Never before, or since, has the world heard music so rendered, and perhaps we may never again hear it equalled.

Guy had it in mind from very early days that what the listeners and dancers wanted was a style that they could understand and love, a style that would embellish the musical line, so that when it was first heard, it would linger in the mind and be repeated and be revered. "Annie Doesn't Live Here Any More" was one such. A person heard it and hummed it over and over. It made sense, and the lyrics told the story of a lover losing his girl to someone new, sad, yes, but the way of the world.

There was a brother nucleus when the Lombardos embarked on their remarkable musical journey, Guy himself, Carmen and Lebert. Each brought a talent: Guy and his leadership; Carmen and his uncanny musicianship, and Lebert and his gorgeous trumpet tones. It was startling how it all came together, with the neighborhood kids all polishing it off on the other instruments as though by order from above. When the Lombardos played in Concord, another brother, Victor, had been added to the sax section. He played the soprano sax.

It was music defined and well executed, and when heard, it was remembered. It stayed with you. "Play it simply," Guy once said, "and they will remember it." They did, as with no other band. Guy had close to 800 song hits in an incredible span of nearly 60 years, and that had to prove the listeners remembered what they heard and started humming the songs the very next day.

For me, it was nothing but sheer luck that I covered the Press Conference that day in Concord and met the young and suave maestro. In many ways, I think my career really started that day, in spite of earlier interviews with several celebrities. Guy gave me a push and a new insight into molding an article. He would add a witticism and a bit of humor, as attest his story on the footballs and grand pianos, and the reader, or the listener, would delight in the account. Guy also charmed his detractors. Once at the Met Theatre in Boston, a fan approached him and said something like, "What you need in this band is a deep bass and an accordian." Guy looked at me and replied, with a smile, "Gee, another guy telling me how to run my band after all these years. I don't know how I ever made it. It must have been by luck."

That was in the early Forties, and Lombardo was very much on top of things in the music world, still the favorite orchestra of millions and millions of listeners. Guy made it palatable, with a danceable beat, and the tone was soft and sweet, easy to hear. Imagine a guy trying to improve on that throbbing tone!

Guy was probably at his best at a dance, and his tempos just demanded the listeners to try a fox trot or waltz or a tango. Guy played them all and made them sound so delectable and dreamy and contagious. He was The Great Guy.

Not only in the world of music was Lombardo a champion. He was constantly voted among the world's best-dressed men by Fashions Institute of America. I remember one year he was selected along with Cary Grant, Anwar Sadat, Gov. Meldrim Thomson of New Hampshire (who dressed for breakfast) and a few others. "Well," Guy said one day, "I was brought up to dress well; my father was a tailor back in London, Ontario days, and he knew what looked smart on a man." In fact, all the Lombardos dressed immaculately, as well as the Royal Canadians. On stage, they were picture-perfect; and that sort of went with their smooth music, with a dapper Guy swinging the baton gracefully. He was the epitome of high-class fashion, and it did not hurt his musical presentation, either. He had it all going for him, and the women just delighted in his smooth appearance and his sparkling music. There was nobody quite like him before he hit the air waves in the Twenties or since his death in the Seventies.

New York City named a street for him in his late years. They called it appropriately, The Lombardo Way, and maybe someone should have put it to music, for certainly, there was a Lombardo way. Carmen, who composed so many song hits over the years, including "Boo Hoo," "Snuggled on Your Shoulder," "Little Coquette," "Return to Me" and many more, might have fitted it to a tango or a lively fox trot, and had them dancing in front of the Waldorf, where the street was situated.

It seems that everything Guy touched became a success. In speedboat racing, he was a Gold Cup champion after a big victory on the Detroit River. Later, he challenged Sir Malcolm Campbell's world speedboat achievements, and still later Sir Donald Campbell's feats. He was Malcolm's son.

One night at the Hampton Casino in Hampton, N.H., Guy asked me to take a look at his brand new jet boat, "Tempo Alcoa," being built in Bay City, Michigan.

Since we were headed for Detroit and a visit with friends we had met earlier in Cuba, we decided one day to drive up to Bay City and look over Guy's new speedster. It was designed largely by Les Staudacher, I believe, and tested by him as well.

"Tempo Alcoa" was completely jet-powered, and just looking at it in the shipyards, it appeared sleek and fast, with sponsons at its sides. The pilot sat near the front, in front of the jet engine. What Guy was attempting to do was set a speed record of up to 300 mph, quite incredible on water, or on land, at that time. Staudacher was not there the day we traveled to Bay City, but I studied the craft carefully and took many pictures. Truthfully, the boat frightened me. I could see it was knifing through the water at those death-defying speeds, and I figured it was dangerous.

I saw Guy a few weeks later, and I told him of my fears. If he insisted on taking it out, much to the discomfort of his family, I mentioned scenic Lake Winnipesaukee in New Hampshire as a good testing area, for the lake is about 30 miles in length. So, Guy sent Larry Owen, his general manager and former saxaphonist-vocalist with the orchestra. Larry was a most trusted adviser and friend, and he recommended, after piloting a speedboat around the lake for a few hours, that it would be better not to try it at Winnipesaukee since that body of water had big waves, and wind con-

BIG BANDLEADER Guy Lombardo, center, is flanked by the Josef Brothers at the Carousel Ballroom in this undated photo.

ditions in the so-called "broads," a wide expanse of water near the northeast sector of the lake.

Thusly, Guy called off any speed attempts there, or any exhibitions. The lake also is very deep, and he figured the waves would be too much to cope with, even on a good day with slight winds. So, the speed attempts were scheduled instead for Pyramid Lake near Reno, Nevada, with Staudacher at the controls. Guy was present for the attempt and watching from shore. In one of the runs, Staudacher was reportedly distracted by someone waving from shore, and in that second, the craft went airborne and crashed, with Guy racing along the shoreline anxiously. Staudacher escaped injury, and the only casualty that day was Mr. Lombardo himself, who fell and bruised his knee.

After that incident, the craft was moved back to Michigan for more trials on Saginaw Bay, and one day it blew up "going close to 300 miles per hour," as Guy told me. The boat was being controlled remotely from shore, and so there were no casualties, and that ended Guy's immediate aspirations for world speed domination, with his brothers breathing a loud collective sigh of relief. Now they could concentrate on the business of music once again, without worrying about their leader.

Guy's main goal in life was, of course, music, but he did enjoy the theatre, and his long stay at Jones Beach, Long Island in producing major hit plays, proved an unparalled success. The stadium held about 8,000 spectators, and, more often than not, was filled to capacity for the big Broadway spectaculars. The evening I was there to present Guy with Governor Thomson's proclamation, Guy immediately had brother Lebert hang it in a prominent place in his office at the stadium. "Take down that old picture of Chicago days," Guy ordered, "and hang the Governor's message there instead." He was resolute. And there it was hung that summer's evening in 1977.

Gov. Thomson sent Guy a supply of New Hampshire maple syrup and told me to tell Guy to use it on his pancakes in the morning. There was also a good supply of bourbon, and we all celebrated for an hour or so before the play, with Guy joining us for a superb performance of "Finian's Rainbow" in the stadium. It was the night Manhattan lost all its electricity, as the city skyline in the background went black, and the towers lost their elevator service. At Jones Beach, however, everything was normal, except for some high winds, and after the show, we all went dancing to "The Sweetest Music This Side of Heaven."

After Guy had played his traditional "Auld Lang Syne," we walked over to his car, with the license plates "GUY", and talked briefly. Guy backed out and waved goodbye: "Well, Bob," he said, "lilliebell is going to make me some waffles in the morning, and I will have this nice maple syrup on them." Guy died in a hospital in Houston four months later, and that was the last conversation I ever had with him. Ironically, he died while the "Royal Canadians" were playing in my home city of Manchester, N.H., actually in Bedford, a suburb, at the Carousel Ballroom. Lebert received the news, along with Kenny Gardner and the others, just after midnight and after they had concluded their theme song. Later that night, Lebert told me: "Bob, you know it's a strange thing. We had just finished playing 'Auld Lang Syne' when Carmen died a few years ago."

It was a sad and subdued evening after that news from Texas. We had planned a little party at my son Bobby's house, with various members of the band, but it was cancelled, of course, and there were some pretty long faces there on Oak Street that night. The wire services contacted me, and I was pretty busy filling them in on Guy, and also his band's performance that night. I called Larry Owen in Florida, and he was crushed. They had just about grown up together from the day Larry joined the orchestra in old Cleveland days. The next day, the editor called and wanted a long, feature-length article on Guy Lombardo and his impact on the world of popular music, so for the next several hours, I was quite busy. Since the editor was Joe McQuaid of the newspaper family, and a youngster I had personally "broken in," (I knew his father, Bernard J. McQuaid, very well, from shortly after his spectacular days in Chicago, to his days as a war correspondent in the South Pacific and the European Theatre of Operations), how could I refuse a request like that on my day off? No way.

I did owe a lot to Guy for his quotes and kindness and his guidance, and to the McQuaids. The next day the information I had given the writers was quoted liberally in newpapers throughout the country, even a quote I had about Guy's lilting music being a Gretna Green of sorts for all the young lovers who danced happily to his beautiful music.

As a friend said recently: "When Guy died, the music stopped."

Indeed it did. It is difficult to pick up the string again when a leader of that calibre passes on. Signs along the funeral route said forlornly "So Long, Guy." And so did a somber America which knew Guy intimately each New Year's Eve, from The Roosevelt Grill and from The Waldorf Astoria and from Time's Square and its seething thousands; all hailing the New Year with Guy.

Guy had no peers whatever in the selection of hit songs. He had but to gaze at one to tell him, and they were all so wonderful. His particular style of music, simple and sweet, lent its charm, also. Great songs just rolled off that Royal Canadian bandstand, sometimes in the old days of Tin Pan Alley as many as five or six a week. He played them as they were written and cloaked them in his own raiment.

One ballad that I especially liked, and Guy never recorded, was something of a novelty, but it really had tune and tempo and story. It was called "The Girl With the Dreamy Eyes," and it was really cute. The lyrics went something like this, and they were sung by the Lombardo Trio:

'Twas in a candy store
    I got my big surprise.
I bumped right in
    To the saucy grin
Of the Girl With the Dreamy Eyes.

She sold the caramels
    I ask you was I wise?
  I bought a few
    Just to say how-do
To the Girl With the Dreamy Eyes.

I didn't know if she could sew
Or if she knew how to cook.
I only know my heart went Oh
    When she gave me that glad to see you look.

Now at the baby shows
My son wins every prize.
    You know who his pretty mother is?
    It's the Girl With the Dreamy Eyes.

The word eyes would be swung on two notes, ey-es. It was cute, and the audiences always applauded when the Trio made its rendition.

Still another in Guy's arsenal was "Sing an Old Fashioned Song to a Young Sophisticated Lady." Very lilting and very pleasing to the ear. But, of course, that was when Tin Pan Alley was cranking them out by the hundreds, and when songwriters were very professional and knew how to handle music and accompanying lyrics. It is truly a forgotten art, and I cannot say that I enjoy the popular music of today. Guy even played excerpts from Grand Opera, such as "My Heart at Thy Sweet Voice" from "Samson et Dalila" I believe, and "Serenade to An Evening Star" from Richard Wagner's immortal "Tannhauser." He played others, too, I recall the Barcorolle from "Les Contes d'Hoffmann" (Tales of Hoffmann), a twin piano rendition, and one of the most sparkling in his repertoire, one constantly demanded by audiences.

In keeping with the mad mid-Thirties, Guy also played often another ballad of sorts. It was called "The Cute Little Hat Check Girl," and this strangely was never recorded. It was typical Lombardo, a ballad of a nightclub habitue who found his love taking hat checks there, and "at 3 a.m.

this dainty little gem" was walked home by her new friend. A classic as a ballad.

Any orchestra today starting out on the long road to fame and fortune, would do well to study the vast Lombardo Library, with very special attention paid to his style of music and the orchestral scores he devised. It would save time, and one might attribute that to Guy's diligence as a young man with music on his mind, and New York City in his sights.

Perhaps the mere presence of Guy Lombardo and his world famous "Royal Canadians" was why we had a Tin Pan Alley in the first place. Guy holds the all-time record of introducing hit songs, and it will never be broken, something like 700 or 800. If anyone could be called a "birth father," it would have been Guy, for he oversaw the lifespan of many a song. He didn't adopt every song he saw, only those that appealed to him, that passed the test of melody, of lyric composition, and of overall astuteness. If it passed Guy's eye, it was in, and it was lasting. Before The Roosevelt Grill Room, patrons even knew the title of "You're Driving Me Crazy" by Walter Donaldson, in fact, they were humming it and whistling it. Lebert, by the way, thought Donaldson was very coy, and that when he wrote the notes on the tablecloth that night at The Roosevelt, he already had the verse, and that it was something of a holdup job. It may have been, but whatever the business rapprochements, the song was a sure-fire hit, and on just about everybody's lips in America once Walter did come up with the lyrics. "I think he had them already that night over the tablecloth," said Lebert, laughing. "He was pretty foxy. He could make a killing once the lyrics were added to the melody, which everyone would know by that time."

Lebert and Guy and Carmen all got a big kick out of Donaldson, but they recognized talent, too.

One of Guy's biggest introductions was "Frankie and Johnny," a play on the old love triangle theme, and it was one of the major hits of the decade. It was introduced, I believe, at the old Metropolitan Theatre in Boston before a capacity audience, and it was played again and again, both on stage and on the coast-to-coast networks of the day that carried Guy's programs. With Kenny Gardner as the vocalist, it needed little further help, save for the beguiling music of the "Royal Canadians" and Kenny's

GUY LOMBARDO, second from right, at the Bedford Carrousel, with Bob Hillard at left, Judge and Mrs. Burnham Davis of Conway, New Hampshire, center, and reporter Martha Donovan of the *The Union Leader* at right.

very own interpretative lyrics, which never failed to send audiences into a storm of laughter. Kenny was a legend too. His enactment of Frankie as she "cried the whole night through," bent over the listeners. Kenny was bent over, too, as he clutched an imaginary skirt and sobbed into it. What a hit! I think Kenny must have crooned that sad tale a million times to listeners who couldn't stop laughing.

It turned out to be a standbye in the Lombardo repertory. Not long after, Guy turned loose another, of old Klondike Days in the Yukon: "Dangerous Dan McGrew." Again, he turned the lyrics over to his brother-in-law Kenny for the usual treatment. Kenny was superlative as the raconteur spying the Royal Canadian Mounted Police arriving. "They're SO big," he crooned, shielding his eyes. "They drew their guns," his own individual saga goes, "and they said, 'Which one?' is Dangerous Dan McGrew." That line got them, as Kenny continued his enactment.

Kenny Gardner was not always with the "Royal Canadians." He joined the band around the time of World War II, later married Guy's sister, Elaine. He was one of the greatest additions Guy ever made, and to me, he was superior in many ways to Bing Crosby himself, in the manner of delivery and stage presence, and tonal quality. It was hard to best Bing, but I think Kenny did just that.

It was a most nostalgic period for me personally, 1934 to the early Forties, and most enriching. It opened a whole new life for me. I met my wife Barbara one cold day in the early winter of 1937. She was involved in a rough game of girl's hockey on the ice at White Park, and I retrieved a ball they were using as a puck for her. It had bounced over the rink boards. I told her: "Rough game." She smiled and agreed. After the game, she came off the ice near where I was standing. I asked her if she still felt like skating, and she replied, "Sure." So, we went for a long skate on the nearby pond and talked of many things. Shortly before she left to go home, I asked her if she ever listened to Guy Lombardo. She answered that she did. "Well," I said, "try to catch his program for Bond Bread this afternoon at 5. I think he will be playing that new song he just introduced, 'Boo-Hoo.'"

He did, and Barbara liked it a lot. The only thing, I forgot to show up the next night to meet Barbara, and I was reminded of it forever after. It was an error, unmistakably, and you can charge that to Bob Hilliard. A real goof. She did, however, tell me that she enjoyed "Boo-Hoo" very much, and she thought that it might be a big hit. She was most accurate. It did become the hit of the year for 1937. We were wed June 18, 1937, and Bobby was born on May 19, 1938. So, it is a nostalgic period for me, still. Barbara died on September 30, 1976, and never a day goes by that I don't think of her, and the day she was playing hockey at White Park. In many ways, Guy should have been the best man. His selection of "Boo Hoo" that day was most appropriate. In a way, too, it became our song and our password into the future.

If I mentioned that Guy Lombardo was a veritable Gretna Green, he proved it with us.

Barbara also saw him that evening in Concord in 1934, and by that time he had come a long way in the music world, and his music, clearly identifiable, was the talk of New York. Where else does one go for success? He had come out of Cleveland's Claremont Tent, the Music Box Cafe and Lake Shore Drive Inn with flying colors, and gone on to Chicago's

Granada, where he was literally discovered by chewing-gum tycoon Philip K. Wrigley, who heard his broadcast one evening and thought that he should be heard coast-to-coast on a national scale.

Wrigley's call early one morning awakened Guy, who told me he had just about gotten to bed at four or five o'clock. Wrigley invited him down to his office for a contract talk. "I didn't mind being awakened at all," Guy smiled. He was signed to a contract, and the rest is history. When Guy walked into the Wrigley Building that morning, workers were pointing him out to one another: "There's Guy Lombardo who was making all that beautiful music last night on the radio." And the word went around and around. Guy had asked the Granada owner to install a radio wire, and the owner, very reluctantly, did so, assuring not only his success, but Guy's as well. The big difference was that Wrigley wanted him coast-to-coast, and that is how Guy's velvety tones were initially introduced to America. So, Phil Wrigley was the big helping hand.

Nightclub owners in those days despised radio hookups under the impression they would render a knockout punch to their place of business, and that people would stay away and hear the music at home instead. This belief proved entirely opposite to the truth: the listeners wanted to hear the band in person, and so they beat a path to the Granada. "Where we were playing for a handful," Guy later told me, "after the installation of that radio wire locally, we were playing to packed audiences each evening. It saved the business, and it saved us."

From that time on, the Lombardos never played to less than full houses wherever they went, and eventually it led to Hollywood, where they made their first movie, "Many Happy Returns," with George Burns and Gracie Allen, with such song hits as "Fare-Thee-Well" and "The Sweetest Music This Side of Heaven." Guy's perception on song selections was uncanny. He picked winners, and soon he was introducing song hits almost nightly. America listened eagerly, and lovingly.

Where has this type of romantic music gone? It has made way, unfortunately, for the beat, the loud beat. Guy observed not long before his death, that "three or four guys beat the hell out of their drums and electric guitars, and palm it off on the public in that fashion, and the meaningful lyrics have disappeared with the music."

Will the old days of Tin Pan Alley be resurrected? Maybe, who knows? One thing that can be said of the Lombardo era: Most Americans can still sing the words and music of the songs preferred, unlike today when all a listener gets is that hard-rock, deafening beat, and you can hear it almost any day from cars racing along city streets, with windows down and all instruments blasting. To this writer it is unsavory, and we pray for deliverance.

Guy's selections on recordings were, for the most part, nearly perfect. There were, however, some songs I wish he had recorded, and one was the aforementioned "The Girl With the Dreamy Eyes." There were others, most of which I believe Guy himself introduced: "I Sailed Away to Treasure Island," "Is It True What They Say About Dixie?" "The Cute Little Hat Check Girl," George Gershwin's "Mine," still one of his best, and largely undiscovered, "Sing an Old Fashioned Song to a Young, Sophisticated Lady," "Thirty Days Has September," "Lies That Made Me Happy, Lies That Made Me Blue," and a few more, "On the Outside Looking In," and "Nice Work If You Can Get It, and You Can Get It If You Try," still another Gershwin ear-caresser.

In my early days, I would stay up to catch the Royal Canadians in their broadcasts from the Empire Room of the Palmer House in Chicago, circa 1935 - 1936, and I would have to call that period, 1932 through 1938, the most bountiful Lombardo Years, with all the hundreds of song hits, and Tin Pan Alley working overtime to keep up with the demand. Most of the composers and lyricists were true professionals, many of them college graduates, and not dropouts and guitar-strummers with little knowledge of line-meters and composition. Maybe some day the Twenties and Thirties will return in a nice, new package of songs with proper and popular arrangements, and metered verse. At the rate we're going, it seems a long way off, with no Lombardos in sight, or Irving Berlins, or Irving Caesars, or Walter Donaldsons, or Jerome Kerns, or Harry Warrens.

Just the other day I pulled from my files a sheet listing the Lombardo Orchestra room arrangements on tour of the United States. It is noteworthy only in the fact that it reveals names of some prominence, like Miss Tonia Bern Campbell (widow of the noted speedboat champion, Sir Donald Campbell), and Tony Cointreau, scion of the famous French liqueur family. Both were vocalists in the early Seventies shortly before Guy's death in 1977, and they were extremely good. Guy would have it no other way, and besides, he and Sir Donald were both speedboat champs. Guy had the best musicians money could buy when it became necessary to make changes as the original members began to drop out, and he never sacrificed tone for totality in his band. Each musician had to be the best in his field to pass Guy's scrutiny. His musicians were tops in their trade, and maybe somewhat spoiled with all the attention lavished upon them, as one onlooker once stated.

The sweet music Guy produced never suffered when changes were made; and to be truthful, it may have been enhanced over the years as a fuller tone emerged, sweeter than sweet. Whoever had this concept of sweet and simple music, and it must have been Guy and Carmen and Lebert in the early days, it hit the nail on the head - just what the public demanded, and Guy had it for the millions of listeners.

Over the many years, I had written hundreds of articles on Guy and his band, and the story was always exciting, from the very way the band started, to the ultimate success and fame it achieved: a neighborhood band up there in London, Ontario, to the bright lights of Broadway and Hollywood. However well I knew Lombardo, only once did I request a recording of one of his numbers, that being Irving Berlin's famed "Easter Parade," and Guy finally did make the recording. I think he had it in mind, anyway. The lilting words and music made it a must for the archives of American music, and Guy always played it at Easter time. Berlin, too, was a Lombardo admirer who frequented the Grill Room of the Roosevelt on Royal Canadian evenings. It was exciting for him to hear his songs played in the Lombardo manner, with Carmen doing the vocals on such as "Easter Parade."

Guy was fastidious in dress and appearance. Being the son of a tailor, he knew how to wear his tux, and he made a lasting impression that way. His bandsmen, too, looked "immaculate always," as Barbara once put it. As his manager, Saul Richman, once told me: "Guy was always one of the ten best-dressed men in the world in Fashion Institute of America, and this didn't hurt his music any with all the female fans." He was, as Barbara said, an "immaculate" dresser.

One night long ago, Guy told me exactly how his band made it to the top. "It was in Cleveland," Guy said, "and we were not doing well at all. We had no bookings, and we had no money. Some of the boys complained and thought we should go home to London, Ontario. Others thought we should stick it out and wait for the break that would do it. We were rehearsing all the time, and after one session, I suggested we take a vote on the issue that night.

"The vote ended, I think, in a deadlock, 4 - 4. One bandsman had not voted, being out for the evening on a date. We said we would sit around waiting for him to show up and break the tie vote. The bandsman was 'Apples' Davies. When he showed up, we told him what we had done, and how the vote had ended in a tie. He replied, 'That's easy for me. I vote to remain here in Cleveland and take a chance. I have just met the most beautiful girl in the world, and I am not leaving her now." His vote, said Guy, "broke the tie and we stayed in Cleveland." Not long after, the Lombardos secured a booking at The Claremont Inn, and they were on their way.

In Cleveland, they had added another member who was going to have some input in the musical direction the Royal Canadians took. He was saxaphonist Larry Owen, also a member of the Lombardo Trio, and an arranger without peer. Much of the Lombardo sound belongs to the arrangements by the same Larry Owen, most of them, in fact, for Larry joined the band at the very outset, and became an invaluable member.

His wife, Marie, told us during a visit to their home in New York City one day, that she was "forever amazed" with Larry. "He will lock himself in his study for hours at a time, and come out with a cluster of arrangements that just sound so beautiful when Guy plays them."

His addition helped put the Lombardos in the big time, his presence and that of impresario Louis Bleet, who suggested in Cleveland the medley-type of presentation, playing four or five songs that otherwise would not make the program. "Run through them once," Guy instructed his men, "then fade into another song." It worked, and requests began to be played in the much shorter version. It became known in time as "Your Lombardo Medley."

So, Cleveland did leave its mark, and then Chicago, his next stopping point. Guy played there at the Granada Cafe, across the street from a cemetery, "and we drew only spooks for a few weeks," Guy mentioned. Guy suggested to the owner that a radio wire be installed, as in Cleveland. When the owner objected, Guy threatened to move the band back to Cleveland. Consent was finally given, and a radio wire installed, and with it came the crowds, as in Cleveland. One of the listeners that first night was Phillip K. Wrigley, the famous chewing gum manufacturer. "He called me the next morning at 8," Guy told me, "and asked whether I could come down to his office right away for a conference. I said 'sure, right on, Mr. Wrigley.' Hell, I didn't mind being awakened at 8 o'clock after about two hours of sleep. So, I went to the Wrigley Building, and as I walked in, I heard some of the office girls saying, 'Oh, there's Mr. Lombardo now. Wow, what a band.' I knew the radio wire had been a success from that moment, and then I found that Mr. Wrigley had been listening in, too. The coast-to-coast radio offer was easy to sign," Guy said laughing. "From that time on, we were made. Chicago, too, was an interesting, if not dangerous, place to play. One night we saw a couple of guys gunned down right while the band was playing. The piano players ducked for cover under their pianos, and the musicians scattered at the sound of gunfire. An exciting place, that Chicago," Guy remembered.

Then came the big offer to go to New York. "I had always said that we weren't made until we could make it in New York," said Guy, "and soon, we were on our way. I picked the Roosevelt out of three choices we had, and we were the band promoting the new advertising concept of MCA (Music Corporation of America), which guaranteed all member bands fees and bookings, which had been a big headache. We loved New York, and we had great success there, unbelievable success."

Today, the original band is all gone, and with it the four famous brothers, Guy, Carmen, Lebert and Victor. Carmen was the first to die, the composer of such hits as "Little Coquette," "Boo-Hoo," "Snuggled On Your Shoulder," "Return to Me," "Power Your Face With Sunshine," "A Sailboat in the Moonlight," "The Goose Hangs High," "Footloose and Fancy-Free," and many more. Guy died on the operating table in Houston while the Royal Canadians were performing in Manchester. Lebert, the celebrated trumpeter, died in Florida in mid-1993, and Victor, the youngest brother, succumbed in January, 1994, also in Florida, where the orchestra had gone in recent years. Only Rose-Marie Lombardo, a vocalist with the band in the mid-Forties, survives, of the Royal Canadians, plus Kenny Gardner, the famed vocalist who married Guy's sister Elaine. "They are all gone," Kenny told me forlornly from his home on

As the years rolled on, there were changes in the roster. Many members, some with nearly 50 years in the orchestra, retired to an easier life, with no traveling around the country and elsewhere. The original pianists were Fred Kreitzer and Hugo D'Ippolito; Buddy Brennan, Francis Vigneau and Bruce Steeg came later. They were all fantastic.

Francis Henry was the original guitarist in the old London days, and he gave the music world the memorable "Little Girl." He died rather young. Bill Flanagan joined the Lombardos later, as did Don Rodney and Ty Lemley (both personal friends). Joe Cipriano became a member of the sax section, and upon Carmen Lombardo's death, he inherited that famous sax, which he guards zealously. There were other changes in the brass section, and on drums, Bill Lombardo, Guy's nephew, took over for George Gowans.

Bruce Steeg played the piano with a lot of bounce and verve, and he kept up the tradition of great pianists in the Lombardo organization. I had a note from Bruce many years ago:

"Dear Bob:

"I received your envelope full of goodies during our rehearsal yesterday for our New Year's Eve Show. I kept the pictures of myself and gave the others to those who had been photographed; we all thank you for your thoughtfulness.

"I remember that we had spoken about Mrs. Hilliard going to the hospital. I sincerely hope that her operation was a complete success and that she has completely recovered by this time.

"Mrs. Steeg and I look forward to seeing both of you again during our next visit to Manchester. We both hope that you and Mrs. Hilliard will have a very happy and healthy New Year.

"Best Regards,

Bruce Steeg"

I had another nice note from Ty Lemley, and two or three from Don Rodney, whose brother, Carmen Ragonese, was quite a football player at the University of New Hampshire, later a member of the Baltimore Colts, and still later, alumni director at UNH. Both of these fellows were fantastic guitarists and not the kind who just strum with little knowledge of music. They knew their music, as did all of Guy's musicians, and Ty's rendition of "Maria Elena" is a veritable classic. Ty's note:

> "Hi Bob,
> Just a short note to say thanks for a terrific writeup in your newspaper, and I really enjoyed our get-together at your home.
> "Joe (Cipriano) really appreciated the article very much. He said that's the best newspaper writeup he ever had. Joe mentioned to me that he would be in touch with you soon.
> "As you can see by this stationary, Bob, we're here in Newburgh, N.Y. We'll be playing the U.S. Military Academy. Should be real nice. Well, Bob, have to run. Take care and let's keep in touch.
> "Sincerely, Ty Lemley."

Ty's letter was postmarked December, 1976. Less than a year later, he and the rest of the Royal Canadians had lost their leader.

There's a letter, too, from my old friend, Larry Owen, whose delightful orchestrations helped put the Royal Canadians in the world spotlight,

> "Dear Bob:
> "Thanks you for the photos, they're very good. Barbara and yourself look great, and I hope you are both in the best of health.
> "I haven't been traveling with the band since March, because there is too much to do in the office. Marie and I are looking forward to my first vacation in 20 years. We are going to Europe for three weeks.
> "Please tell Paul Marston (a photographer) that I will have Guy autograph the small photos when I see him Sunday.
> "Regards, Larry."

That letter was dated June 30, 1972. A few months later, Barbara was in the hospital with pneumonia, later diagnosed as lung cancer, from which she succumbed on Sept. 30, 1976, at Phillips House, Massachusetts General Hospital, on a very sad day.

Saul Richman, Guy's business manager for about 25 years, invited me to write a chapter for the book he was preparing on the Lombardo years. I was in New York to check on a soprano who had been granted a tryout by the Metropolitan Opera, and I wanted to pay my respects to Saul, and the nice job he was doing for the Lombardo Band. Saul told me about his book, and invited me to do a chapter for him. "Bob," he said, "there's no one in this country who knows more about the Lombardo Band than you. Could you spin off a few yarns for me?" I told him I would be delighted to do that, and asked how soon he needed the copy. "I'm in no rush, Bob," he answered, "but I will need it by Wednesday."

When I returned to Manchester, I dashed off a few pages and mailed them to Richman. He wrote back, asking what he could do for me. It was my pleasure, I replied. It's for Guy, a great guy; and too, it was for Saul, a hard-working press agent. Saul never lived to see the finished product. He died shortly before its publication; and I know how much the book meant to him.

The book "Guy" was designed by Scarlett Creech, and she worked diligently to bring it to print. Much of the credit belongs to Scarlett.

The Lombardo tradition exists to this day, both in story form, at the New Year's Time in Times Square, and in the form of a touring orchestra that lends the Lombardo Tone for an evening, minus the vocals of Carmen, Lebert and the others, and minus, too, Guy's smooth stick-handling up front, or should that be baton downbeats? He was the smoothest bandleader.

Irving Caesar—and
"Tea for Two"

While we sat on the tour bus waiting for the passengers to disembark at our hotel in China near the tea-fields, I started to hum a tune that appeared to be appropriate to the occasion, "Tea for Two."

One of the Chinese tour directors overheard the song and came up to me with a broad smile on her face.

"I love that song," she said. "What is the name of it?"

I told her it was a fairly old American song from the musical, "No, No Nanette" that was a hit on the Broadway stage, and that it was by this time a standard in the song market in the United States.

"Could you write the words for me?" she asked.

I told her I had a few hours before lunch, and that I would try to remember the lines as best I could. She seemed pleased and a little excited at the prospects of learning the lyrics. So, I set to the task immediately upon entering our cottage. Now let's see, how does the verse start? Isn't it, "Picture you upon my knee, just tea for two and two for tea. Me for you and you for me, my dear." Or something like that.

Anyway, I plodded on, struggling with the lines made famous by lyricist Irving Caesar so long ago, back in the early Twenties, to the lilting music of Vincent Youmans. It was rather a happy task at that, for that song will never grow old as long as there is a piano and dancing feet. How many of the world's renowned tap-dancers performed to its syncopated beat? Probably thousands upon thousands.

I finished my task in an hour or so at my little table in far-off China, joined Bobby Jr. for lunch, and then stepped outside to find the little girl who made the request. I quickly found her and handed her the lyrics by Irving Caesar that she so desired. She was in seventh heaven as she read them over and over again.

"What a beauiful song," she declared in her labored English. She repeated the lines at the end: "Day will break, and you'll awake, and start to bake a sugar cake, For me to take for all the boys to see. Oh, we will raise a family, a boy for you, a girl for me. Can't you see how happy we will be."

I was somewhat afraid for the girl's personal safety if the American song was discovered in her possession, so I personally gave it a spanking new title (with your permission, Irving), "The China Song." Maybe someday it will come to pass with that subtitle. Well, it made one little girl happy, and when I returned home to the United States, I dropped my friend Caesar a note telling him what I had done to save the day in China. I think Irving must have enjoyed the story, but I never heard from him. There must have been tacit approval.

Irving Caesar and I first met in the famous Brill Building on Broadway in New York, the traditional site of Tin Pan Alley, and in the days of the birth of "Tea for Two" in the mid-Twenties, it must have been bulging with songwriters and musicians. It was the source of thousands upon thousands of American show tunes, and others. They were cranked out literally in staggering figures, and most were professional in every way. Many were ballads that told a story in short terms, like "Annie Doesn't Live Here Anymore," to mention just one.

The same care and class in line-meter is absent today, and the sophisticated lines themselves explaining the story, but then, who is to deny progress? It advances upon us whether good or bad, and in this case, the public seems to be somewhat the loser. Very few of the current melodies will make it very far into the 21st Century, and happily so. The artists who gave us all the great songs that became standards in the trade, have all but disappeared: Irving Berlin, Jerome Kern, Harry Warren, Walter Donaldson, Carmen Lombardo, the Gershwins, Jimmy McHugh and so many others.

Will the musical prowess of these Titans of Song ever return? Who can tell? Maybe the insatiable appetite of the Americans for solid music and catchy tunes will undergo a renaissance of sort in this next century, and we hope it does, for someone is missing out, and that is the eternal Guy and his Gal and a romantic interlude.

To return to Irving Caesar, I only wish we had a photo of Irving and I singing a duet (Saul Richman, business manager of Guy Lombardo's Royal Canadians years ago, termed it the world's worst duet, and he probably was right). The duet was of Irving's song hit of the mid-Thirties, "Is It True What They Say About Dixie," and I will have to say we gave it everything. The only audience we had was my wife, Barbara, and our little 8-year-old granddaughter, Jennifer, now an attorney in Boston, and I hardly would say that they appreciated our work, and the subtlety of our very delivery, arms outstretched, please, but they applauded when we concluded, and probably for that very reason.

One of my favorite songs was that number: "Is it true what they say about Dixie? Does the sun really shine all the time? Do the sweet magnolias blossom on everybody's door? Do folks keep eating possum 'till they can eat no more? Is it true what they say about Swanee? Is a dream by that street so sublime? Do they laugh, do they love, like they say in every song? If it's true, that's where I belong."

Short and sweet, readers; that's what we want.

We pored over many of Irving's masterpieces, and it was a real fun day. He had composed the words to so many song hits of the period, and it was delightful as he recounted them for us musically, including that all-time American favorite, "Tea for Two," and others including "Mammy" and "Is It True What They Say About Dixie," and "I Want To Be Happy," which he also sang with me. I don't know when I had a happier afternoon.

Irving also gave Jennifer a copy of a song he had written especially for the schoolchildren of New York City: "Only a Goof Plays on the Roof" and Jennifer still has it in her collection somewhere, and by this time only her mother would know where. I think Irving autographed it for Jennifer.

When I requested the interview to run with my review on the revival of the big hit of 1924, "No, No, Nanette," I didn't realize the trouble I was causing Irving. Every afternoon, it seems, his chauffeur would drive him to Aqueduct or Belmont for a bout with the ponies, and when he had to cancel his program in mid-afternoon, it must have caused some pain. But he was delivered to the Brill Building promptly at the appointed hour, and it was probably just as well, he said, for the day had not been a total success at the track, and he needed a break.

We talked of many things that day, and one of them was a question that I needed him to answer for me: How long did it take Caesar and Youmans to compose their masterpiece "Tea for Two?"

"Well," said Irving, "it was like this. I had gone home in the early afternoon to catch some sleep. We were having a little party that night with our pal Gertrude Lawrence, and I knew we would be up late. So, I went to bed when I got home, and I had fallen asleep when suddenly I felt someone tugging at my feet, imploring me to wake up. It was Youmans, and I told him to go away; I wanted to be fresh for the party. He said, 'No, no, Caese, you've got to wake up. I just got an idea for a song, and I need some dummy lyrics to see how it sounds.'

"By this time, I am fully awake so I can't get back to sleep again. 'Whadda ya want, Yeomans?'

"'Just some dummy lines,' he pleaded. So, I got up and started toying with some crazy lines: 'Tea for two and two for tea, just me for you, and you for me...' And Yeomans shouted, 'Just what I want, keep going, Caese. It's perfect for the music.'

"He went over to the keyboard, and started tinkling the keys. Ta-ta-ta, and ta-ta-ta. It sounded beautiful. Even Yeomans was singing my crazy lyrics. And we kept at it, Vincent pounding out the music, and I giving him the dummy lines he wanted. Those lines never changed. They weren't dummy lines for long. They became the song."

That was the story of one of the most celebrated popular songs of all time, a song heard often even in today's maelstrom of music; certainly heard as tap-dance accompaniment. And yes, even in China.

Caesar was one of the two best lyricists I have ever known, the other being the inimitable Sammy Cahn, who died several years ago. Those fellows could make a line sing, all by itself.

Irving asked how we liked the show, "No, No, Nanette," and we told him it was fantastic, and all because of those great songs that he helped put together, one when he was half asleep that became one of the all-time greats.

It pleased Irving to know that he had a fan club, and that he didn't mind missing half of the card that day at the race track.

"You have a beautiful state up there in New Hampshire," he told us. "I think I will come up there for another visit," he laughed.

Well, we interjected, what song will you bring up there when you come.

"Don't you have a gorgeous lake up there, Winnipesaukee or something?"

We assured him we did.

"Well," he replied, "how about 'Winnie From Winnipesaukee?'"

Hey, Irving, that connects like "Tea for Two, and two for tea."

We all laughed as we bid the Elder Statesman of Song adieu that sunshiny day in the early Seventies. It was a day of days.

Composers and lyricists have always fascinated me, but none more so than Irving Caesar. He sent me a letter one day, and you could hear his laughter as he wrote, "Render unto Caesar the things that are Caesar's."

He was a dear soul, and what would America be like today were it not for his monumental contributions to music and to the arts, and also all the other super geniuses? It would be a pretty barren place, to be sure.

Bob Hill...
Ambassador

BOB HILL served as ambassador to Spain.

In the late summer of 1971, we made a change in our vacation plans.

Originally, we had planned a two-week tour of the Scandinavian countries. Leon Anderson, a hard-hitting, tell-it-as-it-is columnist with the *Concord Monitor*, suggested a trip to Madrid and an opportunity to speak with the United States Ambassador to Spain, Robert C. Hill, a nice fellow from Littleton, N.H.

Anderson had just completed a journey to Madrid and had conversations with the ambassador about the likelihood of his running for governor of New Hampshire.

Leon said there was a good chance of that happening. "Why don't you spin over there and have a talk with him, Bob."

I thought the suggestion held merit, so I brought it to *The Union Leader*'s publisher, William Loeb.

"I think it is a splendid idea," Loeb said, and so, with Mrs. Hilliard's indulgence, we made a change in our travel plans.

Instead of traveling to Scandinavia, we re-directed our plans to Madrid, with a side trip thrown in to North Africa, to Morocco and Tangiers and the mysterious Casbah. It sounded exciting, and it was. Our plane was hit by lightning en route to Tangiers, and while we held hands and prayed, our four-engine craft made it through the storm over south-central Spain. It was a close call. The lightning bolt hit our craft and everything seemed to turn blue. The resolute pilot just kept going as if nothing had happened, and we circled over the Pillars of Hercules and landed forthwith, no problem.

We lost ourselves in the maze of streets that is Tangiers, toured through the Casbah, noting the mansion Doris Duke built on its outskirts and wondering if on that very day Doris was at home. Our guide told us not to stray from the party in there or it might be "difficult to find you again," so we stayed together and shopped its hole-in-the-wall stores for "goodies," as Barbara described them.

It was a most pleasant interlude, and Barbara bought a colorful native blanket. Then we departed a little after 5 in the afternoon for our home port of Madrid, and that, too, was a stormy, bumpy ride. We landed about 9 or 9:30, and upon arriving at our hotel, there were several messages for me, "from the ambassador" the Spanish hotel operator said excitedly.

Bob wanted to know where the hell we were, and when I told him we had taken a short jaunt to Tangiers, he laughed. "So, that is where you went," he said. "We hardly imagined that."

We made a date for the next morning about 11 at his embassy office, and it was a great deal of fun talking with Bob, a former football player at Dartmouth College, and we made ourselves at ease in his luxurious office.

"The first thing I must tell you, Bob," he began, "is to give you this package from Mrs. Hill." He opened a desk drawer and pulled from its files a large manila envelope. He handed it to me, with Mrs. Hill's warm greetings.

"Open it," Bob said, and I did, while Mrs. Hilliard looked on. It was one of my old columns from several years before, in which I had written about young Graham Hill, their son and a race car driver in, I believe, South America. He also had played sports in prep school, and like his father, he liked winning.

I was somewhat astounded to see my column being shown in Madrid, and I guess I was lost for something to say, and all I could utter was, "Gosh, imagine that." I told Bob to thank Mrs. Hill for her thoughtfulness in making it available to me. It brought some laughter from Bob and Barbara.

We launched into our interview, and Bob told me that he was indeed "interested" in running for the governorship, but that he hadn't fully made up his mind at that time and would have more to say later.

Because of his ability as a football player (prior to a leg injury when hit by Johnny Grigas of Holy Cross in a freshman encounter), and my status as a sports editor, I used the story as a "sports desk" piece, and Mr. Loeb was quite happy with the article, or so he indicated. Later, he labeled Bob Hill as a person "born with a silver spoon in his mouth," and not likely to make a good governor.

Bob Hill never did run for that office if I remember correctly, although I personally thought he would have made a fine leader, with his fine training in college and as an ambassador to various other posts around the globe.

During the interview, Bob made available to me a photo of him taken at one of the nearby farms bull-fighting in practice. In the photo, Bob does not appear unduly nervous and is shown flagging the animal to the side before making a thrust, as a cameraman and aides look on from nearby. Bob seemed to be enjoying the workout. It was a far cry from Dartmouth football, to be sure.

We talked for an hour or so, and Bob answered some questions from Mrs. Hilliard relative to shopping some of Madrid's nice shops, and Bob offered the services of his secretary, but Barbara graciously declined. "I am only interested in purchasing some pearls," she said, "otherwise, I might pick you up on your offer."

She ran into a minor roadblock, however, in making the choice, and a nearby shopper offered her services in making the clerk understand what she had in mind. The pearls are beautiful, and they are now worn by my daughter-in-law with a lot of pride. They could dress up a night at the opera, and I think Shirley has worn them there, too.

Bob bid us goodbye, and told us to enjoy our shopping expedition, and that he and Mrs. Hill would expect us that evening at their home for a visit and cocktails.

At our hotel, the word had spread (from the switchboard operator, I suspect) that the United States Embassy was sending an attaché to pick us up, and the lobby was crowded with Americans anxious to catch a glimpse of the ambassador.

Instead, they had a peek at his first secretary, Arthur V. Diggle, who later visited us at our home in Manchester with a Spanish camera crew covering the famous first-in-the-nation New Hampshire Presidential Primary. It was fun seeing Arthur again, and many times since, I've thought of him, wondering where his adventures have taken him to date.

Robert C. Hill was a most able public servant, employed in many important diplomatic posts, including Spain, before his death several years ago. He arranged for President Nixon's trip to Spain, which was called a great success, and he also arranged for the visit to the United States of Their Royal Highnesses, Prince Juan Carlos and Princess Sophia, in 1971, an overwhelming success, Hill later recounted, because of the "youthful vitality of the Prince and the Princess, their wide-ranging interests and their ability to communicate with people in all segments of society."

While showing us their beautiful home in Madrid, Mrs. Hill told Barbara that that was where Mrs. Jacqueline Kennedy, widow of the slain American president, hid out after his death to escape the media attention. She showed us Jackie's bedroom, and said while the whole world was wondering where she could possibly be, "It was here in our home." She sympathized with Jackie's terrible ordeal in those days.

Mrs. Hill, a top tennis player, played regularly when she was afforded the chance. A forebearer was the founder of Bowdoin College in Maine, by the way, and her family was distinguished by its service in the public domain. Born Cecelia Gordon Bowdoin, she was reared in Paris of a Baltimore family whose members included James Bowdoin, who served as the U.S. minister to Spain from 1804-1814; Louis McLane, who was minister to France and U.S. Secretary of State, a governor of the state of Massachusetts and the founder of Bowdoin College.

Ambassador Hill received many high-ranking decorations and awards during his brilliant career, one of them a doctor of laws degree from his own Dartmouth College, as well as from other colleges and universities.

Bob Hill loved sports, and I believe the rugged action on the field of play often sustained him in later life as he tackled tough problems of one kind or another. He seemed always to ride above them, and come out smiling. It was infectious, too, among his staff and friends. The last time I saw Bob was at *The Union Leader's* big annual baseball dinner, which he followed avidly. He signed as many autographs as some of the great stars of the national pastime who were there that night.

*Andrew Lloyd Webber:
Greatest
of the Great*

TRIBUTE TO ANDREW LLOYD WEB-
BER -- Michael Crawford, right, the original Broadway "Phantom of the Opera,"
shakes hands with Andrew Lloyd Webber
during the curtain call of the opening performance of "The Music of Andrew Lloyd
Webber" at Radio City Music Hall in New
York.
(AP File Photo)

My first introduction to Andrew Lloyd Webber was at St. Thomas Episcopal Church in the heart of New York City, where the famed composer was unveiling his first attempt at classical music, a Requiem, inspired in part by the horrible events in Northern Ireland and by the death of his beloved father.

As I mentioned in my review of the world premiere performance of the work, on Sunday evening, Feb. 24, 1985, it is "moving and touchingly beautiful, especially in the Hosanna, with Sarah Brightman's pretty soprano, and it makes ample use of the choir, in this case, the voices of the Winchester Cathedral Choir, flown here from England, especially for this inaugural performance, and the home-based choir of St. Thomas Church, where the program was presented.

"It also featured the presence of tenor Placido Domingo of the Metropolitan Opera Company and his ringing notes enhanced the Requiem and Kyrie and the Dies Irae that followed."

At the end of the program, which was roundly received by a capacity audience, the principals and the choirs seemed in no hurry to depart the church, and I wondered why. Someone from the technical staff told me: "In certain passages, they picked up a lot of interference from the subway system, and they will have to record that particular portion once again." So that was the reason they were not departing the church earlier. It had to be done again, in certain parts.

This afforded me a chance to congratulate Webber on his fine output and some mighty fine passages. At times, the music was yearning in quality, and it had a distinct appeal. That can be directly attributed to Webber's unique talent, and many times I've wondered whether Irving Berlin or George Gershwin or Jerome Kerns might have been able to bridge the gap between popular and classical, between nice little ditties and the more majestic and serious music, the difference between operetta and grand opera, for example. They had the talent, all of them, but the river between them is wide.

I thanked Andrew Lloyd Webber for an unforgettable evening, and I told him now that he was started on the course, it might not be long before he was ready to tackle opera of the world class.

He shook his head and sort of chuckled. "Well, you know, Mr. Hilliard, I am sure," he said, "that the difference is great, and with all the work I have lined up, it probably would be some time."

Verdi probably comes closest to Webber, for catchy arias were rampant in his inventive mind, as they are in the present-day composer, and they all were received in wild acclaim by audiences. That will provide for thought for many moons, just wondering whether popular music can yet produce another Verdi or Puccini.

The opera I suggested Webber to work on was from the ancient days of England, and it centered on an astonishing character named Boadicea, Queen of the Iceni in what is now Norfolk and Suffolk, and it is said that she was responsible for the deaths of about 50,000 Roman soldiers, some of them personally by her own hand.

She had bright red hair streaming down her back, and the Romans were terrified of her. She led most of the charges personally. A wild woman, she had some pretty wild followers, too. They were the bane of the Roman opposition. She killed herself by poison in a fit of despair when the Romans destroyed her host of 200,000 men, which would have caused anyone to blanch at that stupendous defeat.

I suggested that Webber might somehow make a love story out of it with that tremendous loss, and what was the good Queen to do? I gave him the book on Boadicea, and I know he is still studying its possibilities. After all, Andrew, there is a statue to her on the Thames embankment in London, a short distance from the Towers of London, and she could easily become the Queen of the Female World today, for they would like to set up an all-time champion.

Webber has written so many outstanding musical scores that it is actually difficult to say which is the most popular. I favor "Evita" myself, since there is action from beginning to end and gorgeous musical numbers, including "Don't Cry for Me Argentina," with its beseeching lament. I know Webber will create an opera before his time runs out, and wouldn't it be positively super to have him direct it as well?

The last note I had from Webber was just a few years ago when he was preparing to put "Sunset Boulevard" in motion; that may be one of the most appealing yet.

I personally believe that Webber today is the all-time champion of the world of musicals, and as the composer of all those hits, he has no peers, dead or alive. His "Cats" was inventive, and "Phantom" was just soothing and powerful. I believe he feels he cannot do grand opera, but I beg to differ. I am sure he can, and I hope he accepts the challenge before his intense driving power wears off.

Anyway, most of his works are half there already. The spoken word is all but gone now in favor of the sung word, and this is a definite thrust in favor of the emergence of opera in the theatre today. It is more pleasing to the ear, the sung note, and it is showing up more and more, thanks to Webber's leadership.

Swing into Spring: Of Gators and Grounders

DUGOUT INTERVIEW -- Bob Hilliard
interviews a Toronto Blue Jays coach
prior to an exhibition game with the
Red Sox in Florida.

Without a doubt, one of the most enjoyable experiences for a reporter/baseball fan is taking in the spring training camps in Florida and elsewhere as the baseball teams commence their training for each new season.

Writers are always busy with their chores of picking up notes, of developing feature articles and talking with the stars. Time passes swiftly. Then there's the afternoon game story (in some cases an evening game, which requires added attention).

However, when the game is at 1:05 p.m., it's usually over by 4, and after a post-game conference, we're back at the Holiday Inn, or wherever we're staying, by about 5. The game story takes about an hour, and, after we have filed that back home, we're ready for a leisurely dinner and then a repast at pool side with the baseball crowd, players and fans, and that is where you pick up more fodder for columns.

Game story and column material, that's the format on a given day at camp. When we're at the pool in the evening, the sportswriters swap stories, and there are some humorous ones, to be sure. It's a lifestyle that's slower than when the season begins, for sure. Players are relaxed on the whole, and they join in the general conversation, making for a happy occasion.

Recently (in 2000), I went to visit the new Boston Red Sox camp at Fort Myers, Fla., after spending 15 years or so going to the previous camp at Winter Haven. The new one, City of Palms Park, is gorgeous in every way, a beautiful concourse within the park itself and a parade of Royal Palms surrounding the stadium.

The diamond is every bit as good as old and storied Fenway Park itself in Boston, and its red clay is immaculately kept with real grass, clipped and mowed stylishly, making a vivid contrast. The crews in Fort Meyers all want to come up for a peek at historic Fenway. "We've heard so much about it," they say. To a person, they all inquire about Fenway and its famous history.

There I would say, started the Red Sox' long-time practice of dealing its big stars off to other teams, only to see them winning pennants and World Series for others instead of for the Sox. It started with the trade to New York of Babe Ruth, who at that time was something you rarely see

DINNER FOUNDER -- The late Leo E. Cloutier, right, longtime *Union Leader* sportswriter and founder of The Baseball Dinner in Manchester, the largest in America, is pictured with two friends, Bill and Bobbi Arnold of Manchester.

now, a gifted pitcher and a slugger, to boot.

Even then he could hit tremendous home run blasts that would climb a mile into the sky (or so it seemed) before disappearing into the bleacher seats.

I call the practice of trading their big stars, often for players who are past their prime, or rookies doomed with sore arms, or veterans with knee problems, "outfitting the league," for that seems to be what they are doing.

Anyway, just getting to camp each spring is a tonic for the weary winter-bound writers, particularly from the northern climes, and we all anxiously look forward to the change. After a day's toil, and we use the word with apologies, we have dinner, then gather around the pool in beach chairs and tell stories, not all of them off-color and bawdy, but most of them humorous.

Leo E. Cloutier, also of *The Union Leader*, was a master storyteller, as were various members of the Boston press corps, as well as several of the players themselves.

One story I especially liked was spun by Cloutier. He told of a certain player who was a good friend of his, and Leo had a lot of them, from Ty Cobb to Ted Williams, and to the modern era, all of whom enjoyed com-

ing to his mid-winter
Baseball Dinner in
Manchester, N.H., and it
was by far the largest in
the United States when
it fell victim to the times
after his death, and players would demand
exhorbitant fees.

This good friend of
Leo's told him he want-
ed to buy a new Cadillac,
preferably a pink one
with black leather seats.

THE AUTHOR, left, enjoys the sun and a spring training game with son, Bob, Jr.

He had just received a bonus that would have choked a horse, and he was
anxious to loosen up a bit.

"You know any dealers, Leo?" the friend asked.

Leo said he did. "A guy up in New Hampshire..."

"Well let's go up and see him tomorrow morning, the player suggested. I'll
bring some friends with me."

"Sure, I ll give him a call tonight," Leo said. So the meeting was set up,
and the friend showed up right on time, eager to have a look at a new
Caddy.

"Hop in, Leo, the player said, and we'll all go for a spin to Boston to
see how this car handles. The four of them climbed into the flashy car and
headed for Beantown.

"We went down Interstate 93," Leo remembered, tremulously, "and
my friend roared away like Barney Oldfield at Indianapolis. We were hitting close to 90 when we turned off at Route 128 near Boston, and then he
put it into high gear, and I would say we were going about 110 when I
heard a siren behind us.

"The State Police car, lights flashing, drew alongside as my friend
slowed down, finally, and stopped. The trooper walked over, there for a
second or two at the driver s side, and I finally told my friend, 'Put the

window down, he wants to talk.' So my friend did, and it wasn't too pleasant what he heard. 'say, Pal, where ya headed to, a fire?'

"'What's wrong, officer?' my friend inquired. The officer replied, a bit
astonished at his naiveté, 'You were clipping it off better than 100 miles
per hour, and the speed limit is 55 in this section.'

'Well,' answered Leo s ballplayer friend, 'the sign says 128.' The officer
blew his top. That's the route number, stupid.'

"My friend looked a little abashed at that information," said Leo,
adding, "'I'm damned glad, officer, you caught up with him when you did.
He was gonna try Route 495 next.'"

He did get his Caddy later and was supreme sitting behind the wheel.
He often asked Leo to take a spin with him, and Leo politely demurred
each time, saying he had some errands to do.

Leo, by the way, paid his distinguished guests well for making an
appearance at his dinner, held in mid-January each year, usually in the
midst of a wild snowstorm. It got so the major league stars were begging
to attend the dinner, and he had all the major stars from Cobb and Musial
to Mantle and Williams and Sparky Anderson, the last two several times,
and they all attracted huge throngs. I think his record crowd was something like 2,600.

He never had the Bambino, but I did persuade him to invite The
Great God of baseball himself, Tyrus Raymond Cobb. Everyone had neglected Cobb, even the prestigious New York Dinner, and when finally Leo
did manage to invite Cobb, he answered at once that it would be his pleasure, adding that he did not want any stipend himself, but merely a donation to the hospital Cobb had built in Georgia in memory to his parents.

Leo was against inviting football players to the dinner, saying they ate
too much and cut down on the profit, which was for charity. The dinner
was sponsored for many years by *The Union Leader* Fund, and it was a
pronounced success each year.

Around that pool in Florida was where we picked up many a good
story. Also in Florida, the writers learned not to invite players out to dinner. They always managed to outwait the writers on the bill, even with the
money piling up in their bank accounts. The only dodge was to say you

forgot your wallet, but that didn't last for long.

All the humorous stories did not develop around that pool in the lush of the evening. The road trips to other cities for games was worth a story in its own way of execution.

Do you know where the old guys sit in the station wagons? There are three seats: front, middle and rear. Where would you say sit the guys near retire- ment? Front? No. Rear? No. Middle, yes of course. Why middle

POOLSIDE -- Bob Hilliard, left, and Bobbi Arnold of Manchester are all smiles after the Boston Red Sox post a win at spring training camp in Winter Haven, Fla.

seat for the oldies? Well, because young writers occupy the front and rear seats to watch for the Fuzz, the cops, with their sharp vision. The old guys merely look on. Once, going to a road game in West Palm Beach, we saw one of our cars stopped up the highway as we approached. Overhead cir- cled a police helicopter, and on the side of the road stood a police car. The driver had been nailed. Our driver said, "Don't even wave to him or we will have a police escort ourselves."

The rear gunner was supposed to watch for helicopters, and he fell asleep, and when he awoke, the sun was directly in his eyes, we were told when we arrived in West Palm.

So, the old guys stay out of harm's way and just wave to everyone passing by, whether the Fuzz or whomever. Duke Snider kidded us on that one. It cost the driver dearly. The Fuzz showed no mercy; "No Marcy," as our guide in China would say. "No Marcy." He was from Japan.

On long drives to East and West Coast cities, we would talk of many things. Once, someone told of the story where an alligator slid into the bathing pool at Lakeland, only about 12 miles from Winter Haven. The Detroit Tigers were staying there, and bright and early one morning, one of Sparky Anderson's pitchers was out walking his dog near the pool. As the leashed dog got closer to the pool, he started to growl and dropped down to the concrete. He would not budge and became more and more agitated. Finally the Tiger hurler took a closer look at the water and spied a 10-foot alligator close to the surface. He had dropped in from a nearby lake.

I wrote a feature story on that one about a newcomer at the Detroit Tigers training camp who showed up for a tryout with Sparky. His name, I reported, was Ally Gator, and he had heard that these guys get the best of everything, and he wanted a shot at the gold himself. Sparky looked him over and told him to get lost. The security guards took him for a ride, back to the minors again. Your name is just not right, they said. They told him he would have to put on a few more pounds anyway before he made his next assault, and to try the Yankee camp which was across state. The word spread fast among the denizens of the deep that these players lived high on the hog, and good food was very plentiful at Lakeland.

In Florida, you never know. At Winter Haven, the Red Sox had a long gator who lurked near the worksheds behind the clubhouse, in the woods on the shoreline, and I can tell you, we all kept our eyes open passing that spot, for alligators are faster than a horse on a short spurt of 40 or 50 feet, so they say, and I will take their word on that; and they are mean. Don't try to stroke their heads.

Florida is a land of surprises, and sometimes you might even see a promising Williams or Mantle or DiMaggio to be. Ally Gator wasn't quite in their class.

.

Bobby Orr: The Boy Wonder

BOBBY ORR, the great Boston Bruins defensemen, was a wizard on skates, covering the ice in a flash of moves and artistry. (*Union Leader* file Photo)

I remember with a great deal of fondness my introduction to the skating marvel, Robert Gordon Orr, known today to his millions of fans simply as Bobby Orr.

I heard of this winsome kid from Parry Sound, Ontario in news clips from the sports wire, but they were brief accounts at best, and who knew just what he could do on the ice, with hockey stick in hand.

Many years before, I'd heard of another boy wonder, Jesse Livermore, but that was in the financial world as a winning player on the stock exchange. Jesse won and lost and won fortunes with a skillful hand, and he became the darling of a desperate America.

I had come home late from the office one evening and my wife, Barbara, a devoted hockey fan, was all excited about a player she had seen on the television screen that night. It was, she said, an exhibition game and this kid had stolen the show, as well as the puck, repeatedly, and he had dazzled spectators with his wizardry on the blades. His name was Bobby Orr, she said, and she asked whether I'd heard of him.

I said I had heard a little, and I remember asking, "How good is he?"

She said the kid was "better than anything you have ever seen."

Usually Barbara was a little more cautious in her evaluations, but this time she wasn't. "Bobby Orr can do anything on ice," she said. "He is a wonder. I have never seen another like him, and he is only about 14 or 15."

I was impressed, believe me, because I knew Barbara had seen something out of the ordinary. At that tender age, Orr was skating circles around the other players, and he was scoring. He later told me how he did it.

In Parry Sound, where there is plenty of ice around and where the youngsters can skate for several months of the year, the kids played a game of keeping the puck away from one another, not trying to score, but just ragging the puck and keeping possession. There, Orr learned to keep the puck, and it stood him in good stead in his years ahead in the National Hockey League when it came time to kill off a penalty. Orr could hold the puck forever while opponents strained at the leash. He skated circles around them, taunting them with a boyish grin and leading them on a wild goose chase.

I saw him in action one night at Bobby's place of business, the venerable Boston Garden, against the Los Angeles Kings, and the Bruins rolled Orr out to hold the puck and kill off the two-minute infractions. That particular night I was sitting, not in the Press Box, but at rinkside next to the glass, directly in back of the goal.

It was amazing. I saw the movement from an entirely different perspective, how a player might view it. Orr latched onto the puck almost at once and moved behind his own net, where he stopped, looking eyeball-to-eyeball at Mahoney of the Kings, who was directly in front of the net, afraid to make the slightest mistake against Orr.

They stared at each other as the seconds ticked off, and being up close, I thoght I would goad Mahoney into a little action. "Don't stare at him, you dummy," I shouted, "go in there and take the puck away from him. What are you, afraid of him or something?"

Mahoney picked up the taunt and moved on Orr. They circled the net three times. I counted them while the crowd roared with glee. "Attaboy, Mahoney," the fans shouted, "get that puck."

After holding it for a good minute, Orr gave it a flip to the other end as the frantic Kings raced for it to start a long-delayed power play. It was one of the funniest moments I've ever seen during a professional hockey game. I think Orr could have kept the puck for another 10 minutes, all thanks to that boyhood training on the ice of Parry Sound.

Orr was truly a phenomenal stick-handler. He had a way of holding his arm in front of him to ward off an opposing player, and with his amazing speed, who was to get close? He was perfection as I had never seen it on ice. He even took figure-skating lessons in his spare time to dress up his act. His skating was a thing of beauty, and he could actually do more things than Wayne Gretzky. Gretzky was great, too, but more so in the scoring department.

Orr was an overall spectacular artist, who could also score quite efficiently as his stats would attest.

I can honestly say, I've never seen Bobby make a mistake, and I have never seen a player more confident in action than he. A bad knee cut short his career, but he did manage to play for about 10 years. Like Jesse Livermore with stocks, Orr took care of the money end as well, and he is set for life. He, too, was a boy wonder.

Late one afternoon, I saved Orr from getting struck in the head by the Stanley Cup after the Bruins had beaten St. Louis in the finals of a warm May afternoon at the Garden. Orr was holding the cup for photographers after the wild overtime game, and it slipped a bit from his grasp. I was standing next to him, so I reached over and gave him an assist on the play. It was full of champagne, and I am sure that both of us would have been drenched. It didn't matter much, the champagne was being squirted all over the place anyway, and we were all a little soggy that Sunday afternoon.

Just about that time, the dressing room phone rang, and one of the Bruins answered it. After a second or two, he called over to Orr: "Bobby, your mother's on the phone. The room erupted in laughter as Mrs. Orr checked to see how her little Bobby was doing.

I ve seen many great players in hockey, starting with two of the game's greatest, Eddie Shore, also of the Bruins, and Howie Morenz of the Montreal Canadiens. You can also add to that list the names King Clancy of the Maple Leafs and the brothers Conacher, and another brother act, Maurice and Henri Richard of the classy Canadiens, and little Aurel Joliat, the little playmaker of the Habitants in the 1920s and early 30s.

Orr, however, in my opinion stood above all those superstars—in talent, ability, intelligence and simply as a skater. He was fast at diagnosing plays and disrupting an assault wave, at taking a puck away from an opponent, and, while he wasn't in the class of Eddie Shore in dispelling body checks, he could easily upend an unwary opponent. I saw him deliver some beauties over his playing career.

There was nothing Orr couldn't do in a hockey sense, either in skating or in puck-handling.

One evening at the Garden, I think the same night he totally confused Mahoney on that stall, he was skating around in the pre-game practice, going like the wind behind his own net, when a fan seated about 15 rows from the ice, shouted: "Hi, Bobby." Orr looked up and saw a friend of his. In one lightning-quick motion, he flipped the puck over the glass and directly into his friend's lap. A friend sitting beside me who saw it all, stuttered in amazement, "Di, di, di, did you see that? Ri, ri, ri, ri, right in the guy's la, la, lap? Ho, ho, ho, holy mackerel."

I told coach Don Cherry about it later in the dressing room, and Cherry just laughed.

"That guy never ceases to amaze me," Cherry said. "A few nights ago, I saw him taking his warmup shots, you know, in rapid-fire, one after another, about 20 of them, and one got stuck in his skate. Without stopping, he reached around between his legs and knocked it right into the net and kept up firing. I had to laugh when I saw him do it. That guy is not real."

Cherry, incidentally, was in attendance when we had the dedication of Barbara's cross atop the steeple of St. Paul Episcopal Church in Concord, N.H., across from the State Capitol. Barbara had died the year before on Sept. 30, 1976, and someone had suggested the gift as a most appropriate one since we were married at St. Paul in 1937. I invited Cherry to the event several months before, unaware of when the cross might be made in Boston.

It was finished in early spring, and the dedication was set for May, on a Sunday. It happened to be the Sunday after the Saturday night Stanley Cup showdown between the Bruins and Montreal Canadiens at Boston Garden. Montreal edged the Bruins in that finale, and Cherry, although somewhat exhausted and a bit subdued, still made it to the dedication rites. He was besieged by churchgoers when he strode into St. Paul a few minutes before the ceremonies.

"Hey," one friend remarked to my brother-in-law, Mort Tuttle, "Bob's son looks like Don Cherry." Mort was quick to respond: "That is Don Cherry, you fool, Bob's son is sitting on the other side of him."

Everybody, it seemed, had a word with Don that day, and he was treated like a king, which may have lessened the load a bit.

For all of Bobby Orr's attributes, Foster Hewitt of Toronto still

claimed Eddie Shore the greatest ever, and Foster was and still is considered the ultimate authority on the sport of ice hockey. I was a little astonished when he told me that in an interview at Boston's Copley Plaza Hotel.

"Orr, for all his talents, has played only about six seasons, and a lot
could happen before he retires," Hewitt said at the time. "Shore played a
lifetime and proved it every inch of the way."

That is a valid enough reason, I suppose, although I would have to
rate Bobby Orr No. 1, with the Rocket Richard second and Gordie Howe
third. Theirs' was not a watered-down version of the NHL, although I
would hasten to place Gretzky in the top five. He knew how to find the
net.

In that championship game between the Bruins and St. Louis, it was
sudden-death overtime, and the Bruins were pressing to wrap it up early.
There was a break and a lot of white jerseys flying around the Blues goal,
when suddenly the red light flashed on, and I could see Orr diving headlong toward the ice, and the crowd roaring.

"Who got it?" I asked Ray Valliere, who was sitting beside me and
lending me a hand.

"Who else, but!" he hollered, pointing toward his boy Orr, being
pummeled by his teammates in a mad scene. It was one of the most colorful moments I've ever witnessed at a sporting event, that and Carlton
Fisk's dramatic 12th-inning home run in Game 6 of the 1975 World
Series. They stand out, and for good reasons. They were Boston wins.

That was a memorable windup, of course, but there was the finale in
the Stanley Cup series with the Rangers in New York that was stunning,
and made decisive by Bobby Orr's picture-card goal that cemented the
victory. As I mentioned, Orr had been taking figure skating lessons to
learn turns, and he pulled one of them that night on a surprised Brad
Park.

As Orr sped along the boards, Park approached from the opposite
direction, intent on jamming Orr at the boards and loosening his hold on
the puck. Orr did as pretty a pirouette as you'd ever see on a hockey rink,
and before Park could put his landing brakes on, Orr plunged past him
and went in alone on the poor, defenseless goalie.

And you know what happens when Orr is in all alone on a goalie. No way he's going to be stopped. Unfortunately, it all took place in New York, and Boston fans were deprived of a sterling golden moment. They stormed Logan Airport to meet the flight home later that night and gave modest Bobby his just rewards.

You may have heard the story making the rounds when Bobby Orr, the meteoric merchant on runners was cutting up the ice for Boston.

It seems a hockey mogul had died, and as he ascended into Heaven and stood at the Pearly Gates, St. Peter asked him:

Would you care to see our Heavenly rink, the Celestial Palace? Being a hockey figure, I thought you might enjoy it.

The hockey owner said he would like to see it very much, so the two wandered over to the Palace. The owner was taken by the great beauty of the Palace, and as he stood admiring it, he noticed a solitary figure cutting up the ice, and he asked St. Peter:

"Who's that guy out there, he looks pretty good."

St. Peter replied solemnly:

"Oh, that's Jesus, and he thinks he is Bobby Orr."

A little irreverent, perhaps, but it shows the great regard everyone felt for Bobby. A role model for all, young and old and even the clergy.

What is little known is that Orr has a unique sense of humor. One time at training camp at Fitchburg, Mass., he was resting on the stairs during a break, and *Union Leader* cameraman Alan Jahn, now a copy editor, snapped a photo of Bobby in a most relaxed mood.

"Sir," reproached the hockey star, "we do not allow that type of photo here."

Jahn, somewhat taken aback, replied, "I'm sorry, we won't use it. I'll tell the editors."

Then Bobby broke into a big, jolly laugh: "I was only kidding. Go on and take as many pictures as you like."

Another goal by Bobby Orr.

Bob
MacLeod:
The
Green Ghost

BOB MacLEOD, a collegiate and profes-
sional gridiron great, attended Dartmouth
College and graduated in the Big Green's
Class of 1939. (Photo from Dartmouth
College archives).

One of my all-time favorites on the college and professional grid-iron was Robert (Bob) MacLeod of Dartmouth College stardom. Not just because he was so devastating on offense but because he was also tough on defense. A two-way superstar, a rare breed these days.

Bob was magnificent on the playing field. I saw him in action many times against formidable teams, and I watched him save the day for the Big Green on numerous occasions with a crashing tackle. Early in his days at Dartmouth, he went in with a complaint to his coach, the renowned Red Blaik, about his selection to the second team.

"You wish to see me, Bob?" Blaik asked.

"Yes," MacLeod said in his taciturn style. "I want to know what it takes here to make the first team," he fired succinctly and point blank at the coach.

Blaik had the right answer, one that put MacLeod on everybody's All-America team in 1938.

"You are outstanding on offense," the coach said, "but you lack some defensive skills that some of the other boys have. Once you learn those, you will be promoted."

It took MacLeod less than 24 hours to temper those skills, as he set out to make his case on the Chase Field practice gridiron the next day. It was a terrifying example of a man at work, bringing down a runner. One teammate said he'd never been hit as hard as he was that afternoon.

MacLeod was a rugged 6-2, about 190, and was not about to be denied, especially with his coach watching from the sidelines. He was one of the most determined players I've ever seen.

By the following Saturday, he had been promoted to the first team.

Blaik said later he was impressed by MacLeod's courage in facing the coach and practically demanding to know what it took to make the first team. Blaik told him his side of the story, and MacLeod thanked him and left the office, saying "That's all I wanted to know."

Coach Blaik's wise decision in putting Bob on the first team after such an astounding display on the practice field that day probably won Dartmouth more games than Blaik could calculate, some of those games certainly with Princeton, Harvard and Yale.

Bob went into the U.S. Marine Corps at the advent of World War II and became a pilot, a succesful one, and the lessons he had learned on the gridiron at Hanover, N.H., must have served him in good stead. He was never one to show off or brag, but he had plenty of talent, in the air and on the ground.

MacLeod was a good student in high school, as well as an able athlete, and he worked to go to college. As a teenager, he secured a job in nearby Chicago working as a warehouse boy.

"One day," Bob recalled for some members of our Leather Helmets group (and all that that implies), "we had to load a freight elevator with some goods and take them up to the fourth floor. We overloaded it and the old elevator was creaking and grinding on its way to the fourth floor. It was going slower and slower, then suddenly it let go and dropped almost the full four floors. We bounced off the springs in the bottom of the shaft and went up again almost two fllors, then we settled down and came to a stop at the ground level. The kid I was working with bounded out that door so fast I hardly saw him, and took off down the street. I never saw him again, he was so frightened by what had happened."

Luckily, no one was injured, and shortly after, Bob MacLeod was on his way to Dartmouth and to fame on the college gridiron. Even a four-story fall in an elevator couldn't deter him from his goals in life: To play football at Dartmouth and to get an education. He did both, and today he is the publisher of the widely read *Teen Magazine,* with offices in Hollywood.

He still sings "Men of Dartmouth" and "As the Backs Go Tearing By" and "Dartmouth's in Town Again" with alumni fervor.

Nothing in his career, not even during the war years (and he survived a plane crash in training school), ever frightened him quite like that fall in the runaway elevator, and he never saw his co-worker again, either. He bolted out the door like Man o' War leaving the starting gate.

Two years of professional football with George Halas' Chicago Bears helped prepare him for the rigorous life in the Marine Corps, and after military service, he wound up in the advertising field, thence into life in the publishing field, or life in the fast lane, a highly competitive endeavor. He's keeping up with the challenge as he did with those so long ago on the Dartmouth playing field. I can tell you one thing for sure about MacLeod: he likes challenges, in fact, he thrives on them.

MacLeod resides on fashionable Colony Drive in Malibu, but he still finds the time to visit Dartmouth College just about every year, at about the time that he visits his son in Connecticut while attending the Hall of Fame Football Dinner at the Waldorf-Astoria, where we chatted a few years ago and complimented him for his bright red vest with tux, a sharp target in any league for a quick pass.

MacLeod is well-liked and an excellent storyteller. He recounted the Dartmouth-Stanford game on the West Coast one day on the phone, and how a loudmouth Stanford player kept needling him. Finally, with Dartmouth in possession of the ball, MacLeod addressed the player and snapped: "Listen, watch me on the next play. I'm gonna go all the way. Is that all right with you?"

On the very next play, he took a short pass and raced 75 yards for a touchdown. If Bob MacLeod saw a little light, he could run forever. That spectacular run shut up the loudmouth for the day.

Grantland Rice, the erudite sportswriter of the day, called MacLeod the best defensive back of 1938, and most Dartmouth sources call him the greatest Dartmouth back ever. Swede Oberlander of an earlier day was more the passing genius, while MacLeod was known for his running, his passing and his defensive skills. Both backs were consensus All-Americans.

MacLeod carries a host of memories of Dartmouth and Hanover, N.H., and enjoys returning when time permits. In fact, he probably wouldn't mind living there with all the problems Los Angeles has had in the past couple decades.

It's possible MacLeod might move back to those endearing environs, but it's not probable because of his job affiliations on the West Coast. Certainly, the memories will live with him forever.

I remember one game in particular, the Harvard game of 1938, in which Dartmouth won by a single touchdown. MacLeod was sensational the entire afternoon, as was his teammate, guard Gus Zitrides, who narrowly missed All-American first-team honors.

Most of us took in the Old Howard show in the evening, but Red Blaik herded his team back to Hanover for beddy-check, at least we didn't see any of them there that night for the burlesque show, and I think the Queens were looking for some of those tuffy Dartmouth Boys who roughed up Dear Harvard.

With a bit of whimsy, MacLeod said, "Football today is a lot different than when I played it back in the Thirties. Back then," he said, "a guy oftentimes went from college to college on his football ability. When I was in military training down south, I bumped into a guy I knew from the Boston area, and I called him by his first name. 'Hi, Jack, what are you doing down here?' He jumped on me. 'Hey, Bob,' he said, 'don't call me by my real name; they will find out who I am and bounce me clean out of here.'"

Football hopefuls often played for several schools under assumed names until they grew too old, and yes, too familiar.

What may not be widely known about Bob MacLeod was that he was also an outstanding basketball player in high school and college, and after being graduated by Dartmouth, he played for the old Chicago Bruins of the National Basketball Association.

A truly great athlete, even in the eyes of George Halas and Red Blaik.

*Carlton Fisk:
Classy
Catcher*

CARLTON FISK, by then a member of the Chicago White Sox, acknowledges the crowd after tying Bob Boone's record of catching in 2,225 games in June of 1993. (AP file photo)

I was there at historic Fenway Park the night reserved for Carlton Fisk of the Boston Red Sox, in his greatest game ever, Game Six of the 1975 World Series between the Sox and the Cincinnati Reds, which doubtless made sure of his entrance into baseball's Hall of Fame.

Even a president of the United States was awakened that night to be informed of what had happened in Boston.

It was a warm night for October, unseasonably so, and many fans were in their shirtsleeves. I had passed up my usual seat in the press box to sit with friends in reserved seats behind third base, and it was there that I witnessed the famous home run that rocked the baseball world. It was, as Red Smith and other writers agreed later, the greatest game of baseball ever played, and with every conceivable angle confronted, and when my friend, Freddy Lynn, crashed into the center field wall early on, I thought the end had come.

"Don't look, Frank," I told a friend. "I think he is dead."

Lynn was lying crumpled at the foot of the wall, curled up in sort of a pre-natal ball, and he hadn't moved. I thought he had broken his neck crashing against the wall. Eventually he pulled out of it, and resumed play.

Every continuing inning saw spectacular plays being made. Then in the eighth, with the Red Sox trailing by three runs, outfielder Bernie Carbo came to bat for the Sox with two runners aboard and smashed one into the centerfield bleachers that must have traveled close to 450 feet. It was, in fact, a typical Lou Gehrig home run, a line drive all the way, with little circles of smoke seeming to follow its trail into the seats. The crowd's roar could be heard halfway to Nahant, on Massachusetts' South Shore, or on TV, around the world.

That tied the score, and sent Cincinnati and Boston tumbling into the ninth inning. Earlier, President Gerald Ford, who had been watching the cliff-hanger, had retired to bed with a nasty cold, and with his nerves on edge from Fenway Park. He was rooting, it was said, for the Sox.

At any rate, in the ninth the Reds' Joe Morgan caught a good pitch and sent it toward deep right field. Sox fans moaned. It looked like a sure homer, but there was the all-star sensation, Dwight Evans, racing along with the ball, keeping his sights on it, and leaping high at just the right time to snag it in his glove for a miracle catch. The crowd roared again. This was not the place certainly for a guy with a weak heart; in fact, it was no place for anybody with a heart, for one side or the other. Dwight had grabbed that towering clout just as it was descending into the seats. "Too close for comfort, that," we concurred.

But what about the Sox half of the ninth? The first three batters reached, one way or the other, and suddenly, in the last of the ninth, we're looking at a game about to be decided. Oh, yes? I believed the end was in sight, very definitely, with Denny Doyle, a fast runner, camped on third and pleading with Rico Petrocelli, the next batter, to "get a hold of one, Rico baby."

He did, but it was only to short left field, near to where we sat. Denny was ready to spring to the plate the second it was caught, and then came the play that engulfed the nation. The left fielder took it, and with Doyle springing toward the plate, he let fly with an on-target throw that just nabbed Doyle at the plate. A debate ensued at that point that has lasted for the many years since. Should Denny have attempted to score on such a short fly?

There was one person who had to be asked, and that was the guy coaching at third base on that particular play, Don Zimmer, and we later asked our friend about that play.

"I was yelling no, no, no, and Doyle thought I was saying go, go, go," Zimmer said.

That throw erased the Sox in the ninth as the next batter went out, and the game vaulted into extra innings, with America clinging on. It went down to the 12th, last of the 12th, and with Carlton Fisk, the hometown boy from Charlestown, N.H. striding to the plate, confidence protruding from every pore.

I almost have a heart attack just thinking of that splendid moment in baseball history, almost as if Abner Doubleday invented the game for a scenario just as this. All right, then, Carlton Fisk at the plate, last of the

12th, score tied, and at precisely 12:37, past midnight, the good pitch sailed plateward, and Mr. Fisk did not miss.

He powered a towering drive toward left field, toward the legendary Green Monster, as the crowd gaped. I arched my eyes upward to follow its flight, and just as it passed third base, the thousands leaped to their feet, some (in front of me) standing on their seats, the better to follow it. From that point on, I saw it on television, heard about it on radio, and read about it in the late editions. My view was blocked, but from the tremendous roar from the 37,000 or so present, I knew Mr. Fisk had done it, had hit the home run of the century.

I had a quick view of the blow as it caromed off the yellow post above the fence, fair ball by about an inch, and bounced back onto the playing field. There will never be another game quite like it, and Sparky Anderson himself, the Cincinnati Reds skipper, said it: "What an ending."

The crowd that night would have gladly paid $100 a ticket had it known what was ahead. Fisk was mobbed by the milling fans from the time he circled third base on his way home. He was leaping and jumping all the way home, as a little boy bringing home a report card chock full of A-plusses; a scene never to be forgotten. Many times after this, in my visits to the Red Sox dressing room, I talked with Carlton about that night, about his moment of supreme glory, and I remember one evening two or three years later when a tired Fisk sat in front of his locker, head in hands, and in some pain catchers take from the unceasing battery upon their body, and I reminded him of The Night, and he evoked a little smile. "Right, Bob," he said.

As long as he lives, years after all the homage has been paid to him, that night will reappear in blinding light before him, in Technicolor, every little moment etched on his mind.

Indeed, all America stood at attention that night, from President Ford on down, and applauded, although not so vehemently in Cincinnati and environs as elsewhere, and at the conclusion of the series the very next evening, in which the Red Sox lost the World Series, a gallant Sparky Anderson stated: "It was a series no one won."

What he meant was that it was ALL Baseball, beginning to end, a reminder to millions of what a series is supposed to look like, a series that contained just everything, and anyone who saw only a single game will know that they had witnessed the ultimate. If that series took about 150 years to it birthing, America will doubtless have to wait as long again for a comparable spectacle.

Oh, yes, even before the first game at rainy Fenway Park, it had all the makings of a super Series. I had brought my little granddaughter Jennifer, then 13, to the opener, and I mentioned to Rev. Frank Huntress, our baseball-loving Episcopal parish priest, to keep an eye on her while I took care of my work. A half-hour later I checked back in the reserved section directly behind the Red Sox dugout, where her seat was, on Jennifer and discovered that she was sitting alone, no Father Huntress in sight.

"Where's Father Huntress?" I inquired.

"Oh," replied Jennifer, "he's out at the Green Monster with all the officials. You can see him from here, Papa. He has the blue towel around his neck."

I couldn't believe my eyes. There was Father Huntress as big as life with Sparky Anderson and Darrell Johnson, and officials of the American and National leagues, plus the umpires, going over the ground rules to be followed. From my observation post at first base, it looked like Father Frank was blessing the group on a good series, and I like to think that it did have some sort of divine guidance, or else why would we have had such a series?

Anyway, when he did report in to his post of "keeping an eye on Jennifer," I asked him what "the guys were talking about out there in left field."

"It was the most beautiful thing, Bob," he replied. "They were discussing the ground rules, and Sparky asked Darrell, 'What happens if a ball gets stuck in this ladder on the fence?'

"Johnson answered him, 'Look, Sparky, if that happens, I'll give you a home run. OK?' So I blessed them all and returned to my seat with Jennifer."

That must put Father Huntress in the Hall of Fame, along with Mr. Fisk, for meritorious conduct on the field of play, a special category, perhaps. However, I did think often of that. The series did have something of a divine touch to it, from the first game on, and particularly in that famous Game No. 6, and all I can say is that those who were there that balmy night, please hang on to your ticket stubs. They may be priceless some day.

Although he was on the losing side in the series, Carlton Fisk was the acknowledged hero with that game-ending crack in Game 6, at half-past midnight.   With both of us from New Hampshire, Fisk and I were friends from the start, and I remember him telling me about the early days in Charlestown, and about his high school and American Legion days.

"Do you remember having stories phoned in about my teams up there, Bob?" he once asked me before a game at Fenway.

Of course, I remembered, and even then Fisk was being touted as a long-ball hitter.

I recalled with interest a story he recited one evening at Fenway about the longest home run he ever hit. It wasn't at any of the major league parks where he has played, but right there in Charlestown.

"It went into a big tree way out in the outfield, the longest ball I ever hit, and it took about five minutes to fall through the branches," he laughed.

With his extraordinary record, Carlton Fisk was a virtual shoo-in for Baseball's Hall of Fame, an honor that to date has eluded New Hampshire stars Robert (Red) Rolfe of the New York Yankees, and Mike Flanagan of the Baltimore Orioles. Rolfe played in the Babe Ruth-Lou Gehrig-Tony Lazzeri era, and Manager Joe McCarthy called him one of the greatest third basemen ever, right up there with Pie Traynor of the Pirates. In fact, it was said that McCarthy was grooming the Phillips Exeter-Dartmouth graduate to succeed him as manager of the Bronx Bombers. McCarthy went to the Red Sox, and Rolfe, with a gnawing case of colitis, retired as a player, and later accepted the post of manager of the Detroit Tigers.

Fisk, because of his leadership in both Boston and Chicago, to which he was traded, will have no trouble, I am sure, with those writers who cast their votes for "The Hall."

Although outspoken at times, Fisk has earned it.

"Run it out, you crud" he once told a batter who dogged it on his way to first base, and he has kept his own teammates on their toes with the same peppery treatment. It made no difference to Carlton. "Play 'em all to win," he would say.

I was quite disturbed when the Red Sox lost him to Chicago, for I knew that he was the backbone of the team, even in the years of the big stars like Fred Lynn and Carl Yastrzemski, and it was the latter who succeeded the immortal Ted Williams in left field, and also played a fantastic game at first base. Carlton was a take-charge guy from the outset, and that is precisely what the Red Sox needed. I wouldn't compare the Red Sox teams of the Fisk-Yastrzemski years with the New York Yankees of 1927 exactly, but they had fight and they were good on any diamond, even away from their beloved Fenway, the little park around the corner. And they were truly all-powerful.

I remember Winter Haven, Florida, well, the spring training base of the team for several years, and one morning in particular when Fisk was wandering around the outfield with his mitt chasing fly balls. At a pause in practice, he turned to me and said, "Come on, Bob, let's warm you up; you were an old pitcher, weren't you?"

I laughed and told him, yeah, let's throw a few.

So, we did, and my arm was still pretty good and I threw some fast balls to Fisk.

"Hey, Bob," he yelled, "you still have a pretty good fast ball there," as a pitch smacked into his mitt.

Yeah, I replied, just the kind you could hit for a mile. Carlton laughed.

And how many of those long balls have I seen him golf over that left field fence? They are countless. He had tremendous power in his wrists and body, and it was a delight to see him meet the ball, a pretty picture. Fisk was about 6-3 and close to 200 pounds, and when he picked out a pitch to his liking, well, say goodbye, chum. That ball was gone forever.

There is a big sign in nearby Kenmore Square, the Citgo sign, and it honestly looked like some of his golf shots were going to carom off it and land in the maze of streets at its foot. He was a most dangerous batter. In his final days as a player, Carlton still enjoyed hitting at Fenway, and spoiled many a game for his erstwhile teammates there with those cannon-like blasts.

Fisk was seldom out of shape. He trained with the regimen of a Ty Cobb of an earlier day, and I would say that is why he had such a phenomenal career. He stayed in shape. I can see now in my mind's eye from the old Press Box at Fenway, No. 27 crouched below, directing the pitch, directing the play, looking over the field casually but with perception, moving players with a slight wave of the mitt.

He ran that team, he and Captain Carl, and what a job. Why did they ever trade him? It is a question that still boggles the Boston mind, the one guy that could have led them in. And what is money these days, pray tell? Somebody goofed there, and I don't think it was the Yawkeys.

As a pitcher in the early Thirties, I would never have pitched to Fisk, I would have walked him on four pitches, and taken my chances on the next guy, regardless. I don't think he had any weak spots at the plate, at least I wasn't able to detect any. He covered the plate just right, so that he had his full weight behind every swing. Had Jim Rice moved closer to the plate by only two inches, I think he might have hit the .400 mark once or twice. He, too, had power-plus, but his weakness was very evident, away and low.

To Carlton Fisk we hail one of the very superior beings in the world of baseball. Many fans have asked me why the Red Sox haven't signed him up as the team manager. A good question, that, and some day they might, I hope. It would be a fighting club, for sure, and a winning club.

Casey Stengel:
A bird flew out

"I TOLD him to bunt, and he hit a homerun," says an exasperated Casey Stengel to Bob Hilliard of *The Union Leader* at the annual Baseball Dinner held in Manchester, N.H.

From that day in Brooklyn when Casey Stengel doffed his cap to the crowd and a bird flew out, he was a fan favorite.

Later, he said to a reporter: "We played a few games in Japan, and then we left for the Orient."

Casey Stengel, pure and supreme, the one and only, and none since to match his charm, wit and "Stengelese," a word which yet may find its way into the dictionary.

One winter day, my mother-in-law glanced out the kitchen window, and said, "There's Leo Cloutier with an older man. I wonder who that is?"

"Is he wearing a camel-hair coat?" I asked.

"Yes, he is," mom-in-law said.

"Then that's Casey Stengel," I replied, and just in time for breakfast, which for us was about noon.

My wife, Barbara, her mother and I welcomed them in, and Casey, quick to size up household time schedules as well as hit-and-run situations and double steals, gruffed, "Just in time for a couple of eggs."

He sat down with us and had his second breakfast of the day, which from the schedule Casey was keeping, was probably his lunch.

I recall asking Casey how he and Dave Egan, a Boston columnist, had been hitting it off. Stengel smiled and said, "That guy is murder," a reference to Dave's column reporting that Boston Braves players, when he was manager, carried clippings in their pocket of the day Stengel was hit by a truck. He was not a favorite with the Braves, and the team fared poorly during his tenure, which may not have been all Stengel's fault.

Stengel had a good breakfast that day and left with Leo a half-hour later to finish off his rounds. A good friend of Leo, Stengel appeared at several of the Cloutier Baseball Dinners in Manchester, N.H, and he never failed to steal the show. I thought at the time what a performance he and the the Harvard-educated Dave Egan would have made at the same table, although it appeared that that was Leo's problem, keeping them apart. The two were masters of the word, one in the King's English, the other in his own, and we can leave it up to the reader as to which was the more effective. Both could rain body blows.

On another visit, Cloutier arranged for Stengel and me to have dinner at the China Dragon in nearby Hooksett, and we had a marvelous time. I asked him whether he felt the Japanese were ready for a major league team, noting their prowess in the sport.

He thought for a minute and said, "Yes, I think they are ready right now, but it will still take some years before they have a major league team. You know, they are better fielders than the Americans, but they are not as strong as we are in hitting, and they don't, as a rule, go for the long ball, probably because of their size."

We still do not have a Japanese entry in the major leagues, but we have plenty of Japanese players in the bigs.

How about a fall classic against the Japanese champions for a real World Series? I believe that's the goal of the Japanese: To have their own major league, and then meet the American champion in the final series of the year.

If only we could interest England, France and Italy in such a venture. And Russia, as well. Then it truly could be called a World Series.

Casey Stengel was a real, hard-nosed, successful manager and not a buffoon, as some writers would have you believe, although he did have his moments.

Look at his record as manager of the New York Yankees. He won so many pennants and World Series, it was almost considered perpetual motion on his part, and he had a hard time remembering all his players, in fact. They just responded to his moves on the playing field and his dictates, which were sometimes hard to understand. Stengel's Yankees made all his moves look good, and they dominated their opponents.

I remember one story about Stengel I heard either in the Fenway Park press box or on the street. It seems one of the New York writers wanted to break in a young college kid to the system of visiting the manager before the game for the starting lineups, and for any other news that might be appropriate. So he told the kid one day: "Look, I want you to get in the habit of visiting Mr. Stengel each day in the dressing room and get his starting lineup, then return it to me with anything else that looks news-worthy. OK?"

So the kid took off early one afternoon on his first sally into the dressing room. Upstairs in the press box, the writer waited for his trainee. He waited and waited.

"Where is that dumb kid?" he wondered. "He should have been here a half-hour ago."

The game started, and no kid. The first inning, the second and third.

"Where in hell is he?" the writer fretted.

The fourth inning passed and then the fifth. Finally in the sixth inning, the kid reappeared, glassy-eyed.

"Where have you been, anyway?" the writer demanded. "The game is better than half over already."

"Well," the kid said a little wearily, "we were back in 1910 when I left, and I got away as soon as I could."

"Did you get the lineups as you were supposed to do?"

The boy said he did and showed them to the writer, who looked at them in amazement.

"What the hell is this? I can't read them."

He studied them again, and they were only initials where the players' names should have been.

"What do these mean?" the exasperated writer wanted to know. The boy looked closer.

"Oh, FB, that means Fat Boy. Stengel couldn't remember his name, but I jotted down the initials he gave me."

The writer pondered. "Well, what does this one mean, 'TG?'"

The messenger said, "That one is Tall Guy. I asked Mr. Stengel about it, and he said, 'How am I to know all these guys? I have only been here 10 years. Just write 'em in like I tell ya.'"

And the young man did as he was told, thereby learning of the one and only Casey Stengel. That would have made a great headline: "FB and TG Take Care of Red Sox."

So Casey Stengel lives on in legend and, in fact, is one of the game's best-loved figures.

Stengel had little trouble explaining how Baseball Dinner promoter Cloutier received a new Cadillac from Ted Williams.

"He just knew how to write about him," he told the player-celebrities gathered about him one morning for breakfast at the Locusta Room in Manchester. "Mr. Banks," he said to Ernie Banks, "did anyone ever give you a brand-new Cadillac?"

Banks looked up surprised. "Me, sir?"

"Yes, you," Stengel replied. "Did anyone ever give you a new Cadillac?"

Banks replied abruptly, "Well, no, sir."

Stengel leaned back in his chair. "Well, that is what I mean, you didn't write any stories about Mr. Williams, so you don't get a new car. Do I make myself clear?"

Banks gathered that he did and sat down. He had risen to his feet when addressed by Mr. Stengel, showing his great respect for the man, and that made Ernie an All-Star in my book.

On another visit by Stengel to the Baseball Dinner, the famous manager gave his little speech to the assemblage, explaining how things happened on the ball field and in the front office, as the crowd roared, and then he sat down awaiting the post-prandials, which he loved most of all.

Casey was definitely a student of the old school, from whence he came, and he liked to be first getting there and last to leave. Had he been on that passenger jet bringing in Sparky Anderson one afternoon, he would have been last in getting there and first to leave, with a bathroom close by. The jet tried to land in a terrifying windstorm and came in just above the landing strip, sideways. It had to be rerouted to Boston and delayed Sparky and the other passengers who had to be bussed to Manchester.

Stengel had no such problems on his flights to Manchester and generally was the first guy to cross the plate and the last guy to leave the stadium. It was like that on this particular evening. The crowd gathered around Mr. Stengel at Leo's party afterward and started asking him questions, nothing Stengel liked better. He answered the questions, he explored them, and he expounded on them, appearing as the ole professor in his classroom. That, of course, was a bygone era, a day when professional athletes, retired or not, did have the time of day for their fans and for the sportswriters of the day.

At first it was a roomful of a hundred or so. By 2 a.m., there were 50 or so conversing with Mr. Stengel, and by 3 a.m., when I threw in the towel, there were 20 or 25 dyed-in-the-wool fans with the coach.

Cloutier was among the group and adamant that he would outlast the professor Ah, Leo, if only you knew, Stengel doesn't quit that easily.

So, Cloutier hung on, hoping for a break, hoping for Casey to call it quits.

"When 5:30 came," said Leo, "there were just the two of us, Casey and me. 'Well, what do you say, Case?' I asked, 'Want to get a little shuteye?'

"Stengel spouted back, 'You tired already, Leo? Well, if you insist, I'll turn in then, but I'm not really tired.'"

Cloutier said he went home, and Casey went to his hotel. "It was about 6 a.m. I had just about fallen asleep when the phone rang. 'Hello, Leo, this is Casey. Hey, it's 7:15, and I'm getting hungry. Do you want to have breakfast?'

"That," said Leo, "ended my sleep for the day, and very shortly, Case was bombing around in his usual style. He just wanted to be the hardiest guy on board, and he was."

I can't forget the picture of that night, Stengel sitting at a little table with a dim light, and the gallant Knights of the Round Table gathered around, listening to every word of wisdom uttered by the Grand Knight, a picture that will never grow old.

Another word-picture of the celebrated Mr. Stengel in action came from New York City, with Cloutier as his guest:

"We were on a busy street corner near his hotel, The Essex, when we saw two nuns having trouble trying to cross the street. 'Having some trouble, girls? Just follow me, and we'll get there,'" Stengel said.

"So, Casey barged out in traffic," Leo recounted, "and held up his hand for the traffic to stop, and the brakes started squealing as the cars stopped to let Casey and the nuns and me across. The drivers all recognized Stengel and were yelling to him, 'Nice going, Casey. We love ya.'"

The nuns were grateful and thanked Casey for his kindness. He was

like that. He once gave the Rev. Franklin Huntress, an Episcopal church-
man, a big donation for the priest's youth baseball league. 'He had a big
heart,' said Huntress, 'and we miss him.'"

A one-in-a-million character, to be sure.

One evening when Yankee pitching great Whitey Ford of the New
York Yankees was a dinner guest, I took the opportunity to ask him what
it was Stengel was asking that caused Whitey to smile during the heat of a
game. Ford smiled that same smile once again, reflecting on times past.
Then he really burst out laughing.

"Well," he said, "one day he ambles out to the mound with that worried expression of his and says, 'Hey, Ford, whose side are you really on?
Step aside so I can wave in another guy.'"

A group of listeners laughed. Then Whitey went on.

"That walk of his out to the mound always got me to laughing anyway, and this particular day, here he comes again, and I know I'm gone.
'Ford,' Stengel rasps, 'give me that ball and I'll raise you a thousand
bananas just to get you outta there.'"

There is no telling how many other stories remain of Casey Stengel,
but all of them are memorable, and all are humorous.

Casey was a product of a simpler time, a good-hearted soul who knew
from whence he came. He was grateful for everything he had in life, and
he showed his appreciation to the fans and all who loved him.

He knew he could never be bigger than the game, and that made him
special. Today's pro athletes could take a lesson; there's much to gain from
the spirit of Casey Stengel.

Doug Everett: A road less travelled

NEW HAMPSHIRE hockey legend
Doug Everett, the Dartmouth College
graduate and member of the 1932
U.S. Olympic team. (Photo property
of Edward F. Everett)

Many readers may not readily recognize the name of Douglas N. Everett. That might be because, early on, he elected to a business life after Dartmouth College rather than to a career in professional hockey such as was dangled in front of his eyes by the New York Rangers and Boston Bruins, as Toronto's Maple Leafs watched carefully.

Doug Everett was that good, and just how good we may never know, for he never did take that big step into the pro ranks. Knowing him personally, and seeing him in action literally hundreds of times, he might have been an early Bobby Orr. His stick-handling and skating ability were, to put it simply, dazzling, and he had a bullet shot, a kind that would test any goaltender.

Also, Doug Everett had this going for him: He came from Concord, N.H., where the sport of ice hockey was reputedly first played in America when an Episcopal priest from nearby St. Paul School saw the game played in Montreal and carried it back to Concord with some pretty vague rules.

What is more, Everett lived just across the street from that exotic magnet of sports, White Park, and he sharpened his skating skills there at the rink and pond.

He became very good at the new sport, and at Dartmouth he played on the first team and earned top recognition for his ability. Myles Lane, who went into the pro ranks before a distinguished career in law in New York City, played with Doug in Dartmouth days.

We all knew of Doug's prowess in Concord, also my home town, and we followed his career later with the U.S. Olympic team, and with the powerful University Club team of Boston which was darn near the equal of some of the pro teams of the day.

Once, in a note to me, Everett touched on his career after Dartmouth.

"While playing at the University Club," he noted, "we faced largely Canadian teams, with unusual success. The high point, I believe, was a two-game series with the Canadian Olympic team in 1928 when they defeated us, 2-1, and we them, 1-0. After that, the Canadian team went on

GRANITE STATE hockey notable Doug Everett, center, who lent his name to the
Everett Arena in Concord, N.H., visits with Boston Bruin forward Rick Middleton,
left, and coach Terry O'Reilly at the Bruins' preseason camp in Wilmington, Mass.

to win the Gold Medal without much competition, since the United States
did not send a team that year. I guess my high point while with the
University Club was scoring six goals against Princeton." Where, we might
add, many of its players came from St. Paul School in Doug's hometown
of Concord.

A few years later, while attending a Bruins-Maple Leafs encounter at
Boston Garden, I went into the Toronto dressing room to talk with the
peppery Connie Smythe, one of the top hockey men in the dominion. I
rapped on the dressing room door, and it was flung open with a lot of
vigor.

"Yes?" came the voice from within, "What can I do for you?"

I told him I was looking for Connie Smythe. He replied, "You're looking directly at him, Kid. What do you think of him?" I laughed, and he
said, "Come on in."

We discussed the play of the roughhouse man of the Maple Leafs, Red
Horner, and that speed demon, King Clancy, who was as much a character as Connie Smythe himself. It was a pleasant conversation, and I began
to see what a hockey man Smythe was. I had a question I had wanted to
ask him about Doug Everett.

"You mean the Dartmouth player on the Olympic team?" he asked. I replied in the affirmative. He looked directly at me.

"Well, let me tell you about Doug Everett. He is one of the greatest prospects I have ever seen, and we would have liked having him on the Maple Leafs. He is a terrific stick-handler with a hard shot, but he went into business didn't he?"

I told him he did, and that was the end ofthe Everett saga.

By the way, an arena stands in Concord today bearing the name of Douglas N. Everett Arena. You reach it by taking the Everett Turnpike, named for Doug's late father, Fred Everett, the commissioner of the New Hampshire Highway System in those early years.

Louis Jourdan:
The Flying
Frenchman

FRENCH actor Louis Jourdan, star of stage and screen, also was a fan of Wagnerian grand opera. (File photo.)

On my way to the fights, a hockey game broke out, so the story goes.

Well, on my way to an interview with French film star Louis Jourdan, a Wagnerian concert erupted. Sort of.

As I made my way into Jourdan's suite at the Ritz-Carlton Hotel in Boston that day, he introduced himself to me, shook hands and said:

"Bob, I have some tapes here of Richard Wagner, and I just want to place them back in the case before I lose them. Do you mind?"

"Richard Wagner?" I asked. "Are you familiar with his music?"

He answered yes to both queries. "He is my favorite, in fact," Louis responded. "Would you care to hear 'Tristan und Isolde?'

I told him I did opera for the paper, and had done maybe 500 or so reviews, many of them on Wagner.

"In fact," I told him, "Wagner's granddaughter, Friedelind, was our house guest one year when I secured her an appearance at Dartmouth College."

Louis replied, "Amazing. Then you wouldn't mind hearing Tristan?"

Not at all, I said, this is indeed an unexpected pleasure. So Louis put on the tape, and the overwhelming majesty of Wagner's music pored forth.

The interview was totally incidental to the concert we were hearing. We would converse in between bars and rests and some lengthy passages for which Wagner is familiar, and something of a story developed, and even now some 10 years later, I can't imagine how I was able to manage a comprehensive piece with all that music cascading about us in the suite, but I did, and I must share a few paragraphs I lifted from the article.

Most of all, I remember how grand Wagner really sounded, and how monumental. He was the absolute monarch of all he surveyed, and I thought how delighted Richard would have been himself could he have just seen us that day, playing his music only a few hours before curtain time for "Gigi," Lerner and Loewe's memorable musical.

Louis played the tape at about tonal pit-level, and if the windows in his suite were open that day just before Thanksgiving, passersby on Arlington Street down below were treated to quite a concert.

Press agent Nance Movsesian must have wondered what was going on in that interview, for one other writer awaited. He had a long wait, I must tell you, for Wagner wasn't noted for his brevity.

Jourdan grew up near Cannes, France, and from the outset, he knew that his career would be on the stage.

"I was surrounded by actors," he said that day. "My father ran a hotel in Cannes, and all the actors and actresses stayed there, so there was never any doubt in my mind at all what I intended to do in life, and I had the full support of my mother and father."

When Louis became famous and moved to Hollywood, his mother came out to visit him and his wife. While she was staying with them, Sir Laurence Olivier paid a call one day.

"She stayed in the background, very timidly, just listening to his voice," Jourdan recalled. "She said he had the greatest speaking voice of any actor."

While they were having drinks, she lingered in the ante room, hanging on every word Olivier uttered.

It was curious in "Gigi," for Louis first played the dashing lover Gaston, and restless playboy, and then as he grew older, he essayed the role of Honore, GigI's father, and in that capacity, he had some great Lerner and Loewe songs to work on, among them, "I Remember It Well," and "Thank Heaven for Little Girls." Louis sang them all some 26 years later, as GigI's father. Of course, the film version of 1958 saw the legend, Maurice Chevalier, playing that role to great acclaim.

After listening to Wagner that afternoon, Jourdan was in fine fettle for his appearance that evening at the ornate Colonial Theater on Boylston Street in fashionable Boston. Jourdan is a baritone, and the thought creased the mind that he might have become one of Wagner's boys at the Metropolitan Opera singing in "Tristan" himself. He discounted that immediately, with a knowing smile.

"My voice was way too thin for the rigors of Grand Opera," he said.

Louis had some extraordinarily kind words for his fellow thespian, Marlon Brando.

"No one in the world today," he said, "has had the great influence this actor has. No one in the Western world. Al Pacino and Robert Redford and many others are what they are today thanks to his great talent and personality. He brings it to every single role he plays."

In Boston, Jourdan was literally The Flying Frenchman in the midst of a nationwide tour that still had six months to go.

"You know, Louis," we told him, "opera isn't even that bad, and in spite of a thin voice, you only have to work twice a week."

The Jourdan interview I always considered one of the most pleasant of all. Louis was most affable, and he made it interesting. When my article appeared, he had me visit backstage to meet Mrs. Jourdan, and she was every bit as cordial as her husband—a great team.

Francis Robinson: The Met's Man

GREAT STORY—Francis Robinson, of the Metropolitan Opera, right, likes the story Bob Hilliard spun at an opera party in Boston. The pair enjoyed a laugh. (Metropolitan Opera Photo)

My first recollection of Francis Robinson was at the press window at the old and ornate Metropolitan Opera House at 39th and Broadway, and it was a lasting impression: a cheerful, ruddy face and a most polite and helpful manner.

I had just come in to pick up my press tickets, and Margaret Carson Ruff had stepped out for a few brief moments. Robinson had stepped into the breach to attend to the press.

I introduced myself, and Francis said, "So nice to meet you, Bob," and plucked my tickets from a tray of reservations. "Enjoy the opera," he said, giving us a nice smile. Barbara and Bobby Jr. were with me, and if memory serves correctly, it was one of the first of many visits we were to make to the great lyric house, a few streets away from the hurly-burly of Times Square.

That scene of the past must have been in 1952 or 1953, and it was our introduction to Grand Opera, New York style. From that time until his death in 1980, Francis and I were good friends. Our friendship may have been enhanced by the fact that he, too, was a newspaperman at one time in Tennessee, his home state.

A graduate of Vanderbilt, Francis was fun-loving and something of a practical joker. He could imitate people he knew to a letter, and he often amused his newspaper colleagues with hilarious telephone calls, one in which he imitated the college president getting the football coach on the line, telling him, "You realize the poor season you have just had, and we must make a change at once, so we're going to have to let you go. I am sorry."

The poor coach was absolutely stunned and found it hard to find words in his defense.

As the news staff listened in at various phones around the office, they heard Robinson burst out laughing. He told the coach, "It's only me, coach, Francis Robinson, and you still have your job." I think Robinson avoided the campus for a few weeks after that call.

OPERA TIME -- Francis Robinson, the affable, brilliant director of the Metropolitan Opera, gives a hug to three members of the Met board at a press party in Boston some years ago. From left, Mary Louise Cabot, Joan Larson, Robinson and Bobbi Arnold. (Metropolitan Opera Photo)

Francis was a fine writer and a gifted speaker. He could hold an audience spellbound with his stories, particularly his narrations on the operas themselves. I often wondered why the Metropolitan Opera didn't capitalize on his many talents at intermission time and let him take over. That way the audience could have learned a lot more than they probably did from their programs and librettos, for Francis went deep always in his research, and he always uncovered the most interesting things about the operas, and the artists, too.

He once gave a dinner speech in Boston to members of the Boston Opera Association, in which he told some stories about Enrico Caruso, the fabled tenor. Caruso, too, was a practical joker, and one evening on the set, he nailed a door shut that a soprano was supposed to burst through in confronting the tenor. She gave the door a shove and when it didn't open, she put her full weight behind it, Francis recalled, "and was just about shaking the stage from its foundations. Caruso would have been gonzo had she caught him."

I think it may have been that very night in Boston that I wrote my lead comparing Francis Robinson with St. Francis of Assisi. There was a chapel in the building where the reception was held, St. Francis Chapel, I believe, and I wrote, "When Francis Robinson finished his colorful talk, I think we had witnessed Saint Francis, himself. Come to think of it, he did depart on the Chapel side of the room.

Francis said that as far as he knew, he was the second person to be canonized in his lifetime, the first being Ruth St. Denis by Belasco. In a note on April 29, 1979 to me, he said:

"Dear Bob,

"Your letter and tear sheet to the opera house was forwarded to me here but arrived only this morning or I should have mentioned it last night. Harriet (O'Brien) gave me a copy of the story. Thank you for the elevation. Ruth St. Denis said Belasco canonized her. She was born plain Ruth Dennis.

"I gave Mr. Gniewek a copy of your review and will to Miss Sills when we see her Monday in Atlanta.

"It is always a joy to see you, and I thank you again for your good offices in our behalf. With all high greetings.

"Yours sincerely, Francis."

If it is not too late, we will elevate him once again: "St. Francis Robinson."

For all purposes, Francis just about ran the Metropolitan Opera over the years and, as my friend, Anthony Bliss, once the executive director of the Met, said: "Francis wore many hats during his time with the Met; at various times, director of press, public relations, tour, box office and subscription, assistant general manager and host of 'Live From The Met.'"

That is quite true. He was Mr. Met Opera in all the tour cities, from Boston to Cleveland to Atlanta, wherever the company performed its operatic magic, and when the press went looking for someone to consult, it was Francis Robinson. After Vanderbilt, he bent to the purpose of learning Grand Opera, and he did it well. He was a fountain of fact; he knew opera from every conceivable angle, from story and music to composer and librettist, to the success or failure of a work. He had it at his fingertips, and it is little wonder he was such a pursued figure at opera nights, and by the media in particular. Being a former writer, he was always eager to help those friends of the Met.

I think Francis Robinson at his best would have been in the Rudolf Bing era when the former was pressed into the most demanding service of just about running the "House" itself, as Sir Rudolf took care of his ailing wife. Bing did not call in extra help to look after Mrs. Bing, he did it himself, and this must have been one of the "little things" that my dear Barbara spoke of so eloquently when she advised me: "Always watch the little things, they're what count." How true. Well, if any proving were needed in Bing's case, this was it, when Francis Robinson was his biggest helper and kept the house alive and glowing.

Robinson also saw the great transition, from the old house at 39th and Broadway to the new and glamorous Lincoln Center masterpiece with its sunburst chandeliers and Chagall murals to its luxurious deep red and gold interior. I gasp every time I view the new house, still remembering, of course, the refined beauty of the old, with its elegant proscenium containing the names of the greatest composers.

The old house had history on its side, of course, with Caruso and Galli-Curci having performed on its vast stage to roaring ovations. Francis Robinson missed Caruso and others, of course, but he did see such vocal stalwarts as Mario Del Monaco and Richard Tucker and Jan Peerce, and Renata Tebaldi and Zinki Milanov and Maria Callas and Roberta Peters and Rise Stevens, and many other notables perform there, and just think of all the outstanding vocal enactments he saw. The "Otello" of Del Monaco, the "Carmen" of Rise Stevens, the "Norma" of Callas, the "Lucia" of Lily Pons.

This history he took with him to the new house, where such as Luciano Pavarotti and Placido Domingo were commencing great careers of their own and giving Robinson something to write about, and something to remember.

After Francis' death, I corresponded with his sister, Mrs. Thomas Howe Akin, a schoolteacher in Tennessee, and she wrote to tell me how much she enjoyed my final tribute to her brother, and I thought how sweet of her to let me know, and I remember thinking how like her brother she was.

Francis Robinson is buried in a little cemetery in a little town in Tennessee, far from the glamour of the Metropolitan Opera House in New York City, and may we bless his heart for all the wonderful moments he brought America in his narrations and TV essays; both he and Milton Cross, too, the Texaco Man at both houses.

Francis projected the upcoming seasons for us at Boston Opera Association, and those parties were something to write home about. They were among the highlights of the Boston social season.

I will repeat this: Francis was the raconteur par excellence. One could hear a pin drop as he talked. His stories were the greatest, and we couldn't wait for the "Met in Boston" season to open in the springtime of each year, with the blooming of the magnolias on Beacon Street. That was the spell Francis Robinson cast, with his prologues in person.

Bobbi Arnold, a prominent member of the New Hampshire State Legislature, accompanied us to one of the opera parties in Boston with her arm in a sling. Francis walked over to her and stopped in amazement.

"What on earth happened to you, Bobbi?" he inquired, then gave her a big hug. That cheered up Bobbi and helped make her day. She was one of Francis' loyal supporters. "That man," she once remarked, "was the greatest, and how we miss him."

At one of those pre-opera parties with the New York crowd in attendance, Anthony Bliss, then the president, told me how he had met his wife, a ballerina from Toronto.

"I was in the wings at the Met watching the ballet, and suddenly she leaped toward me," he laughed, "and since there was no one there to catch her, I did, and that's how I caught a wife, very literally."

Incidentally, Bliss and William Loeb, the late publisher of *The Union Leader* and *New Hampshire Sunday News*, were boyhood pals on Long Island. Loeb was a staunch backer of Bliss, and of opera, too. His particular favorite was Wagner's "The Flying Dutchman."

With me at that party was a boyhood friend, Frank Morono of Concord. We were talking with Francis Robinson, and Bliss joined us. We shook hands and I introduced him to Frank.

"He was a Marine," I told Bliss, "on Guam and Iwo Jima, plus Guadalcanal. He shipped home from Guam toward the end of the war."

Bliss asked Frank, "When did you ship back home, Frank?" Frank told him, and gave him the name of his ship. "My God, Frank," he said, "I was the skipper of that ship." They swapped stories for about 10 minutes. "What a very great coincidence that we should meet here in Boston at an opera party," Robinson said.

I agreed, and we all laughed. A small world, at that.

Members of Boston Opera Association tendered a party for Francis Robinson on April 15, 1980 at the Copley Plaza Hotel, but he was unable to attend. It was a gala event, headed by Boston Opera President Lawrence T. Perera, a noted Boston attorney. Some of the distinguished guests were Miss Lillian Gish, Rise Stevens, Jerome Hines, Eleanor Steber (who received her early training at Boston Conservatory of Music), Bunny Rowell and Mary Louise Cabot, among others.

It was to be Francis' last party. He died shortly after in New York City, sending the opera world into mourning.

Friedelind Wagner... famed name

A STERN LECTURE is given in this Christmas card for the benefit of Viennese music critic Hanslick, who rapped a Richard Wagner music drama. Wagner promised to put him in his next work, and he did, as the village idiot in "Die Meistersinger." The striking silhouette is by Dr. Otto Bohler and the card was sent to Bob and Barbara Hilliard in the late '50s. Wagner's granddaughter, Friedelind Wagner, visited the Hilliards and later lectured to an engrossed Dartmouth College audience in Hanover, N.H.

On the wall facing my writing table are three framed Christmas cards. They depict musical scenes, humorous drawings, from the life of the celebrated 19th Century composer, Richard Wagner.

One pictures him lecturing an errant critic, Dr. Hanslick, who incurred Wagner's wrath with a stinging critique. Wagner, with a long suit-coat that reaches to his knees, appears to be telling Dr. Hanslick, whom he is holding in the palm of his hand, that if he doesn't behave, he will cast him in one of his music dramas as the Village Idiot, which he ultimately does in "Die Meistersinger."

In another sketch, Wagner and a dragon are guarding his musical masterpieces, while he shakes hands with an unidentified character, perhaps a conductor, or even a critic, or maybe just a detractor. The third sketch shows a Wagnerian Master Class at work with an energetic conductor, maybe his son, Siegfried.

The Christmas cards were sent to my family several years ago by Wagner's granddaughter, Friedelind, who died a few years ago. She bore a striking resemblance to the composer himself, and it was a pure delight to have her in my home as a guest. She enjoyed lunch with us, telling Barbara that she much preferred eating with us than in a restaurant.

"I get so sick of restaurants, Barbara," she told Mrs. Hilliard. That was in April, 1959 or 1960. After spending three or four hours with us, Barbara drove her to Dartmouth College in Hanover, where she addressed a class on the life and works of her noted grandfather, and the listeners were absolutely spellbound.

We were conversing in the living room before lunch, and telling Friedelind how much we enjoyed "Lohengrin" at the Met a few months before. She was not altogether happy with the presentation itself on that occasion, she said, and she spoke about it. The Bayreuth "Lohengrin" was much superior, she observed, and then she glanced toward our mantelpiece. "Do you see who has the place of honor here?" I asked.

"Yes," she answered. "I see."

She gazed at the bust of a serious Richard Wagner, the bust of Franz Liszt, the great Hungarian pianist, and the father-in-law of Wagner. Wagner and Liszt would doubtless have qualified as the 19th Century's Family of the Year. What credentials!

Wagner revolutionized music with his intense dramas and spectacular leitmotivs in which certain characters, or scenes, take the same musical attention and are thus identified immediately. I suppose it would be possible, though a little unbending, to view an entire Wagner work without once looking up.

"Oh, yes," one might say. "Wotan is out there now."

That was Wagner, and he gave the music world something to talk about, surely. He was an innovator, to be sure, and one who was unequalled in the music world. Beside him, the other masters seem to pale. Oh, yes, and he was a master in art and literature, in architecture (he designed the Festpielhaus at Bayreuth), a student of religion, of warfare strategy (he even led a revolt against his own king), and yes, a master of romance (he was married to Minna Planer before Cosima, and had an affair with at least one other matron, Mathilde Wesendonck, prior to his marriage to Cosima, who was the wife of his conductor, Hans Von Bulow).

That is straying afield a bit, and I wanted to say that "Lohengrin" remains my favorite work still, the most beautiful, the most musical, the most exquisite, and when Swan Boat comes to take him away forever, my heart still sinks in grief. And the Wedding Procession is grander than the Coronation of a King, so grand and so lovely in the reverent tones of the famous Bridal Chorus. Who could not tingle to that?

Still, one producer expunged the Cathedral setting for Elsa's boudoir. Unbelievable. And he wasn't even sent to jail for it. More unbelievable.

Wagner would have been furious at this change. It seems as though someone had given in to the wicked Ortrud and the scheming Telramund and made a shambles of the world-famous Wedding March scene.

We had wanted to take Miss Wagner out to dinner with us, before Barbara drove her to Hanover and Dartmouth College for her speaking engagement, but she wanted it quiet and peaceful, and we had lunch at 331 Oak St., listening the while to Friedelind's graphic account of opera here and abroad, and how they differed in many countries. It was fascinating, and I must say, we were apt listeners.

The trip to Hanover and Dartmouth was frantic, according to Barbara, who did the driving. She was clipping at close to 60 mph and making exceptionally good time, when Friedelind, accustomed to driving on the over-100 mph Autobahn in Germany, leaned over and asked: "What's wrong with your car, Barbara? Can't you go any faster? We'll be late for my talk."

Barbara responded: "I'm going over the speed limit now, Friedelind. Do you want me to get arrested?"

To that, Friedelind replied: "Well, go as fast as you can, anyway, Barbara." And Barbara did, as the scenery flashed past.

Wagner told Barbara that she had hit a deer on the Autobahn going nearly 125 mph, and that it had shaken her up, both mentally and physically, and that she didn't want to go through that again.

The postscript here is that they arrived on time and in good shape in Hanover, in fact in time to have dinner with friends in the area.

We enjoyed Friedelind's visit to our home that day and later we were invited to her apartment in New York City, and we had a lovely time. Friedelind was a refreshing host, and she laughed when she recalled the frantic drive to Hanover. Bobby Jr. was taking a course in music at the University of New Hampshire, where he was a student, and he sang "In Fernem Land" from "Lohengrin" for our distinguished host. She smiled graciously at Bobby, and said: "You did that very well, Bobby. You have a very sweet voice, and it is the first time I have ever heard 'In Fernem Land' in a New England accent. And I will say that it was very fascinating."

Bobby Jr., by the way, had won the state of New Hampshire Episcopal Church's Festival championship at St. Paul Church in Concord (right across from the State Capitol) as a boy soprano several years prior, and he did have a gorgeous voice, sweet and crystal clear.

One of the vestrymen at the church, Dr. Douglas M. Black, told me recently that the Steeple Cross, which I donated in Barbara's memory, looks radiant at night, bathed in the glow from the State House dome across the street, "just like it is hanging up there in the sky." And I know

Barbara is up there somewhere listening to this story of other years, and her trip that day to Hanover with Friedelind Wagner.

Barbara knew piano, and she was able to help me immensely in my features on grand opera, ripping the operas apart and telling me what the composer wished at various stages along the way and desired to convey to the listener. It was invaluable, and it gave my accounts a more luminous passage overall.

I have yet to view the cross at night, and I am planning to do that real soon. The cross is about six feet in height and rests about 125 feet above the sidewalk at the church. When the steeplejack was carrying the cross to the area where it was to be hoisted to the top of the church steeple, a friend, Frank Morono, whispered in my ear: "Bob, does that remind you of anything? Like Jesus carrying the cross through the streets of Jerusalem?" Indeed, it did.

Miss Wagner's visit brings back cherished memories, and I held her in the highest esteem when she told us that day that she preferred dining with us in our own home instead of going out to a restaurant. It always seemed to me that the Wagner brothers should have brought their sister into a more commanding position in the running of Bayreuth than they did. She had some excellent ideas about the staging. She was an intelligent woman and oftentimes spoke her mind, always in a kindly way.

Once when a friend of mine from Manchester, a music teacher named George Gerasi, went abroad for a year on a musical expedition to Europe, I wrote a note of introduction for him to Miss Wagner in case he had any trouble purchasing a ticket. Well, he did have problems: The Festspielhaus was completely sold out for the final performance of the August season.

It was "Lohengrin," and George would have given his bankroll for a ticket. When they told him at the box office that no more tickets existed, he walked away crestfallen. Suddenly, he remembered the note I had given him several weeks before, "in case you have trouble."

Well, George marched back to the box office and told them he had a note for Miss Friedelind Wagner. "You have a note for Miss Wagner?" they repeated. Yes, he told them, pulling the note from an inside pocket.

"Oh, yes," the box office attendant said, "we will page Miss Wagner for you." And they did.

Miss Wagner at Hanover, N. H., with friends and the family dog.

After a few minutes, Miss Wagner appeared.

"Did someone wish to see me?" she asked the attendant. "Yes, that man over there," came the response, and she was directed to George Gerasi himself.

"Yes?" said Miss Wagner, "you wished to see me?" George replied, "Yes, Miss Wagner, I have a note for you from one of your friends in America, Bob Hilliard."

"Oh, yes," she answered. "How are Bob and Barbara and Bobby?"

She read the note I had written, introducing my friend George, and she asked, "What is your problem?"

George replied simply, "I tried to buy a ticket, and I learned they are all sold out, and I have come such a distance just to see an opera here, all the way from New Hampshire."

"Is that your problem?" Miss Wagner asked him. He nodded. "Well," the buoyant Friedelind replied, "I can fix that for you, George. You will sit with me in my private box."

"Bob, it was like a dream," George told me later in a visit to *The Union Leader* newsroom. "I was in a Fairyland. Everybody kept coming up to her asking questions about the production. 'What color in this act, Miss Wagner?' they would ask. 'Blue on blue,' she would reply. It was all so very fascinating. And the 'Lohengrin' there was so much better than our own back here."

The two had dinner during intermission at Bayreuth and talked of opera.

It was an adventure George would never forget, and I know he told his young pupils all about it, and those little ears would long remember the story they had heard, of how their very own teacher had made it into the final opera of the season in far-off Bayreuth, Germany. A fairyland narration, truly.

Cosima, Wagner's second wife (the daughter of Franz Liszt) ran Bayreuth after the composer's death in Venice on Feb. 13, 1883. She ran Bayreuth well and exercised an iron hand in controlling its aims. Once perhaps she went a little bit too far, Friedelind once told me.

Looking over a Wagnerian (what else?) score one day, she thought the music a bit loud in one sequence. When guest conductor Arturo Toscanini was rehearsing the orchestra for an upcoming opera, he noticed that the music differed from what he had played several years before. He stopped the rehearsal abruptly and asked the concert master what had happened to the original music.

"That is the original," he replied.

"Oh no it is not," the conductor retorted. "I know the original music, and this is not it."

Members of the orchestra crowded around and told Arturo that he must be mistaken. "It is the only music we know for this opera."

"Well," Toscanini shot back, "this very definitely is not what Wagner composed. I know because I conducted the original many years ago. Now, I want one of you gentlemen to go over to the museum and bring me the original score. And place it in my own hands."

With that command, the concert master was on his way to the museum to fetch the original manuscript. After some time, he returned and handed the score to the conductor.

Toscanini studied it for a few minutes and finally arrived at the disputed passage. "Ah," breathed the Maestro, "here it is. Here is what I have been telling you. Here is the correct music."

The orchestra members looked in amazement at the original orchestration and surely it was different from what they had been playing all these years.

"Now," said an ired Toscanini, "I intend to find out what happened to the music, and who removed it."

It didn't take long after the maestro had a chance to talk with Cosima herself.

"Someone," he told Wagner's widow, "lifted the original music from his score, and I intend to find the person who did it."

Cosima, a little shocked by the revelation, said quite innocently, "Why, I did that myself. It was too loud, and I removed it."

That ended her defense, and the original music was restored as the Maestro looked on, and brought back to full life once again.

I remember telling Friedelind's story to a group, including conductor Lorin Maazel and Placido Domingo, at a concert featuring Andrew Lloyd Webber's "Requiem" at St. Thomas Episcopal Church in New York City. The "Requiem" was absolutely beautiful, the singing of Domingo and Sarah Brightman heavenly, backed up by the majestic choirs of Winchester Cathedral in England and St. Thomas of the host church, and the treble of Paul Miles-Kingston.

It was a night of music that defied description, and to me, it marked Webber's emergence perhaps into the field of classical music after about 25 years on the Broadway stage with countless hits to his credit. If you can term the "Requiem" a hit, that is what it was, plain and simple. In coming years, it will find its place in musical history, and profound and ear-caressing in a liturgical way. Both principals soared to new heights in this classical endeavor, to heights seldom heard in this day of hard rock and deafening electric guitars.

It was an evening of music by Purcell and Bach, and it marked the world premier performance of the "Requiem." It was a surcease from the world around us, from the roar of the subways to the din of traffic, and it was positively welcomed.

Of Friedelind's amazing story of her grandmother's lifting of that passage by the master himself, Maazel was incredulous. "I had never heard that story, and it is amazing, and it is also humorous," he said. But lift it she did, and it was only by chance that the passage was returned to the original.

Friedelind told us many anecdotes of a life at the family mansion at Bayreuth.

"Cosima was a tartar," she told us, "and we children were scared to death of her. She made us mind, and we did, you can bet."

Friedelind told us, too, of her father, Siegfried, conducting the orchestra at Bayreuth one steamy-hot summer's day in his underwear. "No one could see him," she recounted, "since the pit was under the stage. My grandfather, Richard Wagner, the composer, demanded that the musicians be heard, not seen, and the Festspielhaus was built in that fashion. Also, it was quite impossible to get out once you were seated for the rows were sort of zigzagged.

"Once in, you were there until intermission, and the only people who saw the conductor at work were the musicians themselves. Wagner, a full-flight genius, also designed the opera house at Bayreuth in every aspect, and it is still one of the best in the world. An opera there is unhurried, with dinner served outdoors at intermission. It is a full-dressed affair, tuxedos and evening gowns, and dinner on the terrace; still very magnificent and colorful. Recently television brought coverage of the entire Ring Cycle to America and to world viewers.

The Ring, encompassing four long works, is perhaps the world's most renowned musical masterpiece. It runs for more than 20 hours, and I once asked George Steinbrenner, owner of the New York Yankees, why he didn't stage it at Yankee Stadium in its entirety at one sitting. One opera official at that baseball party said: "Why, of course, Bob, and shall we send the bill to Mrs. Loeb? Let's see," he commented, "there would have to be about three full orchestras, four complete casts, dancers, costumes, technicians, four conductors. Ah-hah. Tired already? Why it's only Tuesday, Bob."

So television takes care of it for us. God Bless TV. And we also get interpretative views and commentary thrown in, and all for free, less the basic monthly television charge.

Wouldn't that be the ultimate at one sitting? Twenty hours of viewing, without even a bed. It may come to pass some day and I hope it is not before the next century. I know some who have seen the Ring Cycle on four consecutive days. But in one sitting? Wow! A record awaiting.

Miss Wagner actually gave two talks at Dartmouth College, the first in late April, 1959, the second in April of 1960, and both were widely acclaimed for her candor and extensive knowledge of the Wagnerian music dramas, and how they should be performed. One season at Bayreuth, if memory serves correctly, Wieland staged the Ring Cycle on a dark and somber stage, without ornamentation of any sort, save for whatever characters the composer decreed at the moment, and attired in the proper costumes of Valhalla. Since the deaths of Friedelind and Wieland, the stately New York Times wonders who will succeed Wolfgang Wagner "as keeper of the family flame at Bayreuth?" ... and conjectures, "It's anyone's guess."

My own personal guess is that it will be the world-famous conductor at the Metropolitan, James Levine, who in recent years has been so helpful and instrumental in his apt leadership at the celebrated Wagnerian shrine. Under his baton, the music dramas have responded in magnificent fashion and have attracted overflow audiences. One name to keep in mind, at least, and one individual who has served his apprenticeship well and honorably.

To return for a moment to Miss Wagner and her captivating lectures at Dartmouth. In the first lecture, Miss Wagner, who fled to England with the help of conductor Arturo Toscanini to gain asylum there during World War II, and who shortly after became an American citizen, dwelled on the life and works of her famous grandfather.

The following year, she discussed "The Lyric Spirit of Wagner," both to very attentive audiences. "Wagner On The Wing" read the caption from *The Union Leader* of a smiling, well-dressed Friedelind Wagner, wearing dark glasses and eagerly anticipating her lecture appearance at Dartmouth. The caption referred to her as "a modern-day Valkyrie" winging in from New York en route to Hanover.

We met her at the airport, and she spent the entire afternoon with us, and I have to confess that it was one of the most exciting days of our lives just listening to her stories of life at the Family Home at "Wahnfried" in Bayreuth, and the presentations of Wagner's great works at the Festspielhaus. Friedelind told us that, although she was very young at the time, she remembers Cosima "very well" and that "she was very strict with us." Cosima died in 1930 at the age of 93 when Friedelind was 12. "She was a tartar," said Friedelind, smiling.

When she was 19, in 1937, she quit Germany after seeing Nazism at close range and ultimately made her way to the United States where she became a citizen. Adolf Hitler visited "Wahnfried" and Friedelind was not enamored of him, or his plans of world conquest, and she did not return to her native country until long after Hitler's death. She returned in 1953 and became immersed in opera and the Bayreuth operations, and she learned her lessons profoundly. She studied music, acting, singing, staging and history in various cities, in London, Paris, Berlin, Buenos Aires and New York, and she brought a wealth of talent to the Bayreuth stage.

In her profile, she bore a striking resemblance to her illustrious grandfather, forehead, nose, chin: the female Wagner. The memories are all most memorable of Friedelind Wagner, and her hometown still has that magical yearning of the Wagner family, at work and at play. She was a vivacious person, pretty and intelligent, and sadly, never known by her grandfather. I think Friedelind would have been a rock for Herr Wagner had she but lived earlier. She brought a fascination for his great works, simply by reciting those great moments in musical history.

By comparison, Beethoven seems to suffer. Wagner invented a whole new concept of music, the leitmotiv, and he composed gigantic works as to almost defy reason and logic, music that has its place even in today's world.

As long as there is his music, the Wagner name will reign supreme, with grandeur, eloquence, mysticism.

Kitty Carlisle: A Hart of Gold

KITTY CARLISLE HART, seated, famous for her movie roles, graced the stage at the Lakes Region Playhouse in Gilford, N.H., in the summer of 1973, performing with her daughter, also pictured. (*Union Leader* file photo)

This writer forever will be awed by pretty Kitty Carlisle Hart, and the abounding energy she displayed in helping the Boston Opera Association through some trying times over the years.

Always it has been with that captivating smile, that vivacious style that seems to say, "We can beat anything."

In addition, she has the bell-like singing voice, probably first heard by America-at-large in the Marx Brothers' "A Night at the Opera," by now an epic unto itself. Kitty charmed everybody, including the zany brothers themselves, with tomes sweet and lovely.

This writer was transported by the quality of her voice, first in that film in the mid-Thirties, then on the theatrical stage, and at the Lakes Region Playhouse in the exotic, tranquil surroundings of Lake Winnipesaukee at Gilford, N.H., where she appeared in the musical production, "You Never Know."

Together with Mrs. Hilliard, we enjoyed a late-evening repast with Kitty after a most delightful evening of theater, and Kitty even hummed a few of the hit songs we discussed that night over dinner.

Kitty made the show sparkle as she performed. It contained some of Cole Porter's most magnificent hits, and the singer was at ease and glorious in all of them. Her voice was suited to some extreme demands, from the rigors of opera to the less-demanding Broadway stage, but the fact remains, Kitty made them all sound ethereal. Her talents did not end on the singing stage, either. She has a way of glamorizing a production, to make it leap out to the view, and in this way by her personal appeal did she help Boston Opera.

She spoke that evening at Gilford of movie-making with the hilarious Marxes, and how difficult it was to keep up with Groucho's constant whims. It seems he changed the lines every time he uttered them. She laughed whenever she mentioned Groucho.

"I don't know how many times he changed the script each day, but it was often, and his lines grew funnier," she remembered. "I could barely keep up with him."

All the time, Groucho, on camera, was racing around with a sheaf of papers in his hand, bent over slightly as if in a terrible hurry, and singing, lustily, "Pagliacci," with that manufactured stage laugh. Enough to throw anybody into convulsions. Then, "I think I will change that line, this one sounds better."

Groucho manufactured lines out of thin air, like the time he snapped off, "I ran outside and saw a man shooting an elephant in my pajamas. What he was doing in my pajamas, I will never know." That's what poor Kitty had to face on the set with the Marxes, but she held up her end.

I met Kitty several times after that Gilford interlude, and each time it was while she was helping The Boston Opera Association in fund-raising functions. I had some years earlier been elected to its Board of Overseers on invitation of Judge Lawrence T. Perera. Our main event each Spring was the week-long visit of the Metropolitan Opera, and the week was just fabulous, with operas each evening and a host of parties; a most colorful time, with the flowers commencing to bloom as the opera stars trekked in. It was really the best of the Met, with the works that had been featured in New York in the season just ended.

Boston viewed all the top operas, from "Aida" to "Die Meistersinger," from Wagner and Verdi and Puccini to Mozart and Strauss and Gounod, all the world composers and their enchanted works. In late April, Boston was indeed a singing city. About every year, Kitty would fly up for the parties, usually at the Ritz-Carlton or at The Park Plaza. They were not only functional, but fun, and Boston geared up for the Met visit. The Met brought its top brass, Rudolf Bing and Francis Robinson and Anthony Bliss (a boyhood friend of our Publisher, William Loeb in New York days) and Bruce Crawford, among many others. Plus all the super-stars of the stage: Del Monaco, Tucker, Pavarotti, Rise Stevens, Renata Tebaldi, Zinka Milanov, and it was hectic but glorious.

Kitty Carlisle Hart's presence at the parties, usually held prior to the season, always proved a gigantic help, and enlivened the proceedings as well with her sparkling presence.

I fear those days are gone forever with the new order of things in New York, and going where the money is most. If they can get it in Tokyo or in

Singapore or in Paris, or wherever, who can really blame them, what with the rising costs of productions? We hope those days will return some day, but at the moment it does not appear that they will. Well, we can hope. The Met in Boston was real shot in the arm for New England, the social highlight of the season, and since Boston was the first tour city ever, it would be nice if the Met inaugurated the endeavor once again.

Harriet E. O'Brien was the Managing Director of Boston Opera Association, and she hustled all the way. She knew everybody, and she hosted a terrific season, in addition to most of the parties. On one occasion, a farewell to Francis Robinson, we had Lillian Gish of the movies as one of our guests, and she loved it. Boston paid homage to her that evening. A few days later, Francis Robinson died, and I lost one of my real close friends, dating to my start in grand opera in the early Fifties, when Francis was the affable Press Director of the Met, and winning new friends every night of the year among the writers and media in general. A great fellow, one who is sadly missed.

I consider Kitty Carlisle Hart, in spite of the fact she is a New Yorker, as one of our crowd from Boston, and I think she does, too. She has done enough in Boston already to earn a lifetime Gold Medal, and was always ready to contribute her time to our projects to keep opera alive in that city, as I mentioned, the first tour city ever of the Met.

I am reprinting a few paragraphs from my initial story on Kitty, for old times sake. The story, in part, follows:

"Kitty Carlisle Recalls Chico, Harpo, Groucho"
By BOB HILLIARD
Sunday News Staff

GILFORD, Aug. 2 --- It appeared at the time that actress-singer Kitty Carlisle might have been doing someone a favor.

"At least, that is the impression I held," said the still vivacious star, appearing at the Lakes Region Playhouse here this week in the musical comedy 'You Never Know.'

"Miss Carlisle aspired then to a career in grand opera, had the voice for it, certainly the looks.

"And here she was cast as an opera singer in some wild and wooly Hollywood laugher that also starred some pretty zany characters.

"Miss Carlisle did manage to score in the film, did hit a high C and came off very well in what appeared to her as a very testing period.

"The picture was the celebrated 'A Night at the Opera,' and the zany guys were none other than the famous Marx Brothers. That film, Miss Carlisle recalled, amidst a lot of laughter and nostalgia, was to become an epic in comedy - one of the finest in this particular field that Hollywood was ever to produce.

"All the time I figured I was doing them a favor, appearing in a silly picture. How was I to know it was to become an all-time classic?' asked the pretty actress as she dined at the Gilford Inn and Motel following a well-received and highly-acclaimed performance in 'You Never Know,' a comedy based on an original musical play by Robert Katcher, Siegfried Geyer and Karl Farkas, and containing many hitherto unpublished Cole Porter tunes, some of them toe-tapping and real catchy, as well they might be coming from the pen of one of the big names of American popular music.

"But there was Miss Carlisle, gamboling in front of the cameras with Groucho, Chico and Harpo, singing it up and just happy to be helping them out, never realizing as they raced through the script that a monumental picture was in the making."

That is the history of a great picture in the making, and of the frenzied action that was taking place. Kitty strung along with the guys Marx, showing that she was a real trouper, as she was years later in helping out Boston Opera Association in its days of need. A real lady, to be sure.

Larry Bird:
The Boy
From Indiana

FAMED NUMBER RETIRED--Boston Celtic great Larry Bird is honored at the Boston Garden before a sellout throng as his number is hoisted to the rafters, as his wife and child look on. He was one of the greatest players in NBA history. (*Union Leader* photo by Jim Schaufenbil)

Until Larry Bird came along, my basketball heroes were people like John Havlicek, Bill Russell, Red Cowens, Bob Cousy and Tommy Heinsohn of the hometown Boston Celtics; (Lew Alcindor) Kareem-Abdul Jabbar, Red Rocha, Wilt the Stilt Chamberlain, Magic Johnson and George Mikan of other teams.

Even before these great shooters and playmakers arrived on the scene, we had others in the late 1920s who were the greats of those early years, barely 36 years after Dr. James Naismith had invented the game of basketball in 1891 at the training school of the YMCA in Springfield, Mass., now Springfield College.

Two of the greatest were known as Nat Holman and Joe Lapchick, and what was the name of their team? The Original Celtics? From Boston? No, no. From New York City. A Celtics team before the Boston Celtics? Indeed, and by about 30 years or so at least.

Nat Holman could do everything on the basketball court, after the towering Joe Lapchick, (6-6) would win the tap and rifle the ball to him. Nat had a wicked set shot, and he never missed at the foul line, or infrequently so. I had been watching the Concord American Legion teams for a couple of years at the old Armory in that city, and they were good. They had speed and good shots and were excellent playmakers. At times, they borrowed players from the Boston Whirlwinds, like Soapy Waters, and they could actually stay with teams like the Philadelphia Colored Giants, the Brockton Okoes and other touring ensembles that knew how to snap the ball in from mid-court. It made for some excellent games.

When the New York Celtics came to town in about 1927 with Holman, Lapchick and Barry & Co, it was almost bigger than the Lindbergh visit, and the Armory was mobbed for the game. The Celtics prevailed, of course, but they had a fight on their hands.

I had a fight on my hands just getting to the game that night. My mother had kept me home from school that day with a bad cold, but when I read in the afternoon paper that the Original Celtics were in town for a

THIS IS HOW WE DO IT —Red Auerbach, of Boston Celtic fame, left, and Bob Hilliard.

game with the Concord American Legion, I had to plan for a quick exit from my bedroom, and this I did by just sneaking out quietly, tip-toeing down the stairs, out the front door at 9 Valley and on down the street, through White Park to the Armory, which was already packed by the time I arrived, without a cent in my pocket. The kind officials let me in, or I never would have seen the great Nat Holman and Johnny Lapchick in person.

Oh, yes, when my mother found out about my spree, she was furious, and she said, "You're going to school tomorrow," which I did, but attending that game made everything worthwhile. I was real happy I got to see the team known then as the world champions.

An old friend of mine, Howie McHugh, named the NBA team as the Boston Celtics, and few today know that the Original Celtics were from New York and not from Boston, in spite of all those incredible championship banners hanging from the Garden rafters. Howie, incidentally, was a goalie for Dartmouth College, and a good one. He later became publicity director for the Boston Celtics and served with me on the Harness Racing Board at Rockingham Park in Salem, N.H. He was just an outstanding guy.

Those years, from 1927 and the New York Celtics to the founding of the new pro league, were in a way the middle years of basketball, and the mark-time period to the future. Just so the readers are aware of how the game of basketball grew, from Nat Holman's days (he threw his foul shots all under-handed) to the heydays of the recent past, and the then new kid in Boston, Larry Bird.

I was present for Bird's first workout with the Celtics at Hellenic College in Brookline, Mass. His coach was Bill Fitch. I remember I remarked in the story how Bill Fitch's slate-gray eyes missed little that day, watching keenly as his new star from Indiana worked out with the team. He was sure he had a winner, and so, too, were the writers.

About 6-10 in height, Larry had the classic moves of a more agile player, and he could also shoot. He was uncanny, easily the find of the year, but of course, Red Auerbach knew all about that a few years before. How else could he reach the Celtics?

I thought I would go over and have a talk with Bird when he was given a respite by the coach. When I reached his side, he was panting heavily.

"Welcome to the Boston Celtics," I said, "and to the NBA." It was, I know now, a little sarcastic, but still Larry held out his hand and we shook. "Larry," I said, "I'll be back when you've had a chance to catch your breath again. I know you're pretty tired."

He wiped his sweaty face with a towel, looked up and said simply, "Thanks."

From that day on, I knew Boston had a real winner and a real gentleman, and I never ceased cheering for him in the fantastic days that followed when Larry was piling up all sorts of records as a Celtic. To top it off was that extraordinary showing in the Olympic Games in Barcelona. That alone provided laughs for the entire year as the Americans bombarded stunned opponents game after game to show them how superior this country's basketball is.

I truly believe that the supermen in Boston history, apart from Paul

Revere and the Adamses, were Ted Williams, Babe Ruth earlier, Eddie Shore, Bobby Orr and a guy named Larry Bird, who could do everything on the court and keep the team going at full-tilt with his selfless contribution.

When I saw Bobby Orr at Red Sox training camp at Fort Myers, Fla. in the spring of 1994, I half expected to see the soft-spoken Bird trailing him. He lived in the area, and he was as much a hero to the Naples community as he was in the Boston area during those great years playing for and leading the Celtics to the several NBA championships and all those green and white banners.

Orr and Bird could look up any game night and feel that their careers as a Bruin and Celtic respectively were amply rewarded. Boston was lucky to have such a distinguished, low-key pair, who sacrificed everything for the team, always. They're still well-known at the Fleet Center, as they were at the Garden, as numbers 4 and 33 on the individual banners and with a great deal of Back Bay pride.

Ah One, Ah Two

BANDLEADER Lawrence Welk with
members of his touring show in this 1986
UPI file photo.

He had the spontaneity many other great figures lacked.

Band leader Lawrence Welk was easy to like, full of life and a good conversationalist. He also liked the people about him, whether they were members of his great orchestra or just fans, and it seemed to me, he treated them all the same, with that effusive charm of his. It was a genuine charm, one he likely inherited in his boyhood days on the family's North Dakota farm. Welk's graciousness never wore off, never in the 20 or so years I knew him.

In many ways, he was more convivial than even Guy Lombardo, whom I knew for about 50 years, starting with that warm, early December day in 1934 when I joined the Lombardos for a little football game in Concord, N.H.

Welk was a most delightful chap, and so he was that night in Portland, Maine, when I met him for the first time. I met him first, introducing myself as a writer and sports editor of The *Manchester Union Leader*. Then I introduced my sister, Betty, and her husband, Mort Tuttle, and my friends, Bill and Bobbi Arnold. It was a jolly evening all around, with some of the most toe-tapping tunes being wafted about the Portland Civic Center, largely a place for ice hockey and boxing matches, but this night it was reserved for the champagne music of Lawrence Welk. It fuzzed up inside you, and though it was a concert, it made you want to dance.

That's probably why Lombardo picked Lawrence and his fabulous team to replace him one summer at the Grill Room of the famous Roosevelt Hotel in New York. He had a catchy style, and his music caught on with the patrons. The next is history, and Lawrence probably outdid Guy in the long run, signing a lucrative contract for television and winning universal praise for his distinctive tunes.

On that night, it was that way with New England fans who heard the music that swept out of the Plains to conquer America. It was a night to cherish.

We talked backstage that evening, and after Lawrence had met us all,

he drew me aside and said: "Bob, we are playing at Boston Garden shortly, and I would like to see you in private if I may. I have something I want
to tell you. I've been working on it for some months, and I want to see
what you think about it."

I said I'd be happy to listen to the plan. Just give me the date of your
Boston concert and I'll be there, I said.

When the date came for the Garden appearance, it was sold out. Now,
for hockey and the Boston Bruins, the seating capacity was 13,909 or
something like that. With the whole Garden floor available, lest the stage
itself, there must have been 17,000 in there that night, all applauding
loudly the sycopated Welk music as they danced about the stage.

It was really catching, and my friends, Frank and Edie Morono,
whirled about endlessly, loving every bit of it. A few years later, Frank died
of a sudden heart attack on the golf course, and I am happy he and Edith
did have that one night of dancing to Welk.

Before his appearance that evening, I went into Welk's dressing room
at the Garden, as he had instructed, to see him before the fun began. He
was jovial and excited to see such a big turnout in Boston.

"Bob, I haven't forgotten what I wanted to see you about tonight, but
I don't want to spoil your fun now before the show, so could we talk about
it after the show?" Welk asked.

That was fine with me, so he said, "I can fix it up if you want to dance
with Cissy." I said, "Do you want to kill me off, Lawrence, before our talk?
Can't you see what a little waist she has. I'd be dead after the first 30 bars."

He laughed and said, "Well, if you change your mind, let me know,
and I will see you right after the show, and I hope you like it, Bob."

Like it??? We loved it, from beginning to end! It was utterly fantastic,
colorful in every way, and real lively with audience participation. The
crowd was ecstatic and loudly applauding each new song Lawrence proffered. Finally came his champagne sign-off, and the evening had ended, at
least on the dance floor.

Frank and Edith and I wended our way along the Boston Garden cor-
ridor, well known to me on hockey nights and interviews with Bobby Orr
and Don Cherry and Phil Esposito and the others, and finally we came to

Lawrence Welk's dressing room, and went in. Welk was waiting with a big smile. "Finally, we can get down to business, Bob," he said.

Frank and Edith went over to the other side of the room while we talked, and Lawrence presented his game plan. "Bob," he began, "we are thinking of starting profit-sharing in our group, and I would like to know what you think of it."

That was what was on his mind, and I put him at ease at once: "Lawrence," I told him, "I am 100 percent for profit-sharing, and I will tell you why. Mr. William Loeb, the owner and publisher of *The Union Leader*, is a charter member of Profit-Sharing Industries of America, and we have had it at the paper for many years, and I personally like it, as do most of us at the paper. It has worked beautifully for us, with good dividends, and it has helped management in a big way."

"Boy," said Welk, "am I glad to hear you say that. I want to get it going and to push us even more toward it. Do you think you could write an introductory story for us in your paper? It would be a big help."

I told him that not only could I write that story in *The Union Leader,* but Mr. Loeb as well would be delighted to learn that Welk was joining the team and welcome him aboard.

So it was that I wrote the Welk story on profit-sharing, but the editors at *The Union Leader* treated the story with a banner headline across the top of the page, about how the swing in the Welk Band is toward profit-sharing. I sent Welk a few tear sheets, and about a week later, I received a beautiful letter from the world-famous band leader.

I have carelessly misplaced it, but it went something like this:

> "Dear Bob, I received your tear sheets on the profit-sharing story, and it was terrific; so good that I am flying out to the West Coast with the story in my brief case, and I will be presenting it at a board meeting we are having on joining the profit-sharing institute. Thanks, Bob, and I don't know how to thank you."

In moving my roll-top desk to my son's house, many of my correspondence was misplaced, including all those letters from Welk, and they were not few in number, so I have had to trust to memory. There was also a delightful letter from actress Arlene Francis in there, as I remember, and she had just written to me from New York telling me how excited she was in a review I did on her in a show that played Boston.

"You have made my day, my week, my year, and I thank you so much for your glowing words." That was the essence of her message, but then a funny thing happened in the newsroom that very morning I received Arlene's lovely letter.

I was just finishing the last paragraph on my column, "The Sports Desk," when someone shouted the dreaded words, "Log off everybody, the system is down," (meaning the computers) and before I could save even a line of what I had just written, I had lost the entire column. I was crushed, and then the office girl came around with the mail and dropped this letter at my desk.

It was the missive from Miss Francis, so before I even attempted to recreate the lost column, I opened the letter and read Arlene's great note. Without wasting another moment on my lost column, which had gone up into the airwaves of nowhere, I dashed off a letter to Miss Francis, which I am sure caused her to laugh. It went something like this:

"Dear Arlene, Thanks for your thoughtful letter. Now it is my turn. Your letter made my day, my week, my year, for you see, shortly before your note arrived, I had just lost my entire sports column on a computer malfunction, and your kind words saved the day. So, thanks Arlene, I always thought you were a special girl."

Who said writing isn't fun. And you meet such wonderful people all the time. No day is the same: New faces, new stories, new ideas.

Lawrence Welk would have liked that story, and indeed, he received thousands of letters each day from his public. I'll bet he had a million stories to tell just in the letters he received.

Lawrence never missed a Christmas after that profit-sharing story. I think in all my list of characters, he was the only one who remembered feature writers, and the gifts from Hollywood were always deeply remembered.

I became a Welk fan myself with millions of other followers around the country, and yes, around the universe. I liked his quick-beat tempos in the bouncy scores, his languid attention to waltzes, his graceful choral work, the various solos, the inspired dancing routines of Bobby and Cissy and all the others.

Welk had a style, like Lombardo, and he capitalized on it. Most bands today have no unique style of their own. They just machine-play the notes, and all have a tendency to sound the same. Guy was different. So was Harry James and Glenn Miller, and Paul Whiteman, and Benny Goodman, and Rudy Valee, and Glen Gray and his Casa Loma band, and the Dorseys, and Lawrence Welk, and perhaps Welk of all of them became the most successful with the eyes of a nationwide television audience trained on him each and every week.

Welk became as popular as Lombardo on the public hearth, but I think the Royal Canadians came out a little ahead with those wonderful orchestrations and style of presentation. That is why Irving Berlin and all the rest brought their songs to that Guy.

In his own presentation of the tones of the different bands of the day, Welk never forgot Lombardo, and as time went on, his band actually sounded like the Royal Canadians.

One day when Lawrence Welk called me from Hollywood where he and his troupe were taping a show, he wanted to tell me how well my story had carried at the board meeting that day. I was overjoyed to hear that, and as we chatted, I suddenly remembered that my granddaughter, Jennifer, was with us that very day, August 12, and I told Lawrence that it was her birthday.

"Is she there, Bob?" he asked, and I told him that she was indeed, right in the same room.

"Put her on the line," he said, and I handed the phone to Jennifer.

"Your grandfather told me this is your birthday, Jennifer. Is that right?"

After she replied in the affirmative, Welk said, "Then listen, Jennifer, I am going to sing you a song." And from that Hollywood set, Welk crooned, "Happy Birthday, Dear Jennifer, Happy Birthday to You," as the cast applauded in the background. She had made the Lawrence Welk Show.

Welk will go down in musical history with me as an individual who loved people and who was loved by people. There was that affection. It worked both ways. Lawrence, too, brought up a whole family in a musical sense, and a most distinguished one. He made them. Their art stood out because of the attention he lavished upon them. He had excellent human qualities, and because of them, he stood out as well. People used to set their clocks by the Welk television show each week, so as not to miss a bar of enchanting music.

I miss Lawrence Welk for his many attributes and for the music he gave America. It enriched the country, to be sure, and maybe some critics said, "Hey, what's this farm kid doing in this business?" and they were partly right. He was a farm kid, but did he know the business, and he kept right up with Dow Jones, as in checking out profit-sharing and investments of a winning kind.

To me, Lawrence Welk was the All-America Boy, with the funny accent. He made it famous: Ah one, ah two. That was his downbeat, and all Americans knew it so well on those Saturday evenings when he and his band took over the airwaves. Revel in Heaven, Lawrence, you've earned it.

Lester Played Royally

IMPECCABLE -- Ballroom conductor Lester Lanin poses for a photograph at the Friars Club, his favorite New York City haunt, wearing his usual impeccable wardrobe. The must-have bandleader for the most important dance occasions, Lanin, contrary to his own dress code, would give dancers souvenir hats like the one in the foreground. (AP File Photo)

To this day, I'm sorry to say, I've never heard in person the great Lester Lanin Orchestra, although it has played many times in Manchester, N.H., which Lester has said is one of the country's best musical cities.

Lester especially liked the Carousel Ballroom with its fine acoustics, and he played many a memorable concert and dance there. He was on pretty much of a par with the world-famous Guy Lombardo Orchestra at the Carousel, and when either of those two bands performed there, it was a forgone conclusion that their performances would be sold out.

Both were primarily dance-oriented bands, and they'd induce dancers by the hundreds to flock to the floor for some head-to-head romantic music. Lester still has a good, danceable beat, with a definite lilt to his style, and that makes him most appealing to dancers wherever, even to Queen Elizabeth II, who enjoys spinning about the floor. In fact, in New York City during a Royal visit, she danced to Guy Lombardo and his Royal Canadians.

The Queen was so enthralled by his sweet style that she asked for one of his albums. Guy went further than that. He recorded a special album just for the Queen, and she still has it among her souvenirs. It is for her ears alone, as well as The Royal Family. As a Canadian, Guy was numbered among her subjects at one time, and the Queen was always one of his favorite fans.

Lanin and Lombardo and Lawrence Welk always had a distinguished, delightful and captivating style that set them apart. Lest you think that these were the only orchestras that attracted my attention, they were not. There was Harry James for one, Glenn Gray for another, Jan Garber, Ray Noble, Fred Waring, the Dorseys, Peanuts Hucko and the Glenn Miller Band, and, of course, Wayne King (the Waltz King), and one of the very first I heard, Claude Hopkins and Cab Calloway, and the Duke himself, Duke Ellington.

They all had their distinctive styles, and it stamped them forever like a mother's kiss, easily identifiable, a real musical trademark, and Lombardo's most of all.

When Lanin came to town, he would always give me a call at *The Union Leader*. I remember once getting a call from Lester.

"Bob," he said, "can we get together?"

"Of course, Lester," I replied, "can you make it on my lunch break at my home?"

Lanin said, "Sure, I'll join you in a few minutes." And he did.

It turned out to be one of the longest lunch breaks ever for me, about two hours, but we had the greatest time, recounting Lester's exciting life and his many memorable visits in London with the Royal Family at the Mayfair. Listen they all know and love Lester as those of us in Manchester do. How do we say it...He is part of the family?

Indeed, he is. Lanin has brought many happy moments to people everywhere, and from all walks of life, and he is one of us, to be sure.

Then why, Bob, have you not seen Lester and his fantastic orchestra perform, one might ask. A good question, and my only defense is that I was working as a sports editor and as a music critic all those years, and I was unable to break away while Lester and his superlative musical arrangements were taking dancers into Lanin Heaven in the shadows of the evening.

Not only did Lester Lanin come to my home for the interview, but after his Carousel concert, he came to *The Union Leader* newsroom and composing room at the old plant on Amherst Street and met all his admirers, and he had an army of them. He brought a lot of extra excitement into many lives, including all those folks at *The Union Leader* that evening.

My article on Lanin that night ran about a column in length, as I recall, and in it, he recollected many of his adventures at home and abroad. Lester was not only successful in this country, but in London and other places where he and his band performed.

Lester Lanin was a wonder of the music world. I interviewed him two or three times and learned of his concept of life: To bring happiness to those about you. He did just that, and about every workday of his life, with his delectable, bouncy music and with that warm and engaging smile. He loved everybody, and all who have come in contact with him loved Lester.

I will always remember Lester Lanin's winning smile and his human touch. My wife, Barbara, I think, took in the Lanin show one year (it was a Saturday night again, and the toughest night on sports, and again I could not make it), and she enjoyed his lively tunes. I hope she had time to dance with Lester.

Lanin sat in the rocking chair in our living room, saying how delighted he was to be in Manchester again. He loved the city, and while here, he walked around visiting its stores and its people, the friendly person that he was. It was always a pleasure to play host to the Lester Lanins of the world, and while at *The Union Leader* that night, he learned how it is done on the other side of the stage, the reporting of an event, the work in the newsroom, the work in the composing room, and finally, the work in the pressroom as the giant presses roar to life. He was dutifully impressed, and it was a distinct pleasure having him as a guest.

I asked him how the dance went, and he replied: "We missed you there, Bob."

Not as much as I missed being there and hearing all that gorgeous music.

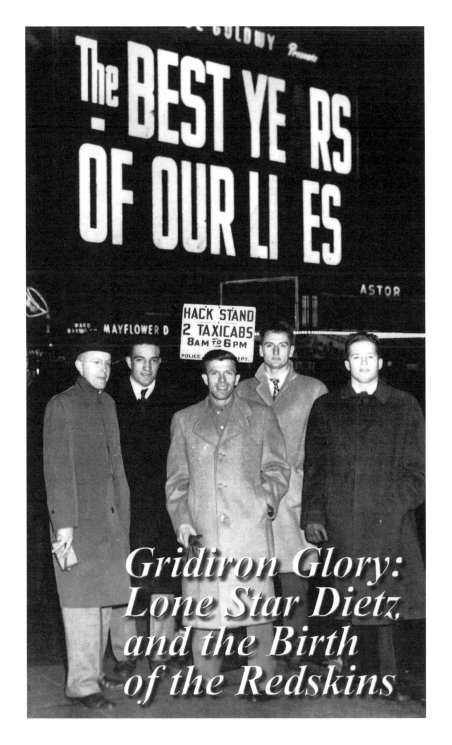

Gridiron Glory:
Lone Star Dietz,
and the Birth
of the Redskins

THE BEST YEARS -- A Manchester Central High School party stands under a sign proclaiming the best of times in New York City. It was, indeed, a welcomed period. The war had ended and everything was looking up for the Central party, which was in New York celebrating the long gridiron coaching tenure of Hubert B. McDonough as he retired. McDonough, earlier in his career, was the coach of a Manchester all-star team that got blasted by the Boston Redskins, coached by Lone Star Dietz. Those Redskins went on to become the vaunted Washington Redskins of the NFL. (AP Photo)

In 1935, New England had its first professional football team. Others had performed, but they were more in the line of semi-pro type teams. The Boston Redskins were bonifide pros.

As such, they sought exhibition games with whatever area teams were available. Manchester, N.H., was a football hotbed at the time, shaped by the coaching of Hubert B. McDonough, who enjoyed a great playing career at Phillips Exeter Academy before moving on to Dartmouth College.

There was a team of college all-stars which reputedly had the class and power of a professional-type club, and they were seeking games.

So, too, was the new team in Boston, the Redskins of the National Football League, which played the league schedule against such teams as the Chicago Bears, the New York Giants and the Green Bay Packers. The Redskins were strong, though not quite yet championship caliber.

It was late summer and the Redskins, which years later became the traditionally strong Washington Redskins, were looking for warmup games with any team close to Boston.

The club's letter to would-be rivals went something like this, a veteran surveyor of the scene recalls:

"Fear not of a high score, or injuries..." and it went on to enumerate plans for its game with that team, which in this case was the Manchester 11, all-stars assembled from local colleges and universities. It wasn't a bad team, either. I had seen many of its members performing on the gridiron at Dartmouth and at the University of New Hampshire and elsewhere, and they were solid performers, though not at the level of the Redskins.

The game that day at Manchester's Athletic Field, formerly Textile Field and now Gill Stadium, drew thousands of fans, many of whom were obviously looking for an upset of the pro club from Boston.

They were hugely disappointed, and with good reason. The Redskins ruined that sunny afternoon by demolishing the local contingent without regard to their letter of assurance not to fear a blowout.

I decided to cover the game for the *Concord Monitor* as a favor to the sports editor, who, it seemed, was interested in my personal observations of the game and who had a personal curiosity.

I made it a point to first meet the Redskins' coach, Lone Star Dietz, a big, bronzed Choctaw Indian who knew his football, offense and defense, and any other way it took to win, although I understand Dietz told his men to take it easy on the all-stars, since they were being decent enough to take on the Redskins in battle to help get them in shape for their regular season.

"Fear not of a high score...."? The pros rolled it up, 82-0, a real frolic for them, scoring at will.

C. Edward Bourassa, a former member of New Hampshire Governor's Council and a close friend of then Gov. Sherman Adams, who went on to become presidential assistant to Eisenhower, had played for the aforementioned Hubie McDonough at Manchester Central High School in its glory years when it was the toast of Football New England.

Bourassa was a fullback with Central and a mighty good one under McDonough's guiding hand. Hubie was regarded as one of the country's best football coaches, a genius of the game whose wizardry, his players attest, led to many plays and formations that later became standard in the sport.

Bourassa was inserted into the game as a fullback about the midway point, and his first instructions from the quarterback were somewhat cryptic: "Let's soften up that fat guy, Turk Edrwards (about 6-2, 260 pounds, which was really big by that days' standards), and we'll start to move."

Bourassa, himself a 6-2, 200-pounder, took the handoff and bulled headlong into Edwards, who slammed Bourassa to the turf.

"I felt my bones were broken, and I had a tough time catching my breath," said Bourassa, a two-time All-Stater and a punishing runner. "I half-crawled back to the huddle, and the quarterback tells me once more: 'O.K., Bourassa, again on the same play, I think we're softening up the Turk.'"

So, once again, Bourassa stormed into Turk's big arms.

"This time," Bourassa later recalled, "he was real vicious, like he was upset that I should even think of running into him a second time. 'You shouldn't try those things, Big Boy' he told me, and from the impact of that last crash, I believed he was right. I crawled on my hands and knees back to the huddle, and when the quarterback told me 'Again,' I said, 'No thanks. I'll pass the ball, but I won't run it for you, or the President of the United States.'"

And he didn't.

In the first or second quarter of that now-infamous game, a lineman for the all-stars wanted to impress the pros with his toughness, so he played without a helmet. They carried him out on a stretcher, and to tell the truth, I thought he was dead. I could see his blond hair, and he wasn't moving a muscle. He had the appearance of a basket case, and I think it was Turk he ran into.

If the Redskins had left Turk at home in Boston, it might have been a bit closer, but not by much. They were all over the place, a real ambush you might say.

Recalled Bourassa: "There was no way we were going to stop those guys. Hell, they were scoring at will, running wild down the field, tossing lateral passes to each other and laughing it up all the way. But it was a comforting letter, anyway, that they wouldn't pile it on."

The letter should have been engraved for posterity. "Fear not of a high score or injuries..."

I went in after the game to get a few notes from the coach, and they were slightly hilarious, as I recall, like "We were lucky those Manchester guys didn't explode on us."

Coach Dietz was pleased with my article, and he wrote me a letter the following week inviting me down for all the Redskins' games. He told me to drop in and see him the next week against the Giants; he wanted to talk with me again. I wrote him a note that I would, and, with a companion from Concord High School, I entered the dressing room shortly after the game with Harry Newman and the Giants, which was a thriller.

I encountered a bit of trouble reaching Dietz, however. The Redskins' trainer, with sloping shoulders and long, powerful arms, and in his under-shirt, stopped me en route:

"Where do you think you are going, sonny?" he asked.

I said I was going to Dietz's office to see the coach.

"Not this day you're not," he barked. "You're the guy who's been swiping all those jerseys."

I told him that this was the first time I was ever in that room.

He replied belligerently, "Horse manure. You're going outta here on the fly."

As I contemplated the door, a player getting ready to step into the shower, said, "Hold on Shorty, let's hear what the young man has to say."

The player was the immortal Cliff Battles, an All-America at West Virginia as a halfback, later a member of the Hall of Fame All-Time All America. I told Battles that Dietz had asked to see me, and that's where I was headed. Battles gave the trainer a dirty look and said, "Come on."

We went to the coach's office, and Battles knocked on the door.

Cliff told Dietz he was with a young man who said the coach wanted to see him. Dietz saw me and said, "Oh, yes, that's the boy from Manchester. Come on in, son."

I thanked Battles from the bottom of my heart, for sparing my any more of a battle with that trainer. We both laughed at that, and I stepped into the room with Dietz.

It was a glorious visit for a fledgling writer barely out of high school and for a school chum who was all agog. We talked of many things, and I still remember one in particular that Coach Dietz took pains to point out.

"No kick should ever be blocked," he said. "It should be kicked on the second step, and at the knees for a quick contact. That way you can get height and leverage."

Since that talk with Dietz, I have watched many kickers taking four and sometimes five steps before even meeting the ball and then wondering what they'd done wrong when it was blocked. With Dietz, the ball was kicked almost at once, and a guy would almost have to be a track star to be able to get in and make the block. It was great advice, and I hope some of today's kickers can learn this lesson, particularly kickers in the NFL who look like they are at a tea party as they make ready to punt the ball out of danger. Dietz would have put them through his chewing machine and ground them into bits.

Remember, guys: At the knees, and on the second step. Got it?

We spoke of the great one, Cliff Battles. There was still another one that afternoon as the Giants nipped the Redskins at Fenway Park. He was the aforementioned Harry Newman, formerly of the University of Michigan. Before the game, I went on the field to watch the players make ready for the game, and I noticed a strange thing. Newman was traversing the gridiron, twisting his shoe into the sod every once in a while.

"What's the pitch?" I asked the former great Big 10 back.

"I'm just looking for slippery spots," he said with a grin. "You know it rained last night, and I want to learn which part of the field is solid and which isn't."

It paid off on the opening kickoff, which Newman caught before bolting 96 yards for the game-winning touchdown. Don't tell me these guys don't notice things, like rain the night before the game and a slippery field. That's called anticipation, and I hear it a lot at spring training camp with the Red Sox and other clubs.

Sometimes it's the little things that make the difference between a good player and a great player. Harry Newman knew that entire field that day, and he proceeded to show the players that he did. It was pretty sensational, as he dashed through the entire Redskins team.

"Newman's Run Beats 'skins," just like that.

On the subject of football, I remember one pretty incredible incident when I was talking with the New York Giants' Hall-of-Fame quarterback Fran Tarkenton before a game at Foxboro, Mass., with the New England Patriots. As we talked, a paymaster I hadn't seen suddenly appeared and handed me a check and also gave one to Fran.

I thought it was a message from the office, and I tore it open, only to find a check inside for a huge sum of money. As I looked further, I discovered the check was for Fran. I don't know whose check Fran was handed, but I handed mine over to Fran, saying, "This belongs to you, Fran." Then I added: "Let's just toss for it."

He got a big laugh out of that. "I didn't even know I had a check coming," he said. "I've been negotiating these past months. Gee, thanks."

Richard McDonald: He Started It All...

CO-FOUNDER OF CHAIN -- Richard McDonald, right, founded the world-famous chain of McDonald's fast-food restaurants with his brother, much against his mother's remonstrations that he go out and find a job. Here, Bob Hilliard interviews him at his Bedford, N.H., home. Richard died in 1999. (*Union Leader* staff photo.)

Try as he might, Richard McDonald couldn't convince his own mother that he had a job, in spite of the fact that he did have a job, a great job at that.

"My Irish mother, God bless her," McDonald said, "would go downtown and talk with all her friends, and they would ask how the boys were doing. She would become exasperated.

"I wish they would go out and find a decent job, instead of sitting around and talking of this quick-lunch business. They're going nowhere, and they are always talking of big money,'" Mrs. McDonald was quoted as saying.

That sounds a bit like any worried mother looking out for the welfare of her children. She wants them to get a good, honest job, and to be sensible about it. Except, that's what they had from the start of their enterprise, a business that paid them in a most stratospheric way, especially when they sold it.

Even then, poor Mrs. McDonald thought her two boys, Richard and Maurice, would have to be looking for work. The money they received for their little hamburger stands wouldn't last forever, and they could flip a pretty mean hamburger with all the experience they had since leaving Manchester, N.H., and looking for some kind of decent work.

Hamburgers were their business, and it brought the brothers McDonald some decent publicity, as well, for they became the world-famous McDonalds, where hamburgers are sold today by the billions under the great golden arches created by the one and same Richard so many years ago.

Maurice died many years ago, but Richard turned a golden 85 on Feb. 16, 1994, the day after we visited him at his home in classy Bedford, a suburb of Manchester. He is alive and very vibrant in his everyday living.

His name, I reminded him, is without a doubt (no recount needed) the most famous in the whole wide world. Many years ago, I looked out a touring bus window in far-away Singapore and saw the golden arches on a busy thoroughfare in that most charming metropolis. I saw others in London during a visit there with my grandchildren. They didn't want to dine at Simpson's-in-the-Strand, or at the Royal Lancaster, they preferred McDonald's near Trafalgar.

It seems the McDonalds did their work well in the big sale to Ray Kroc, who had the milkshake machines and bought the brothers out. Their name, though, lives today in Moscow, as well.

Mrs. McDonald would be pleased today to hear that, for she would have learned that her two boys worked long hours at a good, "decent" job that finally rewarded them quite handsomely. Their original hamburger stand was in San Bernardino, Calif., and that, sadly, is no longer standing, although Richard McDonald points out that the "home in Manchester where I grew up is still standing at 500 South Main Street."

Richard and Maurice's mother would lament over and over to friends on Elm Street in Manchester, "When are they ever going to get a job?" and Richard used to break into a loud laughter as he recounted it. Well, this is a Heavenly message to you, Mrs. McDonald, "Both boys found that job, and did very well, too."

The boys were together in that business venture for about 35 years before Maurice died, and it was a sorrowful scene when death finally parted them. They were close, and the 6-foot-1, silver-haired Richard was heartbroken; he never really got over the loss of his dear brother.

The McDonalds of Manchester were miles ahead of their time, a good seven or eight years, minimum, in the fast-food industry that brought food to the hungry for a small price and helped spread the gospel of the free-enterprise system that even today is spreading to all continents, with the help of Kroc, who worked for the brothers from 1955 to 1961 when he bought the business, with an assist from the owners (exclamation mark, please). They helped him raise the capital (exclamation mark once again). Bill Tansey was the first general manager and had he lived, he would have bought out the business himself, for he knew how lucrative it had become.

I would have to say that the McDonalds have already been anointed: King of the Hamburgers, and Kroc as The Milk Shake King in their endeavors.

Del Monaco: D Above High C

Had powerhouse tenor Mario Del Monaco lived today, he would have blown the world away with his ringing notes. He could hit a D above High C with scant effort and with picture-perfect clarity, one of the wonders of the musical firmament.

My introduction to this man-at-work tenor came on a fall day in 1951 or 1952 on the widely heard Texaco Opera Broadcast, hosted by another wonder of the lyric stage, Milton Cross, a former singer himself.

Cross knew his music, and of course he knew his singing and his Grand Opera as no one else. Del Monaco rated as one of his all-time favorites. He could do things few singers before him, or after him, could do. His stock-in-trade on the operatic stage, or in concert form, was caressing that D above High C.

One evening at the 4,200-seat Wang Center for the Performing Arts in Boston, the famed French tenor, Guy Chauvet, spoke to me about Del Monaco's lofty reputation in the world at large, how his performances were always SRO as audiences clamored to see and hear him in action. He added as in a state of acknowledgement, that Mr. Del Monaco could better him on the musical scale.

"He could reach a strong D above High C," he sputtered, "while I could only manage a High C."

Chauvet thought I didn't get it, so he walked over to the freshly painted wall in his dressing room and proceeded to show me exactly what he meant.

"Like this, monsieur," he said, and he took out of his pocket one of those felt pens and inscribed the staff, lines and spaces, then he placed the High C where it belonged, and said "This is where I reach." Then, to make sure I was keeping an eye on the demonstration, he added, "and this is where Del Monaco goes."

Looking on in almost utter disbelief, he remarked: "I still have this as my official introduction to opera. I will never forget it."

Barbara said with matter-of-fact diligence, "You know the Met comes to Boston each year, and I think this spring they are opening the season there with 'Aida.'"

"Well," I replied, "let's go." I'd love to hear Del Monaco in person."

"It's not all that easy," my wife replied. "They are usually sold out, and with an opera like 'Aida' in town, I doubt if any tickets remain."

By this time, I had been sufficiently challenged, and I said I would write to Anita Davis-Chase, an official with the Boston Opera Association, which staged the opera season in that city. So I wrote.

A few days later, I had my answer. It was succinct, something like: "Thank you for your letter. As you no doubt know, 'Aida' is a first-nighter, and with Mario Del Monaco singing, all tickets are sold out. Thanks again for your note."

Barbara said nothing as I remember it, so I decided to try once more by writing directly to the president of the Boston Opera Association, H. Wendell Endicott, informing him that my request of three tickets was not wholly an idle request, and that I was not just going to the opera to tell friends later that I had seen the opera in Boston. I had to go, I told H. Wendell, because I was doing an in-depth interview with Mr. Del Monaco that day for *The Union Leader* in Manchester, and that I must see him in action in order to do a comprehensive story.

His reply was forthright. "By all means," Endicott intoned, "I will set aside three seats for you in Box 34. Please send me a check for $25.50."

Imagine, for Met Opera box seats. Now they are well over $100 apiece at Lincoln Center in New York.

We sent the check along, and received our tickets.

Then Barbara asked, "What are you going to do now about that interview with Del Monaco?"

"Yes," I answered, "I have been thinking about that."

That very day, I took care of the matter. I sent a telegram directly to Del Monaco at the Met, and the very next day I had my answer. It was short and to the point, I recall, and it stated: "Meet me Monday afternoon at 1 o'clock at the Ritz-Carlton for drinks."

That was the best news yet, and so we followed instructions, dressing

up for the first-nighter, and taking off for Boston. We met Mr. And Mrs.
Del Monaco in the dining room, and sat around a small table. I hardly
knew what to talk about, this being my first-ever excursion into the world
of opera, but both Mario and Mrs. Rina Fedora Del Monaco put us at ease
at once. Barbara and Fedora moved to the far end of the table, and Bobby,
Mario and I talked.

I asked first about Mario and his work in mastering 47 different roles
in opera, most of them three or four hours in length.

"You must have to train very hard, Mario," I suggested.

"Train?" he responded.

Trying to think of an appropriate synonym, I said, "You must have to
condition quite a bit for all those roles."

He was completely lost, understanding about as much English as I did
Italian.

"Train, condition?"

He looked to his wife for some help. She touched her forehead and
thought a minute.

"Oh, yes," she smiled, "air-conditioned trains, all over Italy.
Everywhere you go, air-conditioned trains."

We labored past that portion of the interview, and progressed to the
part where I inquired to individual operas, and poor Mario had to spell
hem out, dumb me. I knew very few, and he spelled them out painstak-
ingly. I will tell you this, it took about 15 minutes for Lucia di
Lammermoor. Mario did not hurry, he gave us plenty of time for the
interview, and when it was through, I had a pretty good story from the
tenor ranked No. 1 in the world.

After that day at the Ritz-Carlton, Mario and Rina, and Barbara,
Bobby Jr. and I were friends for life.

"Don't forget to drop in to the dressing room to see us after the
opera," he said.

During the interview, in which Mario indicated his favorite opera was
Giordano's "Andrea Chenier," he sat next to Bobby Jr., who earlier had
won the State Episcopal Choir Festival at St. Paul in Concord. On the way
home about midnight, Bobby was chewing on a candy bar when sudden-

ly his throat felt very sore. He opened the car window and tossed his candy out, then closed it and sat quietly all the way home. He went to bed at once after arriving back in Manchester, and Barbara summoned the doctor the next morning. He checked Bobby, and said with a grin, "He has the mumps."

"What," I said, "and yesterday he was sitting right beside a Metropolitan Opera tenor, the greatest singer in the world."

I could see the headlines the next day in the New York papers: "Met Tenor Down With Mumps."

I hurriedly sent a telegram to Mario at the Met Opera House, telling him to have a checkup at once, for Bobby had come down with the mumps, and I was afraid he might have caught them as well.

Mario let us know that he had had mumps as a child, and was feeling all right. And for that, we thanked the Lord. We always mentioned that incident whenever we met at the opera, in New York or Boston.

Today, Bobby is married with two lovely children, Jennifer, and attorney, and Robby III, a stockbroker, both in Boston. Bobby Jr. and Shirley reside in Marco Island, Florida, where he has his office for Chicago Stock Trade.

I have never heard "Radames" sung as brilliantly, or as powerfully, as Mario sang it that night, and I thought he put a little extra effort into it for us. In any event, he brought down the house in that "Aida" and won, with Zinka Milanov singing the title role, a tidal wave of curtain calls for some 10 minutes. The Boston papers hailed the performance the very next day in all the late editions, and it was truly a night to remember.

Over the years, we heard Mario many times, both in Boston and New York (at the old house), and he had a list of triumphs as long as your arm. I don't think Mario ever had a lackluster performance. In his favorite opera, "Andrea Chenier," his voice took on a rather mellow hue, and was so rich in overall quality.

In "Carmen," with Rise Stevens, they earned 24 curtain calls, and enough bouquets to stock a flower shop. They came pouring onto the stage, bouquet after bouquet. It was a sight to remember, and with his lemon-yellow uniform and black shiny boots, Del Monaco was a commanding soldier figure. His rendition of "The Flower Song" was sensational, and it brought down the house, and in the finale, Miss Stevens took over, mortally wounded by the flashing knife of Don Jose, tearing down the drapes as she slumped to the floor. What an opera, and what a combination.

"Carmen" and "Aida" were triumphs of the first order, of course, but I always thought Del Monaco's greatest role was that of the crazed "Otello" in which he strangles his Desdemona, and then takes his own life by a dagger, and as he sinks to the floor, sings softly the immortal lines, "I kissed thee ere I killed thee; no way but this, killing myself..."

Del Monaco put so much fervor into his singing, and acting, that the opera became a living, realistic thing right there on the stage. Shakespeare, and yes, Verdi, would have been proud of that type of acting. It brought the chills, really, and damn Iago anyway. Why did Shakespeare have to invent a character like that?

I have reviewed "Otello" many times, but I have yet to see the equal of Del Monaco's Met performance, nor will I ever. A Desdemona so fair, so truthful and honest and loving, to meet that terrible end, one cannot help but feel a wrenching pain as she lies so still on her deathbed.

Del Monaco had the great ability to enact any operatic role to the fullest, bringing into play that voluminous, powerful voice, so rich, so clear. VerdI's musical touch enlivens the work, making it quite superior to the staged "Othello," especially with Del Monaco in the title role.

The first opera I ever saw was that "Aida" with Zinka Milanov in the title role, opposite Del Monaco as Radames, her lover, and they are both destined to end their lives, deep in that tomb, from which no escape is possible. They sing, locked in each others arms, a farewell to earth, "O terra addio," which is very plaintive and touching. It is a dramatic ending. VerdI's music is gorgeous, from the Nile Scene early on, with the harp solo envisioning life in Egypt, the Land of the Pharaohs, to the death scene in that tomb.

Backstage that night, it was a bedlam. Zinka was running around, half-dressed, one shoe on, one shoe off, and her brother, Baldisar, beret on, and cigarette holder in hand, was wandering about leisurely. Suddenly he hit a key on a piano in his sister's dressing room, and she let out a blast that could have been heard the length of Tremont Street. Baldisar, a musician, smiled. His sister was right on the money; and she was right on the money in the four-hour long presentation.

Del Monaco was a tired, near exhausted, performer at the end, and as he had asked, we went back to see him and Rina Fedora, his wife, and offer our excited congratulations. People were streaming in, and we stayed only a short time as we wanted Mario to rest and relax a bit after that sort of a wild evening. We drove the relatively short distance to Manchester, discussing the opera every way, and also Bobby's terribly sore throat.

It was for us an introduction into a whole new world of glamour and excitement, and we loved it thoroughly. Mario and Rina spoke that afternoon of their little boy back home in Europe. He was only about eight or nine at the time, and he was attending school I believe somewhere in Switzerland.

Obviously, he could not tour with his parents because of the schooling. That was little Giancarlo, now a world-renown operatic producer, and the intendant of the prestigious Bonn Opera Company in Germany.

Since father and son were directed to the opera stage in different generations, I thought it might be appropriate to quote from my tribute in The Union Leader of October 24, 1982, and from my review of Giancarlo's presentation of "Stiffelio" at the Met Opera in The Union Leader of Nov. 1, 1993, and also the obituary of Giancarlo's dear mother, Rina, in Opera News of September, 1991.

They were important dates in The Family Del Monaco: a father bowing out of the world after an astonishing career, a son commencing a world career, and a devoted wife and mother, relinquishing an operatic career of her own, to care for both, dying at the age of 73, two months shy of her 74th birthday. A noble family, and as a woman remarked to me in the dining room of the Mayflower Hotel near Central Park when I introduced her to Giancarlo, Italy's First Family.

The headline read: "Tales of a Tenor. Mario Del Monaco: A Voice to Remember."

A paragraph or two from my tribute follow:

"Mario Del Monaco died the other day at his villa near Venice. He was 67, and he had known the greatest artistic triumphs. Before Pavarotti, Del Monaco had been London Record's leading tenor. He sang gloriously and powerfully. One critic, indeed, characterized his style as roaring tenor. One thing is certain. He could be heard in all corners of any opera house in the world. Please make that ballpark, had that been where he was performing.

"Those were the golden days at the Metropolitan in Mr. Bing's retinue of colossal superstars. Those were the days of such as Rise Stevens, Richard Tucker, Leonard Warren, Jerome Hines, Robert Merrill, Jan Peerce, and of course, Mr. Del Monaco. Giants of the industry.

"Of them all, however, Mario Del Monaco was perhaps the big gun. He was known and loved and respected the world over, wherever in fact a lyric house stood. He was the one.

Del Monaco was an exciting person, kindly disposed, a gentleman in every way, courteous, well-mannered, exceptionally humble. A perfect type to be called the greatest, the champion. He was just that."

On Giancarlo:

"This was the Editor's Note in *The Union Leader*.

"Critic-at-Large Bob Hilliard, at the invitation of Producer Giancarlo del Monaco, attended last week's premiere performance at the Metropolitan Opera of VerdI's stirring "Stiffelio," a controversial work first heard in 1850. His review-essay follows. The opera received glowing praise in the media. --Editors.

"**By BOB HILLIARD**
Critic-at-Large
"**NEW YORK** -- Had Giancarlo del Monaco but listened a bit more attentively to his little daughter's baby singing at rehearsals a few days earlier of Giuseppe VerdI's stirring Stiffelio, he might have known what awaited him at the Metropolitan Opera's recent colorful premiere.

Little Fedora, named for Giancarlo's late opera-singing mother of the 1940s, Rina Fedora Del Monaco, began singing so loudly at the rehearsal, imitating the principals, that her mother, Marissa, had to carry her off the stage, while her noted producer-father tried to hush her.

"Little Fedora had it right. The audience loved the 1850 work, staged about the time of VerdI's great masterpiece, "Rigoletto," and surprisingly neglected to this date. Like Little Fedora, the listeners, too, whipped up a whirlwind of applause after the final curtain, convinced that they had witnessed a bit of history, and a whole lot of vocal and musical artistry.

"Why not a storm of applause? The title role was sung gloriously and with distinguished fervor by Mr. Placido Domingo himself (of the trio known to the world as The Three Tenors). It was positively enchanting and with Placido's friend, Maestro James Levine at the helm in the pit, it was an evening to be long remembered and savored. Even the cab drivers were talking of it out in the streets. "Hey," said one, "what singing in there tonight. A woman fare was telling me all about it." Yes, and thats what the talk was all about over coffee the next a.m.

"That is how is was for the premiere in New York City, and Verdi himself would have been proud. His opera had finally found itself, through the help, too, of a little child at rehearsal who gave him an unexpected assist, and revved up the cast.

And finally, the obit on Rina Del Monaco:

"RINA DEL MONACO, September 19, 1917, in Genoa, Italy, soprano who performed such roles as Musetta and Lola under the name of Fedora Solveni, later relinquishing her career to devote herself to that of her husband, tenor Mario Del Monaco, on July 12, 1991, in Pesaro.

As mentioned, that was from the *Opera News* of September, 1991.

Thus, as two of the Del Monaco Family departed, another took up his position on the firing line, and it looks like still another is on her way.

A New del Monaco

THE WORD IS OPERA -- Singers and author Bob Hilliard party with opera director Giancarlo del Monaco, son of the great operatic tenor, Mario Del Monaco, in New York. (Sally Corcoran Photo)

One morning about 7, a few years back, I was routed from my sleep by a telephone call. The operator asked my name, and then said "You have a call from Bonn, Germany."

The voice on the other end wanted to make sure of things. He asked, "Is this Bob Hilliard?"

I replied that it was, and he identified himself as the attorney for Giancarlo del Monaco.

"We over here have read your wonderful tribute to his late father, Mario Del Monaco, and his son is very desirous of meeting you." he said.

I replied that I too was anxious to meet Giancarlo, and is he right there?

"Oh no," the caller answered. "He is in New York to direct the opera at the Met. He has given me all the directions for the meeting."

"Well," I inquired, "when am I supposed to meet Mr. Del Monaco?"

"Tomorrow at noon at the Mayflower Hotel in Central Park West," he replied.

The meeting was arranged just like that; yes, even before breakfast and a chance for a cup of coffee. I told the caller I would try to be in New York the following noon, and I tried to clear up another bit of a mystery that bothered me.

"Is this really Mario's son? I notice he spells his name with a small del."

"Oh, yes," the caller replied, "he likes it better that way than with the capital D."

I thanked the caller for getting in touch with me, and thought back to the day when first I met the great Mario Del Monaco at the Ritz-Carlton in Boston, and discovered what a wonderful person he was, so kind and polite and so thoughtful. A lawyer friend with me on another occasion when Mario and his wife, Fedora, got together with Barbara and me at the Ritz, remarked "What a great guy, and what a great talent."

Indeed, he had a touch of greatness, and it showed wherever he went—at the Ritz, on the stage. He was so very kind, and you know, he never charged other singers who had talent a cent for helping them. There was never a question about Mario's greatness.

As the Met and other great opera companies around the world continue their search for lyric talent, del Monaco is rapidly soaring to the top in another category, that of a producer, and it seems he has few peers. His many productions to date have reached a preeminence few attain in this competitive world of strife. His are at once novel and colorful and moving.

How could I have been so fortunate in meeting, first Mario and Fedora, then Giancarlo and his lovely South African wife, blonde Marissa, an opera singer herself. Ask a ballplayer whether he would like to be lucky or great, and he will respond lucky about every time. So it is with writers; you can be great and not hit the connections. Lucky is the right word, and so it has been with me.

Mario was the very first of my operatic friends, and the object of my initial flight into the world of music and glamour.

There is little doubt in my mind that Giancarlo will equal his great father in the world of opera, though in a different approach, that of producer, and to this writer, that means boss-man. He runs it, and to run things one has to be extremely talented. I would like to see Giancarlo some day change his base of operations to New York City so I could see, and review, more of his works. He has invited me to Bonn, but that is too distant to harbor weekend reviews.

Breaking In:
Of Butlers and
a Famous Violinist

A YOUTHFUL DAY -- Author Bob
Hilliard, right, and his brother, John, circa
1934. Bob Hilliard was just starting his
long career in journalism at that point.

I broke into Boston's famous cultural life at a tender age. I believe I was about 17 at the time, and it was pretty darn exciting.

It happened like this. I had been informed that Miss Ruth Posselt, a young violinist hailed by many critics as the greatest woman violinist in the world, was to be feted at the ornate home on Beacon Street of Gov. Alvan T. Fuller. It was to be in the form of a late-afternoon musicale, with Miss Posselt at center-stage.

Earlier on the day of the concert, I made arrangements to meet Miss Posselt at the Ondricek Studios in Boston, where an older sister gave lessons to the most promising students. At the last minute, however, the interview was shifted to Gov. Fuller's mansion, and a sister told me to meet Ruthie over there.

At that age, I didn't even know where Beacon Street was in Boston, let alone a particular address. Marjorie, who gave me the information, was Ruth's older sister.

So I picked up a cab from the North Station to 150 Beacon St. It was fairly close by, and as the cabbie let me out, he asked: "What are you after, Buddy, a job?"

"No, sir," I replied, "I'm after a story."

When I saw the imposing home, I was somewhat awestruck. It left its mark on me, and even today, when I'm returning from a review at the theater, I look its way and tell friends, "That's where I interviewed Ruth Posselt, the great violinist."

I rang the bell, and a butler answered the door. He was most properly attired.

"Whom did you wish to see?" he asked.

"Miss Posselt," I said.

He bowed, not saying a word, and I followed him inside. He bowed again, and I entered a side-room, with beautiful Oriental carpets and paintings just about everywhere, it seemed. I took a small chair and waited.

A few minutes later, he reappeared and bowed again, not saying a word. I followed him up a winding marble stairway, past still more gorgeous paintings. It seemed they were everywhere. What beauty!

We went down a hall for a short distance and came to the Music Room, which seemed to this ogling teenager the size of a small football field, with three concert grand pianos placed at vantage points around the room. A pianist was playing one of them.

My new friend escorted me across the room to a sofa, where Miss Posselt sat, smiling and beautiful in her blonde tresses. She was stunning, and she put me at ease immediately, making the interview an easy, almost effortless one. She filled me in with a description of her triumphant St. Petersburg, Russia concert, and she told me how the audience cheered her playing for several minutes after she had concluded. In fact, the Russians went wild. Seldom had they heard such genius by an American artist, and that pleased Ruth Posselt immeasureably.

"Are you hungry, Bob?" she asked. "You look thin, why don't you try some goodies?"

In short order, my plate was piled high, and Miss Posselt and her friends could not do enough for me. It was a little embarrassing, but I suppose I brought it on myself, weighing only about 125 pounds (baseball wet in high school). To a woman, they thought I was underweight.

I want the public to know, however, how attentive these so-called Bluebloods of Boston were to me that afternoon at 150 Beacon St., and how much I enjoyed doing my story. If memory serves correctly, the interview was conducted sometime in 1935, when Miss Posselt was at the very top of her famous career.

The story ran in my Aunt Addie's paper, the *Franklin*, (N.H.) *Journal Transcript*, where I forwarded many of my early adventures. Addie attended and later taught German at exclusive Mt. Holyoke College in Massachusetts. She was a close friend of Miss Frances Perkins, secretary of labor under President Roosevelt.

Addie ran the story in its entirety, and I was pleased with her deft handling. She would have made an excellent big-time editor had she so chosen. She also used my articles on Guy Lombardo and actress Elissa Landi, who portrayed the lead role in "The Count of Monte Christo."

All in all, it was a most rewarding day in Boston. I completed my interview and listened to a day of the most glorious music—Ruth Posselt at her very best, and I knew then why the Russian audience was so enthralled with the young artist.

It was all somewhat dampened the next day, however, when I read an article in the *Boston Post* telling how the Fuller Estate had been plundered of some rare paintings some time earlier that week, and how sorry I felt for the Fuller family.

Son Peter Fuller remembers well the musicales his mother used to present, and they were just wonderful, he recalls.

Miss Posselt married the concert master of the famous Boston Symphony Orchestra, Richard Burger, one of the most renowned musicians of his time. Ruth resides in Gulfport, Fla.

I would have to say that the Posselt interview was one of the first such in my career of interviewing Boston and New York personalities, and it still stands out in my mind. They were all so kind to me that day, perhaps because I was so underweight in the year 1935. My own career went on from there, to The Metropolitan Opera, and it led to my coverage of nearly 500 operas in the intervening years, all a lot of fun, and to coverage also of about 600 Broadway plays.

In fact, the game has to be fun. I joined the Board of Overseers with The Met in Boston, and that has always been a great joy, being with my dear Boston friends. Ruth Posselt would have been a super addition on that board, with her musical ability and knowledge.

Mr. Bojangles and Joe Penner

One of my youthful expeditions was to go Boston to see the world famous tap-dancer, Bill Robinson of Shirley Temple fame, and to chat with him in his dressing room about life on the theater front in Hollywood.

We asked him how things were going in the film capital, and he said, "Oh fine, thanks to that Shirley Temple film."

"You are pretty close to Shirley, Bill," I said. "If anyone harmed little Shirley, Bill, what would you do to that person?"

His answer was a classic: "Why, Bob, I would carve him long, deep and consecutive, and leave him out in the street to die."

He loved that little girl, and he spoke, I remember, endearingly of her. He tapped his way into the heart of theatre-goers that day, and into the heart of this writer for granting the time he did for a feature. His nimble feet flew that afternoon as they beat a soft staccato on the stage, barely touching the floor, but crisp and quick to the shuffle.

There has never been a tap-dancer his equal since, and for that reason, he will go down in stage history as the greatest ever. He was smooth and ever so graceful as he glided across the stage at the Boston theatre that day, cane in hand, and all dressed up, with that great smile on his beaming face.

Anyone who ever saw Bojangles in person, surely saw an immortal. His feet seemed barely to leave the floor, yet there was that syncopation. Fred Astaire must have taken lessons from Bill, for he, too, had that easy glide.

Several years after the Boston interview, after I had gone to work for Col. Frank Knox (who was Landon's running mate), I had a chance to renew old times with Mr. Bojangles, who was performing in vaudeville in Manchester. It was a hurry-up job, inasmuch as I was late for the interview and had to run from the train station to the theater, where I just managed to catch Bill, who himself was leaving via train for Boston and New York.

He said, assuringly, "Bob, I'll make it easy for you on this interview. Jump in the car with us guys, and we'll talk on the way to the station."

Thanks to the B&M Railroad,they got me to Manchester from Concord, and Bill to his next appearance in good time. That was in the days before air travel took over, and where train time between Boston and New York, where Bill was headed, consumed a good four hours. So, he was hustling that day and not tap-dancing his way to the station.

He remembered our first interview, and said he was always at the ready. Bless his heart. He was really one of the early superstars of the legitimate stage, well-loved by co-stars and fans alike. When he died in 1949, the heart of show business stopped beating. He was a gentle soul, and so considerate that he would put a young cub reporter ahead of his own trying schedule.

Luther (Bill) Robinson was a true friend, and with a talent that has not been seen since.

Ask the kids today if they've ever heard of Bill Robinson, and they will shake their heads. But ask them if they've heard of "Bojangles," and they'll answer yes. Bill would have loved that.

One other figure that compelled attention on the stage was Joe Penner, the ludicrous figure with a little pointed hat who carried a basket under his arm with a duck perched in it, and who asked everyone the silly question, "Ya wanna buy a duck?" For a period of time, in the Jack Benny era, he took over the radio networks with his gags and funny lines, and he knocked other front-liners flying. Everybody in America tuned in to the escapades of Joe Penner, and when this writer asked for an interview, it was quickly granted.

So we hit out for Boston and a look at Joe Penner.

He was one of the most gracious personalities I have ever encountered; he made the interview come alive. I met Joe backstage. He was clad in a red bathrobe, his black hair held neatly in place with the help of some hair tonic. He ushered us into his dressing room, and we fell into a long talk on the status of the living stage and what made it tick.

I had one question for Joe, which I asked almost at the outset. "How much do you want for that duck, Joe?"

Bob, he said, it's not for sale, but for you I will give it to you for a special price, two eggs I can fry tomorrow morning for breakfast.

Joe autographed a photo of himself for me, which I have misplaced, and which may be found 20 years after my death, with somebody asking, " Now, who in hell is that guy, carrying a toy duck in a grocery basket?"

Well, that duck probably earned Joe Penner a million dollars in radio and personal appearances around the country.

Penner had another great line, often repeated by those who listened to him each week on his coast-to-coast radio show: "You nasty man."

He spoke the line so humorously, that it became one of his trademarks.

One wag, with unpardonable effrontery, suggested Joe died trying to eat his beloved duck. You may duck that one, if you please.At one time, he was giving Jack Benny and the Marx Brothers and Ed Wynn a run for their money.

He died a relatively young man.

On Getting There:
A Personal Note...

LAST TRAIN -- A B&M Railroad train rumbles into the Manchester train station. This photo, taken in 1967, marked the end of passenger train service to New Hampshire's Queen City.
(Jimarjon/*Union Leader* File Photo)

A Funny Thing Happened on the Way to the Forum," or so they say.

In this case, the forum was *The Union Leader* newsroom, where daily news was the business. After a busy day, the editors and writers would jack it and head for the home fires, three of us on the bus bound for nearby Concord.

The three included Tom McKoan, George Connell and the author. On this one early evening commute, history of sorts was made. In *The Union Leader* edition the next day, a headline writer referred to it as the saga of "the balky bus." And, truly, it was just that—a balky bus.

We had stopped in Hooksett, a hamlett just north of Manchester, to let off a few riders, and as our driver shifted to go forward, the bus lurched backward. We laughed at that, but it only became hysterical in the moments that followed.

The driver looked a little puzzled and decided to have another crack at it. He shifted again, to go forward onto the highway. The bus balked again. The driver, astounded at his bucking bronco, jammed on the brakes so as not to hit any vehicle behind us, or any unwary pedestrian. He gave it one more try. Shift to go forward, that's it, easy now, easy on the pedal. Again, the balky bus bounced backward.

By this time, the driver, thoroughly annoyed, called out to the passengers: "Everybody out; we're changing buses."

So, laughing at the antics of that crazy bus of ours, we disembarked, and stood around in little knots awaiting the reserve bus. In 10 or 15 minutes, it heaved, and I remember thinking at the time, I hope this driver doesn't park too closely to the bus in front of him," and that, of course, is just what he did. He inched up to within two feet or so of the "Balky Bus."

We filed aboard again for the trip to Concord and our driver clambered aboard, and went through the motions as before, although this time it was in reverse fashion. The substitute driver who had brought the second bus to the scene had inched up to the first bus, and thus had given the original driver only two feet or so of room to play with as he made his move.

205

Now he was forced to back up to clear his way by the balky bus. As he did so, the bus moved forward. The driver jammed on the brakes at once to avoid hitting Bus No. 1. He had only about a foot at the most of space between the two vehicles. One more shot, please, as the passengers looked on in disbelief. He gave it the old college try this time; foot lightly on the gas pedal, foot heavily on the brake and a shift backward to clear Bus No. 1.

Once again, the second bus jumped forward, so close to the first bus that they looked like Siamese twins. By this time, the passengers could not restrain themselves and broke into frenzied laughter.

The bus driver alighted, as did the others, and made his way to a near-by telephone, which "Someone Higher Up must have placed there for the benefit of discouraged bus drivers.

This time, as before, a second bus came to the rescue of some harried commuters and a bus that did not work, but this time, the driver, fully conversant with what already had transpired, parked the third bus a good distance from the other two. All filed aboard once again, took our seats, and watched closely as the driver made his third attempt of the day to get airborne, or onto the northbound highway. When he shifted to go forward, that is what happened; we went forward and some mighty cheers rent the air.

Bus company officials refused to believe the incredible story of "The Balky Bus" but were shot down by the accounts of all aboard the three buses that afternoon. We were delayed perhaps by 45 minutes or so, but it was better than B.F. Keith Vaudeville. A welcome committee did not meet us in Concord that late afternoon, and luckily, no search parties were undertaken.

Getting to work always seemed the better part of the day for me, and getting to Manchester was made by train, bus and car at various intervals. No dull moments, ever.

On another occasion, arising late one morning, we discovered only 20 minutes remaining to catch the 9:30 train for Manchester and Boston. We made a hurried trip to the kitchen for a fast cup of coffee and to comb our hair; not even time to turn on the faucet with a pan of water already there in the sink. We scooped up the water, thoroughly pouring it over our head, combed our hair, and with a goodbye kiss for Barbara, dashed for the station about a half-mile away.

The train was already there, and we clambered aboard the last car, as was our custom; nearer to our home in Concord, nearer to the office in Manchester. Very good thinking, there.

About 20 minutes later, the train roared into Manchester, and we alighted and headed for the newsroom, and whatever was news for the day. As comedian Bob Newhart would say, "It was a slow news day," and there were no major problems, at least not on the surface, not until about 4 p.m., or close to closing time. I went in to the men's room, and departing, glanced in the mirror. Something looked wrong. I looked once again. Not a hair out of place, but startlingly white. I thought about this as I departed the men's room and prepared to catch the train for home.

"Gosh," I thought, "my hair looked funny, all in place, and so white."

I arrived home at 13 Center St. and spoke to Barbara about the picture I had seen in the mirror at work. She said, "Let me take a look." Her face fell.

"Gee, that is white," she said, before asking me a question. "Did you comb your hair this morning at the sink?"

I said that I had, indeed, combed my hair at the sink in my haste to catch the 9:30. She broke into laughter.

"Well, Buddy," she said, "I must tell you now that you used the very same water I was using to starch the curtains. It's no wonder you looked about 80."

Lesson there: Don't use any water to comb your hair when you are late for the office. Imagine if I had shaved with it!

Another time while I hurried to catch the 9:30 a.m. for Manchester, Nashua and Boston, I barely made it, and strangely, there were many faces aboard I knew. The train thundered on to Manchester, and I got up to leave, only to find the platform still closed. I asked the trainman to please open the platform so that I could get off to go to work.

"What are you trying to be, a wise guy?" he angrily asked. "This platform is only to be opened at Fort Devens, and that goes for you as well as for all those other draftees you see this morning."

My heart sank. I could hear the bugles blowing at Devens from way up there in Manchester. What would Barbara say—"He didn't tell me he was going into service."

I looked for the regular conductor, Henry Donovan, and saw him sauntering down the aisle in the car ahead, fortunately coming in my direction. I motioned to him to save me, and he wore a knowing grin. He had only a few wise words.

"Don't take this car again, Bob, however close it is to your work in Manchester. It is reserved for the inductees to Fort Devens."

He let me off, and I scooted for the office, and my job then as military editor. It was a good story, and my old friend, Reg Abbott, a Dartmouth man, who turned the job over to me shortly after my arrival at the paper, saw that it made the editions.

Reg used to start the stories about me in this fashion: "You know our friend with the two left feet? Well, he is at it again this day..." or similarly.

One story Reg did not exploit was my account of a visit to the dentist, probably because it was a little too gory.

On my way to work one sunny day, I stopped at my dentist's office in Concord to have some work done on an impacted wisdom tooth, hardly realizing what I was getting into. The dentist took a preliminary look, and then set to work. After two hours, he was little more advanced than at the beginning but with a swollen cheek to show for his work, and the wisdom tooth still very much in place.

"I can't get the tooth to budge," he said despairingly. "You will have to see a dentist in Manchester, first thing tomorrow. I will get you an appointment."

He did just that, and I stopped in to see that dentist the following morning.

"We've got to get at that tooth," he promised, and after the two-hour probing the day before, I promised the Manchester dentist I would make an appointment to see him in a very few days.

"You will do nothing of the sort," he snapped. "There is already infection started, and we will have to extract it today, at once."

I was given permission to go back to the office and tell them I would have to have the day off but would return the following day.

After what happened in that office, I should have told the managing editor I wouldn't be in for the next several weeks.

The dentist sat me in the chair and gave me a few shots that he said would deaden the pain.

"Oh, there will be pain?" I questioned.

"A little," he replied.

He set to work, and pulled and pulled and pulled. The tooth showed no signs of giving. The doctor, sweating profusely, removed his white jacket and set to work again. He had been pulling at the tooth for an hour, with little progress.

Then he stopped, and sat down for a minute. He produced a chisel-like apparatus and a small hammer, and started in again, trying to dislodge it in that fashion. After 15 minutes or so, and little progress, but with plenty of blood to show for his work, he gave up on that approach.

"We will have to go at it in another way," he said.

This had the ominous touch of finality about it, and as he looked at me, I could see the headlines the next day: "Man Succumbs in Dentist Chair." More accurately, it might have read: "Man Passes Out on Dentist Floor," for that is where I wound up, on the dentist's floor, with the doctor with his knees on my chest, and his nurse on her knees beside me, wiping my brow every few minutes.

Before I wound up on the floor, the dentist showed me the secret instrument that was going to do the trick.

"This is what it looks like," he explained, and it was not unlike a simple pencil, with a blunt hitting edge. "I will try it at first so you get used to it, and please don't get your tongue in the way or you might lose it."

He said it could hit a thousand or so times every minute, and it beat the old technique of hammering it out by hand. The tooth, he said, was locked around my jawbone and would have to be broken out. He snapped on the electric current, and the apparatus began to whir. Then he placed it beside the gum in which was rooted the tooth.

The first impact jolted me so much, I almost fell out of the chair.

"You'll have to lie on the floor," he said. "I will just have to keep hitting it until it is broken out of there."

With his knees on my chest, and the poor nurse trying to console me, he set to work once again. The blood was spurting all over the room, when suddenly the door was opened, and there stood my shocked wife.

"What are you doing to him?" she screamed, seeing all the blood. "You're killing him."

The doctor waved her off and told her to have a chair in the waiting room. He had work to do, and Barbara wasn't totally convinced he wasn't trying to knock me off.

Anyway, that is how I spent the next 15 minutes, on my back, with the dentist breaking the tooth out in little pieces. I remember him saying, "God, where did that piece go? It must have gone out the window," which by that time was wide open to give the patient some air. "It hit a guy walking by," the doctor suggested.

At last the job was done, and the dentist and nurse got to their feet and helped me to mine. It was battlefield heroism of the first order.

Poor Barbara, a nervous wreck after witnessing that operation, ordered a cab to pick us up and got me to the railroad station. Her ordeal was still not over after helping me to our seat on the afternoon train. Across the aisle sat two elderly ladies, busy stealing glances our way.

"That poor woman," they whispered. "Imagine having a drunkard for a husband and having to tend to him like a baby."

"Oh, yeah?" I said under my breath. "I hope you never have an impacted wisdom tooth. I have just the doctor for you."

I was out of work for three days, as I recall.

Parties:
Say When

LATE ARRIVAL -- Famous actor Richard Harris puts in a late appearance at a party in Boston, looking rather haggard. He stole the show that night.

Oftentimes, in our roles as critics, we're invited to attend post-performance parties, which, for the most part, are elegant affairs.

I can think of four or five of them that have been standouts. They bring the writers and newscasters together at last, and they can compare notes if they wish, although most of us have other things on our minds by midnight.

The most gorgeous party I believe I ever attended was in October, 1993 at the flower-bedecked Grand Tier of the Metropolitan Opera House in New York City, and let me say this: New York soirees differ a bit from those thrown on Beacon Hill in Boston, or Pier 4, or over at Harvard, in that they are done on a bigger scale.

Seldom in the Hub do parties last beyond 2 a.m., although I can remember one that was blasting away at 3 in the morning when I left, and everybody was out on the dance floor after finishing their lobsters. That was directed by Nance Movsesian, one of the best press representatives in the land. It featured four casts that just happened to be playing Boston theatres at the time, a band for dancing and chorus girls that knew their way about the floor. Attorney Bob Woolf and his wife were there, and he showed them a thing or two as he bobbed and bounced about the floor.

I warned him that he was taking his life in his own hands with that list of stage dancers on hand. "Don t worry, no sweat," he said. "I ll show them some brand-new steps." And he did, surprisingly. He wasn t even panting.

The party at the Met last October was easily the biggest and probably the grandest of them all. Placido Domingo, one of those three famous world tenors, had just finished singing the title role in Giuseppe Verdi s dramatic "Stiffelio," and he was greeting old friends and many new ones from Germany who had come across to back up their world-renowned producer, Giancarlo del Monaco, in his Night of Triumph. He is the Intendent of Bonn Opera Company in Germany, and those people got an eyeful of New York after dark. Conductor James Levine, who conducted

REMEMBERED FILM -- Lillian Gish, right, was the featured star in the first major Hollywood hit, "Birth of a Nation." Here, she chats with author Bob Hilliard and his friend, Bobbi Arnold of Manchester, N.H. (Sam Greenwald Photo)

the work, being staged for the very first time at the Met, also was present.

I will never forget that night, how beautiful the house looked, with those sun-burst chandeliers shining brightly, with flowers everywhere.

Del Monaco invited me to tell the gathering about the first time I met his famous father, tenor Mario Del Monaco, and his wife, Fedora, the mother of Giancarlo, then a little boy of about seven in school in France or Switzerland.

"You mean the time at the Ritz-Carlton in Boston?" I asked.

"Yes," he replied, "that one."

I told them the story which I have mentioned previously, and they burst out laughing.

About 12:30 or 1 a.m., we were served a roast beef dinner, and when I left at 3 or 3:15, the party was still going on. They had locked the doors at the Met when the last opera-goers had left, so we had the whole beautiful place to ourselves. It was something like Richard Helliburton had

OPERA PRODUCER -- Beverly Sills, left, in Boston to discuss Metropolitan Opera plans. Here, she's with author Bob Hilliard, a member of the Boston Opera Association board at the time.

written in his "Royal Road to Romance" when he was at the Taj Mahal in India, and secreted himself on the grounds when the last visitor had departed, and he had the beautiful Taj all to himself, to swim in the placid pool, and to dream the dream of romance.

It could not have been more beatiful at the Met that night. It was a pretty hard-to-believe story, and I'm glad I knew the del Monacos so well, and if there is such a thing as a Service Wire to Heaven, I would send the following message to Mario and Fedora: "The Kid is doing Just Fine. He'll pass his Father some day."

That party will be difficult to top. Deedee Chereton had the one at Pier 4 that had as its guest Richard Burton and his former wife, Liz Taylor, the Kennedys and everybody else in leadership in Boston, including my friend, Billy Bulger. Liz has the prettiest lavender eyes, and I asked her for a dance.

She replied "Sure," and just as we were about to tango, some cameraman slipped out of the dark and engaged me in a conversation about cameras. By this time, Miss Taylor, with her eyelashes fluttering, had left the scene and wandered back to Richard. My luck had deserted me, thanks to that dumb cameraman.

That party in New York will be No. 1. Nance Movsesian's lavish the-ater affair in Cambridge, with four casts playing Boston at the time, will be No. 2 on the list, with a lot of celebrities present, including Jimmy Belushi. No. 3 on the list will be the Pier 4 frolic, at which I missed a chance to tip-toe with Liz Taylor. Drat my luck.

All of them are good, let's face it, and it gives everybody a chance to cut loose, even some of those word-bound critics who are wrapped up in cocoons of their own choice and color.

That party in New York was novel in that when we did depart the Met Opera House, there was hardly a cab in sight. Most of them had probably fallen asleep in Central Park nearby.

Porgy &
Bess &
Born in N.H.

FAMOUS TRIO -- Legendary dancer and movie star Fred Astaire, far left, tickles the ivories with reknown songwriters George Gershwin, center, and his brother, Ira. (Courtesy Photo)

From the moment composer Irving Berlin first talked with him, he knew George Gershwin, the young man who had just applied for a job in his office, was destined for great things. He was right.

Berlin was happy to take him on, of course, and he told him that; but he could see that this intense young man would make it big on the musical front some day, and that day was not too distant.

Gershwin was also a composer, albeit a newcomer and with his own ideas about popular music, although he seemed to be interested in bending the present to a more sophisticated symphonic style, believing that there was ample room for both. It was this marriage, ultimately, that gave the world the George Gershwin style, substance with class, and with a beat.

George studied piano and harmony, and at the tender age of 16 he became a song-plugger, promoting singers and name orchestras to play and croon the firm's most presentable scores. Little did he know at that time that his articulated style would soon be all the rage in a growing America. His brother, Ira, two years older and very easy-going, was to provide the lyrics for George.

In 1924, George came up with his first great success, "Rhapsody in Blue," a work for piano and a jazz orchestra. It was orchestrated by Ferde Grofe and played by Paul Whiteman and his famous band at Aeolian Hall in New York City. That probably was the major impetus for his notable career in music. He became famous overnight. Irving Berlin was proved right.

He turned out many musicals, among them the "George White Scandals," 1920-1924; "Lady Be Good," 1924; "Funny Face," 1927; "Girl Crazy," 1930; "Of Thee I Sing," 1931, and "Let 'Em Eat Cake," 1933.

The blockbuster was to come, making use of the jazz idiom in something of an operatic work, the story of "Porgy and Bess."

About this early time, a young man was in residence at the famous MacDowell Colony in Peterborough, N.H. His name was DuBose

Heyward, and he was a most enterprising artist. He was at the colony from 1921-1928, and later in 1938. While in residence at MacDowell, he met and married his girlfriend, Dorothy, and she encouraged her husband to work on "Porgy and Bess," and she, according to the colony, "even wrote the script herself."

I remember when "Porgy and Bess" first blossomed forth on Broadway. It was about the year 1935. It was being hailed as the biggest thing to reach the Great White Way in years. The great songs emanating from it were, I believe, first introduced to America by Guy Lombardo and His Royal Canadians in one of his coast-to-coast broadcasts. Gershwin was a close personal friend of Lombardo, and turned his apartment on Riverside Drive over to the conductor, himself, since Guy was looking for a place in New York City closer than his residence at that time in Connecticut, and that might have been how Lombardo introduced the "Porgy and Bess" numbers to a listening America. I know I first ever heard "It Ain't Necessarily So" and "I Got Plenty of Nuttin'" and "Summertime" on Guy's widely heard radio show, and they sounded beautiful.

Gershwin had a lot of substance and style, and Lombardo was just the individual to bring it forth on the radio network. It paid George to let Guy take the apartment, but the music of Gershwin was destined for worldly attention, regardless of who played the music.

George also did many individual numbers, such as "Mine" (with patter), and "Nice Work If You Can Get It," which came along in the mid-Thirties. I never did meet the Gershwins, but I felt that I knew them a little bit from what Lombardo told me, and they were class all the way. Everything they touched seemed to turn up gold for them, and George's music was positively entrancing, with Ira providing the enchanting lyrics, such as on "Mine."

Poor George died in Hollywood in 1937 at the age of 39, while writing scores for the movie industry. His brother George died many years later.

With the Gershwins went an era, and the world must be delighted that DuBose Heyward had a couple of good allies in Dorothy and the two musical brothers from New York City. Otherwise, we might not have had the sad story of "Porgy and Bess."

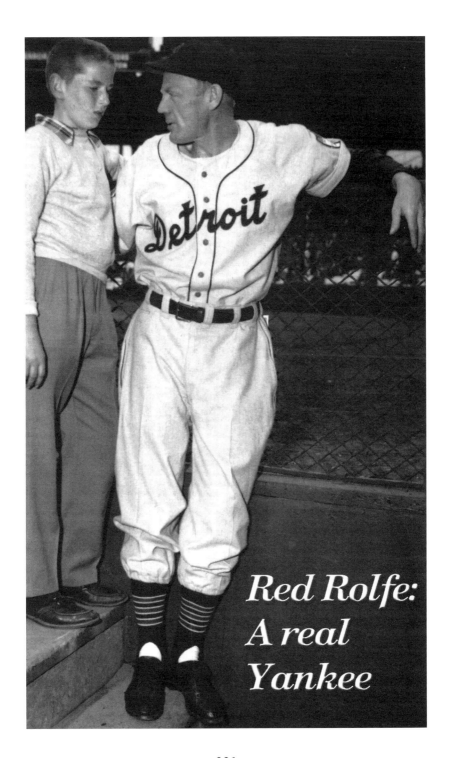

Red Rolfe:
A real
Yankee

DUGOUT VISIT -- Bob Hilliard Jr., left, son of the author, enjoys a dugout visit with Robert (Red) Rolfe, manager of the Detroit Tigers at the time, at Boston's Fenway Park. Rolfe made his name as a ballplayer with the New York Yankees in the Lou Gehrif-Babe Ruth era.

In the early days in Concord, N.H., we knew him as Bobby Rolfe.

That was when he was a student at the Phillips Exeter Academy, and later while he was attending Dartmouth College, from which he was graduated. His first love at Exeter and at Dartmouth was baseball, and while his home was in nearby Penacook (Ward One of Concord), he frequented the famous White Park in the Capital City, where its diamond was immaculately kept and was hailed as one of the best in the State of New Hampshire.

The diamond is still there, and well cared for, except that it has been turned around completely from Rolfe's days, and where he once batted is now center field. This was done to save homes nearby from damage from foul balls, although I cannot recall Rolfe hitting many foul balls. He usually crashed them into the outfield, and most were of the line-drive variety. He was a vicious hitter even then, as a schoolboy, and he practiced at it more than anyone I knew.

From my earliest days, I knew Rolfe, and there was no one I respected more. He was polite and courteous and good-natured, and everyone liked him.

One summer's day I wandered to the park. I must have been 13 or 14, and I frequented the diamond hoping that the older guys there would let me into their games. Rolfe, of course, was older than I was and he also knew my brother Harry very well. They were good friends. Even then, Rolfe was just about the best player in town, and most townspeople knew that he someday would make the grade in baseball, if that indeed was his intention. The time he devoted to baseball, most of us were sure that someday Bobby would wind up in the major leagues. He was a shortstop then, before Joe McCarthy took him under his wing, and he was sure-handed, with a tremendous throwing arm. He whistled them across the diamond, and on the mark every time.

He wasn't even at Dartmouth when I first met him, and he played summers in the famous Concord Sunset League, oldest such in the United

States, and where many major league players first developed, including Rolfe. He was a completely dedicated person, and he worked at baseball. I would call it his first love. One thing he taught the young fellows around the park was never to get waterlogged, no matter how sultry the weather. Rinse your mouth out, and expectorate. That was it. Don't swallow the water.

On a day I dropped by in the hopes of finding a game going, there was none. Rolfe was one of the few there, and they were playing catch and hitting fly balls to one another. Bobby saw me and said: "Hey, Bob, I want to get some hitting practice, could you throw me a few?" I was delighted to see some action, for that was why I had come to the park in the first place, hoping to get involved in a scrub game. Even then, I had done some pitching, so I was not entirely foreign to it. Only in pickup games, of course. This day I was the only guy there who had done any pitching, so I was singled out by Rolfe to serve them up, and I did.

I threw the ball in for him to hit, and man, could he hit! They were going by me like bullets on a battlefield. All the time I am admiring his skill as a hitter, and happy I didn't have to pitch to him in a game. I remember thinking at the time I would walk him if that were the case. I had thrown him maybe 20 or 30 pitches, soft ones for him to hit, when suddenly he caught one flush and sent it screeching back toward the box. It hit me in rather a glancing blow, and bounced clear out to the outfield. I thought my leg was broken, it hurt so. The blow had knocked me to the ground, and Rolfe came running out to the mound to make sure I was all right. I was hanging on to my leg like it was going to fall off.

The pain subsided shortly, and I got to my feet. Bobby helped me over to the bench, and that ended the hitting practice for the day. The ball hit me a glancing blow, and I think that saved me from a broken leg. It had smoke coming from it, I tell you. Rolfe always reminded me of that incident, and we would laugh over it. One day at the World Series between the Boston Braves and the Cleveland Indians at old Braves Field, he told some friend about it.

I was covering the game that day, and I had just stepped into the dinner line with other newsmen and reception guests to get my lobsters and other delicacies, and someone tapped me on the back. I looked around, and it was Red Rolfe himself, the all-time third baseman of the New York Yankees, retired by then, but still a magnet for writers and fans.

"Where you sitting, Bob?" he asked.

I replied I hadn't even had time to look, and he said "Why don't you join my table, I want you to meet a couple of friends."

I said I would be delighted.

"I'm sitting over in that corner of the room," and he pointed it out. "I will stand up and wave when you get through the line, and you can come on over."

I finally made it through the line at Lou Perinl's big World Series luncheon for the writers and broadcasters, and looked up toward Red Rolfe's table. He was standing up waving and shouting "Over here, Bob," and I steered my way through the tables.

Rolfe shook hands as I reached the table, and promptly introduced me to his guests.

"Bob, I would like you to meet the famous writer, Grantland Rice."

My mouth fell open, I am sure.

"So nice to meet you, Bob," and I replied what a wonderful surprise this is, and I added "the greatest of them all."

Rice smiled and said, "I don't know about that, Bob," and I repeated, "the greatest."

Then Rolfe introduced me to his other guest. "Bob, please shake hands with Rogers Hornsby, one of the great hitters of all time."

I had hit the jackpot for sure, and Robert Abial Rolfe had not forgotten those early days at White Park. Hornsby and Rice, and of course Rolfe, proved the most interesting and adept table companions a sports writer could have sought, and quotes were flying everywhere.

That was the famous series that featured the "Spahn and Sain, and Pray for Rain" exercise for the Braves, versus the Feller and Wynn tandem for the Cleveland Indians, and the Indians wielded the Tomahawk on their brother Braves from Boston. I had been pulling for an all-Boston series, but the Red Sox lost out in a special one-game playoff against the same Indians over at Fenway Park. Someone should work up a quiz on that one.

A few years later, Red Rolfe had been named manager of the Detroit Tigers. Joe McCarthy had groomed Rolfe for the post of Yankee manager, it was rumored, and it would have been a fine choice for Red was popular with the fans and his teammates, and had the Ivy League class to go with it. Instead, he went to the Tigers, and proved himself an apt pilot, in spite of the colitis that troubled him to the end. He had courage, and he showed it every day to the end. As Red Smith wrote in his final tribute to Rolfe: "That man looked at class every day that he shaved."

When the Rolfe-Tigers deal was announced, in 1949 or 1950, the paper sent me up to his camp at Blackwater, not far from Concord, and we talked for a couple of hours or more after Isabel Rolfe had prepared a tasty lunch for us. We talked of plans for the next baseball season, and after I had asked a few questions, Rolfe said: "Wait a minute, Bob, and I'll get my little black book to check out some of these things."

I have never seen a more factual man in my life. Everything pertaining to his squad was written down in that book. It looked like he was cramming for a test at Dartmouth. Every rundown on every player was covered in that little notebook of his, good and bad, and believe me, Rolfe knew that squad from top to bottom.

Well, I asked, how are you set on pitchers? Do you think you have a competent staff? He replied that he did, with possibly one exception. What is that, I asked him.

He pondered a minute, then told me: "I really need a good left-hander. If I had a good lefty, I think we might win the pennant."

Out of a clear sky, I blurted, "I think I know just the pitcher for you."

He looked a little surprised, and asked me who that was. "Bobby Cain," I answered.

He repeated his name, "Bobby Cain, how did you know about him?"

I told him that in 1946 I had covered the Class B Manchester Giants of the New England League, and in mid-season Cain joined the squad and pitched some beautiful games, and faced many heavy hitters, including Roy Campanella of the Nashua Dodgers, and looked pretty sharp against all of them. On top of that, I went on, Cain is a real scrapper and a hard guy to beat.

Rolfe asked me one question: "Do you think I should try to get him?" I answered in the affirmative. "Absolutely," I said.

From that moment on, Rolfe had his sights set on Cain, and he managed to land him. The way things turned out that first year for Rolfe and his Tigers, I am glad I mentioned Cain's name that day. He beat the Yankees five or six times, as the Tigers raced that same team for the American League championship. If memory serves correctly, the Yanks won the title by one game, I believe, just edging out the Tigers. It was one of the hottest races in years, all thanks to Cain's pitching wizardry, and Rolfe's uncanny leadership.

Rolfe invited me to Boston to see a game right after he had landed Cain, and set me up with dugout seats behind the Tigers' bench. I went on the field as usual before the game to renew friendships with my old pal Cain, and he was happy to see me.

"Gee, Bob, what the hell am I doing with this great club?" he asked.

"You're looking at the guy," I laughed.

"You?" he said. "I don't understand," and I told him I was a friend of Rolfe's for most of my lifetime, and when he told me at his camp during the winter that he needed a good left-hander, I recommended Cain.

"There's a guy who has guts," I told him, "and this guy Cain is not fazed at all by these fence-busters of today. So that is how you are here today, Cain."

Bobby Cain was in almost complete shock as I told him the story. I haven't heard from Bobby since that time, and I suppose he returned to his home in Salina, Kansas after his major league fling. He was the guy who pitched to Bill Veeck's midget pinch-hitter one balmy day, Eddie Gazda, before joining Red Rolfe's Tigers.

"How big was his strike zone?" I asked Cain that day. "Mighty small, Bob, about the size of a playing card." He walked him, of course. "He went into a crouch on me, too," Cain added.

After a few seasons with the Tigers, Rolfe retired from the game. He was with the New York Yankees from 1931 to 1942, when the colitis forced his retirement as a player, and he compiled a lifetime mark of .289. It is puzzling that he has not been voted into the Hall of Fame at

Cooperstown, N.Y., for he still is the all-time New York Yankees third baseman, and the acknowledged finest bunter in the game. I once saw him
beat out three bunts in a game with the Boston Red Sox. He was in six
World Series with the Yanks, and batted .284. Rolfe authored at my behest
a long column on the art of bunting, which appeared in longtime *Union
Leader* sports editor Joe Barnea's widely read "Barnstorming" column, and
which is a must for any young player looking for a career in baseball.

When Rolfe joined the Yankees after a few seasons at Albany and
Newark, he was converted to a third baseman by Joe McCarthy, the astute
manager, with Frank Crosetti at short, Tony (Poosh-em-up) Lazzeri at
second, and the powerful Lou Gehrig at first. Man-for-man, that team
almost rivaled the 1927 team of Babe Ruth, et al. What is more, the infield
featured two Ivy Leaguers, Rolfe and Gehrig (Dartmouth and Columbia),
and it was high-class all around. In at least one season, Babe Ruth himself
played on the same team.

A one-minute quiz: What famous major league team starred two
members who married countries?

Answer: The New York Yankees, whose Red Rolfe married a girl
named Isabel Africa, and Johnny Broaca via Yale who married a lassie
named Ireland.

After the Tigers, Rolfe went back to his alma mater, Dartmouth, and
became one of that school's finest athletic directors ever. On assignments
to Dartmouth during the football season particularly, I would enjoy long
talks with Bobby in his office, and we would recreate the old days at White
Park.

"Where the heck is this White Park you guys talk about?" Red Smith
of the New York Times once asked me during a late-night party at Fenway
Park.

I was having a drink with Peter Falk of TV and the movies, and Cedric
Tallis, general manager of the Yankees at the time, with George
Steinbrenner and Yogi Berra nearby.

"What," said Tallis, "you have never heard of White Park? Why, it's
more famous than The Mound in St. Louis where Yogi and Garagiola grew
up, and surely you have heard of Joe Lefebvre and Red Rolfe and Bob
Tewksbury and Cedric Tallis? They all played there, Red."

"My word," said Red Smith, "I should have known that."

We all had another drink on that, God Bless the bartender, Walter Underhill, who joined in. Walter went to his reward a few years ago. He is the same fellow who used to sit with Carl YastrzemskI's father in the press box, just above my seat, and once observed on one occasion as Yaz was kicking dirt on the plate after an ump had call him out on a third strike: "Sit down, Yastrzemski, your act is over; you're slowing up this game." His father was taking it all in, and chuckling. Walter was about as ornery as they come, and he didn't spare the horses.

That same night, Steinbrenner and Bill Crowley, then press director of the Red Sox and a former Holy Cross professor, tried to teach me German, the "better to sing 'Lohengrin' with," he croaked.

I always loved the New York crowd: big league all the way. Maybe it was because Rolfe and his prodigy Tallis once played in the Sunset League at White Park. There are more Yankee fans around the park than there are Red Sox rooters. And they are fervent. For a few seasons, Bob Tewksbury, now of the St. Louis Cardinals, kept the string going.

Red Rolfe was my ideal as a player, always giving it the old college try, and he was just about the smoothest third sacker I have ever seen, in the same class with Pie Traynor of the Pirates, another New Englander. On one occasion, Rolfe came to Manchester from Hanover to handle a baseball clinic for youngsters, and he and his co-host, Tom Padden, of Manchester, treated the kids as equals, which impressed me no end. Kids 12 or 13 like to be treated as grownups, and not as children.

Rolfe showed them how to make the throws from third, and Padden, now deceased, told them the posture behind the plate "is that which makes you comfortable."

I think Mike Lavalliere was one of the kids there that day. He later caught for the Phillies, Cardinals and Pirates.

Red Rolfe was perhaps the greatest third baseman of all time, certainly the all-time New York Yankee at the hot corner. Another great was Pie Traynor, and ironically, both were New Englanders, Rolfe from Penacook, N.H., Traynor from Somerville, Mass.

One day, a worker at the Rumford Printing Company in Concord,

N.H., whispered in an official's ear that "Mr. Traynor in the Composing Room has a son who is an excellent third baseman. Why don't you try to get him to play on the Rumford Press team? He could really help you out."

The worker wrote the name on a small slip of paper and the address of Mr. Traynor's son, so the official wrote him a letter forthwith.

"Dear Mr. Traynor:

"I understand from friends here that you are quite a third baseman. We can offer you a job in the shipping department, and $25 a week salary, if you would care to play two or three games a week for the Rumford team.

"I hope all is well, and please let me know on the offer."

The official soon had his answer.

"I am pretty content here playing third base for the Pittsburgh Pirates each day, and I am afraid that I will have to turn down your kind offer," the note stated.

It was signed Pie Traynor, Pittsburgh Pirates.

The official was not too perturbed, for he not only hadn't heard of Pie Traynor, but he assumed the Pittsburgh Pirates was some kind of a vaudeville team, and he wasn't anxious to get mixed up with any actors.

That is the story, anyway, that made the rounds around the printing plant long ago.

Red Rolfe, like Pie Traynor, was interested in teaching youngsters, as most of the major leaguers are, and Rolfe's forte was bunting and place-hitting. One day I approached Rolfe and asked him if he had any objections to turning out a piece on the art of bunting for Joe Barnea's column in *The Union Leader*. "You can let it run at will," I told him. "If it's too long, we can run it over two days, as a message to the kids on the skill of bunting and maybe for grownup players, as well." Rolfe agreed at once. "I am all for it," he said. "When do I have to turn it in?"

As soon as possible, he was informed.

A few days later we had Rolfe's informative column on bunting, and shortly it appeared in *The Union Leader* and was widely received. Many players cut it out and posted it on their bedroom walls. Periodically, it is still published near the start of the Major League season.

There you have it, managers and coaches and hopeful major leaguers, right from the pen of Robert (Red) Rolfe, all-time third baseman of the New York Yankees, and former manager of the Detroit Tigers until colitis forced his early retirement from the game. He should by all rights be in the Hall of Fame.

Rolfe was a dear friend from my very youth, and when he puts a treatise like this on paper, for all the kids of the nation, and for coaches and managers, and yes, for many major leaguers themselves (who should know), he is in fact leaving a legacy of true greatness, and a supreme willingness to help those who are willing to learn the game of baseball, and some of its finer, more delicate, deployments.

Red Rolfe truly belongs in the hallowed halls of Cooperstown, and may I here and now excoriate those writers and sportscasters who have the task of choosing such people for their lack of good judgment.

Remember, kids, the words of Tyrus Raymond Cobb and Robert Abial (Red) Rolfe, the two necessary adjuncts to a Major League career: Hold your hands about two inches apart on the bat to direct your hits more accurately; and this above all other:

Learn To Bunt.

Just this millenium, Dartmouth College paid one final tribute to its famous son. It named its baseball field for him, a fitting gesture for a personality who played alongside such as Lou Gehrig and helped the Yankees win several pennants and World Series championships, and rightfully belongs in baseball's Hall of Fame at Cooperstown, N.Y.

Someday, perhaps.

Moe Berg: Catcher and Patriot

Perhaps the most fascinating story of them all is that of one Moe Berg.

Major League followers may remember Berg as a catcher with the old Washington Senators, the Chicago White Sox, and the Boston Red Sox. They may also remember Moe as a catcher at Princeton.

Berg was a brilliant student at Princeton, spoke several languages, and was a Phi Beta Kappa. You cannot ascend the educational ladder much higher than that. Moe was a rugged fellow, a good catcher, and a fairly good hitter.

Following Princeton, Moe embarked on a career in law. It didn't satisfy his tastes, however, and one day he reported to his father that he was giving up the practice for the sport of professional baseball. He was from a most learned family, and one can only guess how that pronouncement fell on the home hearth. It is said that relations were strained somewhat between Moe and his father.

Be that as it may, Moe went for a baseball career, and as I have said, he was pretty successful at it. He knew how to handle pitchers (in any language), and it was like having a manager behind the plate. He knew every batter like a book, and the bench manager was probably content to let his burly Princeton catcher handle things on the field of play. So, he caught his share of games.

One evening, Leo E. Cloutier brought Moe into *The Union Leader* newsroom for a visit with the writers and it was most entertaining. I was the Night Sports Editor at that time, and I queried Moe about the big lens cameras of the TV networks, and how they were stealing Yogi Berra's signs from center field.

"That's a lot of hogwash," Moe retorted. "How can they possibly be stealing his signs?" He went on, as the baseball fans gathered about. "Look," he said, "you're standing right next to me, you couldn't get much closer. You pick up my signs, and repeat them to me." I said sure, you tapped one knee, then the other. You banged your mitt a couple of times, then you went to the fingers, two, one, three, and two. Then you gave the pitcher the target of where you wanted the pitch. Right?

"No, of course not. I'm not even giving the pitcher the signal with my fingers, or the slams into the mitt, or where I want the ball pitched."

Well, where? we persisted.

Moe answered. "I'm surprised you didn't notice. I'm giving the signals with my left foot, and then my right. My right foot will name the pitch. Straight ahead, a fast ball. Foot to the right, a slider. Foot inward to the left, a knuckle ball. All the other signs are simply decoys to mislead some in the ballpark, probably not the coaches, for those guys are real sharks. They steal anything."

It is true, they do steal signs from one another, but not as adeptly as Moe Berg stole the signs from the threatening Japanese Empire in the Early Thirties when that country was beginning to become a problem with the United States Government. Moe was picked as a backup catcher for the touring American team with Babe Ruth and all those other stars, and a week's series was arranged in Japan.

As Casey Stengel once declared: "After we left Japan, we headed for the Orient."

That may have been right, Casey, depending on how you were looking at the map. At any rate, the touring Major League stars were in Japan for about a week, with exhibitions scheduled for every day. The Japanese are crazy about baseball, and it too, is their National Pastime. One morning, Moe Berg called the manager, and told him he wasn't feeling too well, and wouldn't be able to make it that day. "Gosh," the manager replied, "you looked great yesterday. Well, if it gets worse, call me and we'll get a doctor to you to look you over."

Moe hung up the phone, put on his hat and coat, and went out the door. He walked down the street to the nearest flower shop, went in and bought a large bouquet, and then continued along to the American Hospital in Tokyo. Entering with his large bouquet, he advanced to the desk and asked, smilingly, if there was a patient there named Mrs. Lyons.

Told that there was indeed a patient registered in maternity named

Mrs. Lyons, he replied: "I'm an old family friend, and I understand she has just had a little baby, and I want to pay my respects."

"Oh, yes," the nurses smiled, "a very pretty little baby."

"What room?" Moe asked.

"Oh," said a nurse, "we will take you to her."

"No," he replied, "that won't be necessary at all. I'm a healthy American, you give me her room number, and I will find it."

So they did, and Moe entered the elevator with his bouquet for Mrs. Lyons.

"It was on the tenth floor, I think, and I went whizzing along, six, eight, ten, thirteen, fifteen, eighteen, twenty, to the final floor. I think it was 20 or 21. I got off the elevator, went over to a trash barrel, and threw the bouquet in. Then I went over to the side of the building and said to myself, 'What a sign.' I pulled my tie over and started shooting pictures. There was Fuji in all its glory off to the left, and there on the horizon, were big oil tanks and what could have been a series of military installations. I photographed for several minutes, and then left, without saying any good byes. I had the pictures I wanted."

With those pictures leading his squadron on, Jimmy Doolittle some years later bombed Tokyo, and Moe's fellow ballplayers never knew a thing about it until Berg released the information in a book of his adventurous life some years after World War II. Moe told me the story himself, sitting in my living room, and before some astonished guests.

Incidentally, at the receiving line, the Emperor Hirohito met all the famous ballplayers, and stopped short when Moe Berg spoke to him in Japanese. "He did a retake," Moe said, "and came back and talked with me for about five minutes, in Japanese. He was startled that a ballplayer would know the Japanese language. "Moe wasn't particularly worried about baseball, he wanted to do his ultra-secret job for the U.S. Government, and he did it, and very well as Doolittle would have noted. Fuji was the perfect landmark.

The bouquet Mrs. Lyons, whose father was U.S. Ambassador Joseph Grew, did not receive that day, somehow got to Mrs. Lyons at a party several years later in Virginia. Moe never forgot. Certainly not Mrs. Lyons, whose husband, a Harvard graduate, Cecil Lyons, worked in the ambassadorial service of the U.S. Government, as well.

One day at sunny Fenway Park, Manager Joe Cronin was stuck for a pitcher as the visiting Yankees threatened. "Tell Moe Berg, if his nose isn't in a text book," he barked, "to warm up a pitcher for me, we're gonna need one in a hurry." Moe could also do that.

To me, Moe was the grandest patriot of them all. He also had a hand in the "heavy water" incident in the NazI's hydrogen bomb buildup in, I think, Norway. He had the plant blown up, and to think, his father didn't want him to become a ballplayer. Had that been so, U.S. Intelligence might have been deprived of his services .I liked Moe that night. He was relaxed, and he told us some wondrous stores, as all listened intently. It seemed to me that Moe was something of a lonely fellow. He had never married, and probably had scarce chance for romance, and he seemed such a happy guy. He bought stacks of newspapers each day, and read them avidly, from the sports pages through all the sections. It is said, when he died, newspapers were piled to the ceiling. Moe was an inveterate reader, allowing no one to touch his supply of daily papers until he had read them thoroughly. Possibly he picked up ideas in their contents, maybe he was just checking major league averages with the idea of future trades and swaps.

Moe was a handsome individual, with black, curly hair, always a flashing smile, and a warm, engaging personality. In spite of his attributes, I felt that Moe Berg was somewhat the lonely man. He never married, and maybe this was the reason for his melancholic state occasionally. At other times, however, he was a delight at gathering.

When I think of Moe Berg, I think not of him as a catcher for the Boston Red Sox, as I knew him, nor as a scholarly student at Princeton, but as an American Patriot.He fit that symbol clearly, a solid American, and very proud of it. I admired Moe Berg for his many fine attributes; he was just good at anything he attempted, though he didn't care especially for law, which he gave up for baseball, much to his father's dismay. At old Fenway Park, textbooks were very much a part of his daily equipment, as much so as his catcher's togs, mask, shinguards, chest protector and mitt.

In more than 60 years of writing, I have never met a person quite of

Moe's equal. He studied not only at Princeton, but at the Sorbonne as well. He was first a scholar, then a ballplayer. Then why not a teaching career? Apparently that did not carry the same degree of excitement that baseball did, and baseball opened a lot of exciting doors to him, such as meeting the Emperor of Japan one fine day.

Sammy Cahn:
Let It
Snow

SONGWRITER Sammy Cahn had more music copyrighted than anyone else in the United States. "Let It Snow" was one, "Three Coins in the Fountain" another. (Courtesy Photo)

It was in 1937 or 1938 that I first became familiar with the name Sammy Cahn. Bandleader Guy Lombardo, a friend of mine for about 50 years, mentioned a song he had just introduced, I believe, in his coast-to-coast radio program, and he described it like this, "Sammy Cahn's 'Bei Mir Bist Du Schon.'"

I didn't know what the song title meant until I heard Guy's trio singing it one night, and then I knew. A subtitle explained it: "It Means That You're Grand."

That song may have marked the emergence of Sammy Cahn as a big-time songwriter (he did the lyrics) on Tin Pan Alley, and one day Sammy told me how it was all done.

He said a friend had invited him out to dinner one night at the Roosevelt Hotel in New York, saying, "We can dine in the Grill Room and hear some of the good music you like, by Guy Lombardo and His Royal Canadians," and that sounded real good to Sammy.

"So, we got dressed up and headed out for the Roosevelt," said Sammy. "What he didn't tell me was that Guy had made an arrangement of 'Bei Mir Bist Du Schon' especially for me, and he was going to play it when my friend brought me to the Grill Room.

"We ordered our dinner and then Guy stepped up to the mike and announced that he was going to play Sammy Cahn's 'Bei Mir Bist Du Schon.' What a surprise for me, and did it sound beautiful, you know, the way Guy played all of them. The orchestration was perfect, and the trio was fantastic. The song drew much applause that night, and I think I got up and took a bow. It was a thrilling night for me."

More and more after Guy introduced the song to America, the name of Sammy Cahn was being mentioned by people who liked their music sweet and soft and swingy, and that is what Guy gave them in this partic-ular number.

As good as that song was, it could not be matched by some of Sammy's later blockbusters, such as "Let It Snow," "Three Coins in a

Fountain," "It's Magic," "Five Minutes More," "It's Been a Long, Long Time," "I'll Walk Alone," "I Should Care," "Call Me Irresponsible," and a few others.

Sammy had a way with words, and with phrases, and most likely had he chosen, he would have been an A-plus writer, but he chose songwriting, and he was in his element.

I asked him one day how "Let It Snow" ever came into being, words and music. That was one of Sammy's touring shows, I believe, "Words and Music." He said it was Julie Styne's idea for the song.

"It was the hottest day of the year in southern California, and we were on the beach under a blazing sun when Julie turned to me and said, 'Let's write a song about the cold winter we're having and all the snow.'"

From my feature article in the New Hampshire Sunday News of Nov. 18, 1990, I quote:

"Sammy, never one to be caught lagging, responded at once: 'I'm with you, pal. When do we start?' His friend replied, 'Now.' And they did, and winter arrived almost instantly, that is, from the time Sammy had a chance to write the first words of his lyrics to the last:

'Oh, the weather outside is frightful. And the fire is so delightful. And since we've no place to go, let it snow, let it snow, let it snow.'"

That was the start of a song all America sings as the winter weather and Christmas approach, and its beautiful lines captivate all, young and old alike. It is one of Sammy Cahn's most celebrated songs, and the lyrics really sing out of the advent of winter, of the chance for a little romance where "the fire is so delightful," to the end of the evening, "When we finally kiss goodnight, How I'll hate going out in the storm. But if you really hold me tight, All the way home I'll be warm," and then the assurance, "The fire is slowly dying, And, my dear, we're still good-byeing. But as long as you love me so, let it snow, let it snow, let it snow."

Where could one find more touching lyrics than that? And yet, I think Sammy Cahn felt it was not his best. He spoke of others, all exceptional of course, but hardly of that caliber. Still, I believe his two greatest hit songs were "Let It Snow" and "Three Coins in the Fountain," for they told a simple, direct, heart-warming story, and that's what the public likes best, and

TOP OF HIS WORLD -- Songwriter Sammy Cahn sits atop a piano with note for Bob Hilliard: "For Bob Hiliard - Here I am on 'Top of my World' - with 'High Hopes!' (plus) '3 Coins for the Fountain!!!'"

even to this day, everyone knows them, song and verse. They just tumble out.

Sammy Cahn was a genius in every way. Nothing could seemingly get him down. He loved his wife, his family and his work, which for him was something akin to play. Verses poured out. He could put anything to verse in a matter of seconds, match up improbable words within the meter and make the song sound so elegant and so clever.

There was not another lyricist like Cahn, although Irving Berlin was a master of lines, too, as well as music, which he also composed. Berlin did words and music both, and for that reason, must be hailed as the finest, although my friend Sammy is not that far behind. I oftentimes have wondered how Sammy might have fared were he writing his own music, for he was exceptionally talented at the keyboard.

The question will go unanswered, but the world knows well that

Berlin and Cahn were geniuses in their field, angels of a kind that flutter down only once and leave their magic wands behind. Their work will live wherever songs are sung.

Sammy told me in one of our last conversations that he understood he held the record for song copyrights. "I put on my show in Washington," he said, "and an official in the government came up to me and said, 'You know, Sammy, you hold the copyright record for songs, 2,600.'" That's a lot of songwriting, and a lot of time, a lifetime, in fact, where ideas blossom every day of the year.

Sammy was always spilling over with ideas for songs, and his were pleasantly catchy, all of them. I remember another of his big hits, "If That Isn't Love, It Will Have To Do Until the Real Thing Comes Along," another lilting tune with the right kind of words.

I wondered how Sammy was on the golf course, and over the recent years, I attempted to set up a foursome where he and I would take on Bob MacLeod, the Dartmouth All-America grid star (1938), and Warren Girard, a former foreign editor of the Los Angeles Times and another Dartmouth Man, a fellow I broke in to the newspaper game. Try as we might, it never came to fruition.

MacLeod was the publisher of *Teen Magazine.* Three of them resided in the Los Angeles area, and I in New Hampshire. I think I was the bottleneck, for Sammy was looking forward to a match, and I know the others would have been eager to play. Cahn often asked for Warren Girard. I think he wanted to go fishing on Girard's palatial yacht and go after "The Great White Shark." He was always one for the exciting life and a gentleman to the end.

A couple of years before he died, Sammy dropped me a line, citing a few plans he had in mind. The letter follows:

"Dear Bob:

Even as I was chatting here in my home with two VIP men from Boston, Drs. Hoard R. Hall and Kenneth Quickel, president of Joslin Diabetes Center, your letter arrived.

"Coincidentally, they were hopeful I could do a benefit performance of "Words and Music" for the hospital in Boston.

"In any case, I have put them in touch with Paul Blake, my producer, and maybe between us all, you and David Balsom, we might make it to Boston one of these days.

"Chicago was beyond imagining. The town really belonged to me, and I left beginning to realize why it really and truly was My Kind of Town.

"There is talk of me taking it to New York (there always is), but I am just taking it easy here at home, preparing for the ASCAP memorial tribute to James Van Heusen.

"I am not sure if I heard from Warren Girard, but I am always standing by for any reunion. Belated Happy New Year and all nice things..... Sammy."

There were several other letters Sammy and I exchanged, and I am sorry to say we couldn't get together. One of them is a thank-you note on his book, I *Should Care*. It follows:

"Dear Bob:

"I should have known anyone called Bob Hilliard would be simpatico to anyone who is called Sammy Cahn, because a Bob Hilliard I knew wrote marvelous songs and was a marvelous guy.

"My beautiful bride Tita and I just were sitting here reading your warm and lovely review of "I Should Care," and I must say it is reviews like yours that make it all worthwhile.

"Right now, there are plans for me to tour my one-man show, plans to make a film of my life, and well, many things, and one way or another, I may make it to your city, and if and when I do, I'll say things like over a booze and thank you personally. Mainly, I Should Care— and I do. — Sammy."

That letter was dated November, 1974, and that is when I got to know Sammy Cahn for the great, fun-loving human being he was. I wrote two or three features for *The Union Leader* after that on Cahn, and I tried unsuccessfully, I am distressed to say, to bring him to Boston and to

Manchester. My work went for naught in my own hometown, but the Boston press agents, David Balsom, Nance Movsesian and Deedee Chereton put up a good fight to bring him in and failed. You win some, you lose some, and that is how it was.

In December of 1990, I received this note from Sammy about a feature I did on him in the *New Hampshire Sunday News, Union Leader* of Nov. 18, 1990, the same story I quoted from previously. His letter follows:

"Dear Bob -

"I get this eerie feeling when I write to Bob Hilliard (because I knew the lyric writer so well.)

"In any case, I love the story and have sent XEROX copies to all good chums. You, sir, are one helluva writer (I know because of the countless articles I have read about me that aren't quite accurate or even fair reporting.

"Chicago (My Kind of Town) is again very kind to me (read enclosed story of performance there). I was going to leave here today, but they are making me remain through New Year's Eve.

"I won't be back in Beverly Hills until January 15 or so. Have your friend, Warren Girard, call me, and maybe we'll meet for a coffee or whatever.

"Again, you are a talented fellow, and I wish for you and yours all the nice lyrics in all the nice songs.

HAPPY HOLIDAYS ..... Sammy."

The one thing that is very painful to me is that I never was able to meet my dear friend Sammy, and he was such a happy guy. While we were talking on his birthday, he said, "Excuse it a moment, Bob, I've got to tell Tita what I want for a drink. What will you have Bob?" I told him to make mine bourbon and ginger, and through the courtesy of Transcontinental service, New England Telephone, I wished him a Happy Birthday, though with a bourbon. His was a gin and tonic, I believe.

It is a dreary task to talk of the death of a friend, especially one of Sammy's magnitude, but he was a giant in his own trade. One has only to

listen to some of those thousands of songs that the little guy propelled like
the wind into worldwide hits. He was a Titan among his peers, and you
have Bob Hilliard and the late Guy Lombardo to thank for that.

Here is the Associated Press release on his death on Jan. 15, 1993:

Sammy Cahn Dies at 79
Lyricist Won Several Academy Awards
LOS ANGELES (AP) -- Sammy Cahn, the prolific lyricist whose
Oscar-winning songs included "Call Me Irresponsible," "Three Coins in
the Fountain" and "High Hopes," died yesterday. He was 79.

Cahn died of congestive heart failure at Cedars-Sinai Medical Center,
hospital spokesman Ron Wise said. Cahn had been hospitalized since
December 30.

Cahn collaborated with Saul Chaplin, Jimmy Van Heusen and Jule
Styne on hundreds of popular songs.

Frank Sinatra immortalized many of Cahn's tunes, including "Love
and Marriage," now heard on television's "Married... With Children." The
song was awarded a special Emmy from a musical version of Thornton
Wilder's "Our Town." Cahn also wrote music for the children's television
show, "Sesame Street."

Among his best known works were "Rhythm Is Our Business," "Let It
Snow, Let It Snow, Let It Snow," "I'll Walk Alone," "Love and Marriage,"
"Second Time Around," "Pocketful of Miracles," "My Kind of Town" and
"All That Love Went to Waste."

As a film composer, his credits included "Anchors Aweigh," "April in
Paris," "Meet Me in Las Vegas," "The Tender Trap" and "Thoroughly
Modern Millie."

And on Broadway, Cahn worked on "High Button Shoes," "Two's
Company," "Skyscraper," "Walking Happy," "Words and Music" and
"Falling in Love Again."

He won Academy Awards in 1954 for "Three Coins in the Fountain,"
from the film of the same name, in 1957 for "All the Way" from the film
"The Joker is Wild," in 1959 for "High Hopes," from "A Hole in the Head"
and in 1963 for "Call Me Irresponsible" from "Papa's Delicate Condition."
"Call Me Irresponsible" also won an Emmy award.

He was nominated for Oscars many other times.

The songwriter was born Samuel Cohen in New York City. An early student of the violin, Cahn started playing in a local orchestra at weddings, bar mitzvahs and other parties.

He continued playing the violin at burlesque houses and wrote his first lyrics at age 16. Before coming to Hollywood, he scored short films.

He was a president of the National Academy of Popular Music and was a member of the board of the American Society of Composers, Authors and Publishers.

OPERA SOPRANO star Roberta Peters
was a frequent visitor to Boston and a featured guest at an opera party in Newport,
R.I. attended by author Bob Hilliard several years ago.

It isn't all work.

The opera party in Newport, R.I., several years ago was so much fun, it ought to be repeated every few years for the full enjoyment of its distinguished patrons.

It probably won't be, for money beckons, and that's the mover these days, as always. It is, however, a pleasant thought that won't go away.

I received my invitation from Mrs. John Barry Ryan, one of the Met's honorary directors, and had tossed it on the credenza for filing away. The thing that bothers me is that I didn't give it another thought —that is, until my sister and her husband, Betty and Mort Tuttle, dropped in for a visit one afternoon. Betty saw the invitation and picked it up, and naturally read it.

It was from Mrs. Ryan in New York, and it invited Barbara and me to a bash being held in Newport.

"Barbara," Betty inquired, "are you and Bob going to this nice affair in Newport?"

"I don't think so," Barbara replied, "Bob hasn't said anything about it."

"Gosh," Betty said, "I think you should go. It sounds like a marvelous affair."

"Ask Bob about it," Barbara said. And Betty did. So then I asked Barbara if she'd like to go. Her reply: "Of course."

Mort chimed in with, "I'll help you out, Bob. I'll drive you to the party —and back." Fast travel plans, there.

I telephoned Mrs. John Barry Ryan in New York to ask if it was all right to bring my sister and her husband. She agreed with the girls.

"Of course, Bob," she said, "bring them along. I'll look forward to seeing all of you in Newport."

And we did just that. In the receiving line that sunny late afternoon was Mrs. Ryan, and she beamed when she saw us.

"Bob, you and Barbara finally made it—I'm so happy," she said. I introduced my sister and Mort to Sir Rudolf Bing and, of course, to the next in line, the very own Mrs. Ryan, and they all broke into wide smiles, and Mrs. Ryan spoke to Barbara and Betty. "I'm glad you were all there that day. What gives with Bob? she asked.

It was the most enjoyable party I have ever attended, and I have been to hundreds following plays and operas and to private ones, but none equaled this one. Everybody from the Met was there, including conductors (if we wished to sing a few lines). And to think I might have missed it.

At the luncheon, we sat at the table next to Mrs. Auchincloss and the Browns (of Brown University), and we had a great time just talking. I remember asking Mrs. Auchincloss about "that stylish yacht tied up nearby close to shore."

She said, "Oh, that belongs to the Mosbachers. They moor it here. Would you like to see it, Bob?"

I said I'd love to, and my brother-in-law, Mort, piped in, "I went to college with a Mosbacher at Dartmouth."

Mrs. Auchincloss said she thaught that was the same one.

"Mort," Mrs. Auchincloss declared, "you will be happy to see that Mosbacher has put a Dartmouth-green carpet on deck just to remind him of his days at Hanover."

We all laughed with that, and we trooped on down to the water's edge to inspect the trim craft.

That is how it went at Newport, plenty of music, plenty of great singing (as you might suppose with all those artists present), and I knew many of them from all those years of covering Grand Opera and New York stage plays.

What a night! We talked with Roberta Peters and Robert Merrill and others of the Met—and just mingling with them all produced many a story, I can truthfully say.

Mrs. Ryan was so delighted, for she knew it would represent attention in the day's press, for many of the Boston papers were represented as well. It was a banner day for the Dear Old Met.

I really hope the Met can restore this exciting interlude in the near future, to bring a new rapture to the works of Verdi and Wagner and Puccini, yes, and to the many other gilded works of the Metropolitan Opera as well.

There at Newport, with all those gorgeous mansions nearby, we approached Opera Week with great excitement, and it was fulfilled with soaring tones of the greatest beauty.

I for one cast my vote for the restoration of the Newport Week, with all speed, with secondary casts if necessary—but to get it back once again.

And to think I might have passed it up once upon a time.

Tammy Grimes:
One Ired Girl

BROADWAY actress Tammy Grimes: Her tough voice sent theater-goers sprawling...(UPI File Photo)

When Tammy Grimes wrote me that letter so many years ago after Hollywood had bypassed her for Debbie Reynolds for the title role in "The Unsinkable Molly Brown," she was steamed, and I think rightfully so. Not at Debbie, but at the Hollywood think-tankers who make those astounding decisions. Better that they were farmed out in the beginning to West Waco.

Tammy was stunning in this role, which she created for Broadway, and the whole world lay at her feet. She played it so realistically and so humorously. To theatre-goers, there was no one else for the role of Molly than Tammy, the fresh and saucy, "Never Say Down" sprite who would never let her pesky brothers get the best of her, nor for that matter, any of Europe s nobility when she and her husband, Johnny Brown, "Leadville Johnny," went abroad.

Her tough voice sent them all sprawling, and it was cultured right out of a barroom. That was Tammy and Molly, one and the same. Had I been Tammy, I would have brought a suit for a million bucks against Hollywood for their bypass. Molly was her role, with all due regard to Debbie's talents, and she didn't get it. Well, neither did Julie Andrews in "My Fair Lady," which she truly deserved, and which she had earned. Well, that's Hollywood, a compelling fairyland but a fiercely competitive one.

By being denied her true role, Tammy Grimes lost her one big shot at lasting fame in Glitterland. I would have been seething, and I know that Tammy was, from the tenor of her long letter to me shortly after Debbie Reynolds was picked as Molly. Tammy's mother used to visit us in *The Union Leader* newsroom (which has seen many celebrities since our "First in the Nation" presidential primary was inaugurated in the early 1950s), and we were hearing all about the Molly choice from two good sources, Tammy and her Mom. What is more, they were right. Tammy Grimes and Julie Andrews both should have been awarded these roles, and they weren't.

That is life, I guess, in the Celluloid Capital of the World, where there are as many heartbreaks as there are tremors and earthquakes.

Tammy's portrayal of Molly lives on, and it must be richly rewarding to her after these many years of laboring in the vineyards of playmaking. She made "Unsinkable Molly Brown" one of my own personal all-time favorites in the family of musicals, topped only in this field by "My Fair Lady" and "Camelot," which writers have compared with John F. Kennedy's presidential years.

Ted Williams:
The Splendid
Splinter

BOSTON RED SOX great Ted
Williams hits some balls to
Boston fielders during Spring
Training. Williams was one of
the greatest hitters of all time.

It was rather a quiet, sunny morning at Winter Haven, Fla. as I stepped into the dressing room of the Boston Red Sox.

Ted Williams had already shown up for his business day with the promising farm hands, ready to teach them the important lessons that need to be learned in the majors and the things one needs to know by rote.

Sitting just outside the door was little Jerry Remy, having an early morning smoke. As he sat there on the stoop, he looked a lot like a junior high student sneaking a butt behind his mom's back.

He and Yaz smoked a lot, and it didn't seem to bother them. Of course, times have changed, and today the team doctor would have approached them for a word about the harmful effects of smoking.

I made a note to myself to ask Ted when I saw him if it was true that Ty Cobb, the famed "Georgia Peach," had actually come up to Boston to see him about his batting style.

"See you for a minute, Ted?" I asked.

"Sure," he said, "good time to talk."

I asked him about Ty Cobb's visit to Fenway Park that day.

"Well," he said, "it wasn't actually Fenway Park where he visited me, it was Yankee Stadium, and we were in for a series with the Yankees. He told me he thought that I could get more hits and raise my batting average much higher by the placement of my hands on the bat. I listened to him, and he made a lot of sense. He picked up a bat and showed me, his hands two inches apart.

"I told him right away that wasn't for me. I liked to slug, hands at the end of the bat, not apart, and go for the long hit.

"'Well,' Ty said, 'hitting my way, you could place-hit better and probably boost your batting average by several points.'

"I told him it was probably true, I could do that, but it would not be my style of hitting and might bring on a prolonged slump. Ty agreed with me, but told me to experiment with it some time.

"When the Lou Boudreau Shift of stacking the diamond for a left-handed batter came into being, I accepted the challenge and would try to hammer the ball through the infielders. Probably, batting with my hands two inches apart would have enabled me to place-hit better, but I didn't do it, and I don't think my average suffered that much. But I did appreciate Mr. Cobb coming up to tell me that."

Maybe Williams was a little obstinate in rejecting Cobb's tip on batting, and possibly he could have had a lifetime mark of close to .370, but Ted isn't complaining. He hit a lifetime mark of about .344. Rogers Hornsby was second to Cobb in lifetime batting with a mark of just better than .350, and I consider those three the greatest hitters ever.

Williams not only hit for average, he hit for distance, belting 521 home runs. One big argument in Ted Williams' favor is that he lost five years of playing time serving as a Marine pilot in World War II. There is no telling what he might have done, for those five years were in the prime of his baseball life.

He might easily have picked up percentage points on Ty Cobb had he not volunteered for duty with Uncle Same...who knows.

Williams, like Cobb, was smart, discerning and athletic. He had, and still has, unsurpassed vision. At Fenway, the writers all felt that Ted called the pitch, not the umpires. If he let one go by, it must have been a bad pitch. This wasn't always true, he did wait out some pitchers on occasion and pass up some perfectly fine strikes, but it was the norm.

He had a quick and powerful swing and was the classic antithesis of Yogi Berra...Ted's swing was termed perfect by many baseball men, although I liked Joe DiMaggio's better, level and parallel with the ground, and hefty. He also hit for distance.

I would have to call Ted Williams the greatest hitter of "modern" times, along with Stan Musial of the Cardinals, with the edge going to Ted on the basis of pure octane.

Ted was a close friend of Leo E. Cloutier, the late sports editor of *The Union Leader, N.H. Sunday News,* and also for nearly 50 years the Baseball Dinner director, largest in the United States. Ted was Leo's pal and often came up to Manchester and to Wells Beach, Maine, where Leo and Laura Cloutier had their beautiful seaside home.

SPRING CHAT -- Red Sox great Ted Williams, left, stops to chat with the author and friend John Buckley at Spring Training in Winter Haven, Fla. in March 1980. Frank A. Morono Jr. photo

On one visit, he reportedly bequeathed a new Cadillac to Leo. He liked a column Leo had written on him and told Leo he already had two or three cars... "what do I need another one for?"

On hearing this, Shirley Povich, the famed Washington writer, sprang into action with a piece about what a nice guy Ted Williams was and how he took care of his friends, ending the articlet with this: "Come to think of it, I knew Ted pretty well, too."

Leo stamped his new car with the now famous license plate: "LC - 9." Leo Cloutier's initials, Ted's immortal No. 9. Everyone around the baseball circuit knew that number, and Leo always was given preferred parking. "Friend of Ted's," they would say.

After Leo's death in the late 1980s, Ted would still stop in for visits with Laura and his buddies in New Hampshire and Maine.

Someone asked me once, "Did Ted ever bunt?" A good question. Offhand, I can't remember that he did, although the percentages would not dictate a bunt from Ted with his sure-fire hitting ability. The odds, I would think, would be for hitting away.

The year Ted was flirting with that .400 average, manager Joe Cronin told him to sit out the final two games and preserve the mark. Ted would have nothing to do with it, and told Cronin there was no way, he was going to play in both games. He came up with about seven hits and went soaring over the .400 mark, to .406, the last since Ted accomplished it that anybody has caressed that almost unattainable average.

He did it in 1941, without Joe Cronin's approval. He hit. 356 the following season, and then went into military service.

I know Ted quite well, and I always admired his readiness to speak up on any subject. In some respects, he and Carlton Fisk were cut from the same mold. Once when George Scott was tossing off some remarks on the topic of hitting, Williams joked: "That's the trouble with you, George. You're suspect from the neck up. You don't hit a ball like that at all. You wait for the proper good pitch. Have you got that, Georgie?"

We had a lot of fun at the training camp. The mood was generally relaxed and light. Ted likes to play tennis, and I told him my grandson was a member of the tennis team at Clemson University in South Carolina.

"Gee, I'd like to play him a few sets when he is with you in camp. Can you arrange it?" I said sure, and the following year, Robby did come with me to camp on a break from school, and I told Ted. Williams said, "Let's set it up for this afternoon," which we did on the courts Ted preferred, near where he was staying.

The match drew a bigger gallery than most college contests, and that afternoon all Ted did was lob high shots back to Robby, who had some trouble controlling his serves as well as his return shots. In the end, Ted prevailed, much to his son's displeasure. He lost ten bucks on the match. Robby went over and shook hands with Ted afterward and complimented him on his game. In an earlier time, Ted might have been a champion, Robby ventured, "with that lob technique." The crowd gave both a big hand.

Ted enjoyed fishing in the wild rivers of New Brunswick, and after one such expedition, he stopped in Manchester, N.H. to view The Manchester Historic Association's tribute to Leo's big Baseball Dinners over the years, and he stole the show, naturally. He laughed at many of the photos which showed him tieless amongst a tuxedo crowd. "Well," he proffered, "that's me, I guess."

Ted will forever be a champion of the crowd, and he was that night to be sure.

I liked the story Birdie Tebbetts, the former major league catcher and manager, told at the Baseball Dinner on a cold night in January many years ago. He was retracing the career of "The Splendid Splinter" on his first visit to Detroit, and I am sure it was at this dinner he told the story.

Said Birdie: "I looked up from my catching position, and coming up to the plate was the young and sensational Ted Williams of the Boston Red Sox. I was a catcher for the Detroit Tigers and later on I became a teammate of the very same Ted Williams on the Red Sox. I spoke to him:

"Well, if it isn't the celebrated Mr. Williams himself. Welcome to Detroit. Where would you like the pitch, Mr. Williams? I will try to help you.

'Right about so high,' he answered. So I called for it in that spot. In no time, it was in the center field stands.

Then, a couple of innings later, Ted came up again.

Why, hello again, Mr. Williams. That was some clout. Where, by the way, do you want this pitch?

'About in the same place,' he answered. So I called for it in that spot, and bam, it was gone again.

And that was the last time I ever asked his advice; two times at bat, two home runs. Even I knew when to quit."

In that brief period, Birdie knew he had seen an immortal in the making.

The foregoing was a recreation of Birdie's speech as best I can remember. Ted was there that night, and he roared with laughter, along with the 2,000-plus audience.

I miss seeing Ted Williams at Fenway, and I miss the old press box where we plotted the games and checked out the players' bad habits. One night, we were checking out Denny Eckersly's faulty pitching habits with a runner on first base. A righthander, Denny would come down to his groin practically in his stretch, and by the time he fired, the runner was well on his way to second for a stolen base. The catcher, however good, had no chance at all of nailing him.

My press box companion, Bill Arnold, checked it out for me on the nights Eck was pitching, and one evening Bill discovered that Willie Wilson was taking five steps before Eck even threw the ball, a stolen base in any league.

A few nights later, I told Eck to drop his arms only to the shoulder, but way back to get the impetus for the pitch, and he said he couldn't do it that way, he couldn't get enough leverage. I told him that he could, for we worked on that style even in high school, and if done right, Willie Wilson or whoever was on base, would be a dead duck at second in an attempted steal. Eck, by the way, modified his stance, and runners weren't taking the same liberty later in his career.

I miss those nights, and I really miss the play and hitting of Ted Williams, Esquire. And by the way, may we say it now: The Fenway Park Press Box is the worst one in the league, and I told one of the guys not long ago that it was even inferior to the one at Hopkinton Fair, which must have been built at the turn of the century.

Teo Fabi:
Fabi Likes It Fast

FABULOUS FABI -- IndyCar racer Teo Fabi poses in this 1993 file photo. Fabi raced at the New Hampshire International Speedway in the early 1990s.

It isn't true that Teo Fabi, the affable Italian race car driver, sings a lusty "Pagliacci" as he hurtles along the race course at 180 miles per hour, although it wouldn't be startling if he did.

He comes from a musical family in the very musical city of Milano, which houses the famed temple of opera, La Scala, and where native sons are more or less expected to gravitate toward the Grand Opera stage than toward the Grand Circuit racing tracks.

"My grandfather was a conductor," he said, smiling with pride. "I never knew him; he died 20 years before I was born." Fabi loves speed and action, belying his placid mien when he's strapped into his yellow Lola Chevrolet, and he's right at home roaring along the straight-aways and into the banked curves at dizzying speeds, completely at home.

There's no telling what his musical grandfather might have said, or thought, could he have seen his grandson in action one weekend in the PPG Indy Car World Series action at New Hampshire International Speedway in Loudon, N.H. He probably would have required a sedative and a visit to the nearest church.

Although Teo likes music, as most Milanese do, his major at the esteemed Institute of Technology at Milan was aeronautical engineering, and it didn't contain any musical components. "Yes," he said, "I do like music, and I plan to see many operas. I saw the opera 'Don Carlo,' and I enjoyed it." His grandfather would have enjoyed hearing that.

Teo is a careful driver, and on this particular Friday in the mid '90s, he elected many pit stops in the car trials as he checked out a few trouble spots in his racer. He is a smooth driver, and one who will seldom beat himself. At the terrifying speeds these drivers go, one cannot be too careful. Checks should be made all the time.

Fabi is in Car No. 8, and it is electrifying to see him bolt out of the pits onto the track itself. He does it with a sturdy hand and a very clear mind. It would not be surprising to see him in constant conention Sunday in the feature event. He ranks ninth in the driver standings, and is considered a

TEO FABI brings his Pennzoil-sponsored race car to the attention of the Hall
Racing Team as they test at New Hampshire International Speedway in this 1994
photo. (NHIS Photo by John Owens)

perpetual threat by fellow drivers who recognize his latent ability. Teo is a
quiet, thoughtful individual with the sparkling blue eyes of a northern
Italian. He is kind and very patient with interviewers as this reporter discovered, and he exudes a definit charm, as though perhaps he was, after
all, an opera star emerging from La Scala after a hard night of "Aida," and
pushing around a sumptuous soprano much larger than himself.

In that respect, he would have found car racing much easier, and
more to his liking.

Friday was a big day at the track as drivers made ready for Sunday and
jockeyed for strong pole positions. There were many racing celebrities in
the infield awaiting the time trials. At one point, we paused near a pit and
there was Emerson Fittipaldi, secured in his racer and ready to go. Many
drivers stood around their brightly colored machines, set for the grueling
day of time trials; Paul Tracy, Britain's Nigel Mansell, Raul Boesel of Brazil.

The day was beautiful, the track fast. For the most part, drivers gave
the course high marks, although Turn One was described as a bit slippery

due to some work done there after the Winston Cup race. Some sliding was noted, but it was not overly alarming.

One famous personality watching the Friday trials was the silver-maned Tom Carnegie, track announcer at Indianapolis. He greeted *The Union Leader*'s Kevin Provencher and cowboy-hatted Jack Ratta, an old friend from way back, most affably. Leaning against the cement retaining wall, he was doing a little announcing himself.

The thunder of the engines shattered the stillness of the serene view as the drivers tested their sleek machines. It is a wonder how well their reflexes work at the screeching speeds they attain, but as Provencher pointed out: "Their best friend is the brake." On the straight-aways, the drivers were blurs in their cars, clipping it off at 180 or so.

The writer showed Carnegie the names of three or four drivers of the past who competed at the old board track at Rockingham Park in the mid-Twenties, and he knew them all: Frank Lockhart, Ralph DePalma, Pete DePolo. "Great drivers," he remarked, "every one of them."

It was a memorable day, made so in large part by many of the old-timers, including Carnegie and Deke Houlgate of the *Los Angeles Times*, and various officials. Houlgate inquired for Joe Barnea, retired executive sports Editor of *The Union Leader*, and he took the time to drop him a note.

Today is the big day, and look for some lightning-fast times. Movie star Paul Newman was not present at Friday's trials, but was expected to check in from his Connecticut home during the weekend. Newman is a veteran of the track wars, and well respected by his fellow drivers.

Cooke and the Chinese Halfback

Of the many millions of inhabitants calling New York home, only one, an erudite New York City sports editor by the name of Bob Cooke, was able to uncover a hoax played on hundreds of thousands of readers by a will-o-the-wisp jokester who called in the football results each Saturday evening, faithfully and like clockwork, and then laughed himself to sleep.

The caller lured the rewrite man in with his exciting accounts, and the stories began attracting the sports-minded people of the city, entranced by the heroics of a 140-pound halfback named Johnny Chung, who had the speed of lightning in his legs, and the twisting and turning of a modern-day Ray MacLean or Albie Booth, enough maybe to get him into the Hall of Fame.

The first story really bugged the readers. "Johnny Chung raced to five touchdowns today as Plainfield Teachers romped to a one-sided win."

Just enough to get everyone thinking of Johnny Chung, as the perpetrator wished. The rest is rather history in a warped sort of way, for Johnny Chung, the celebrated and dapper Chinese running back, was stealing every show on Saturday afternoons. Readers began following the exploits of Chung instead of the school, Plainfield Teachers.

"How many did Chung get today?" they would ask the sports editor.

Once, Bob Cooke replied, "Only three today; he had an off day."

At the time, Bob was sports editor of the *New York Herald-Tribune*, one of New York's best, with hundreds of thousands of readers, and Bob kept his readers well posted on sports matters, something he had learned at fashionable St. Paul School, where kids prepped for Harvard and Yale and Princeton. It's situated in my home town of Concord, N.H.

I didn't know Bob until many years later, when our paths crossed in correspondence, and he remarked that he had spent some memorable years at St. Paul, probably at the very same time I was struggling with my French and math at nearby Concord High School, the same school where astronaut Christa McAuliffe, years later, was a science teacher about to take that tragic ride into space.

Bob Cooke went on to the sports editor's post and became one of the best known in the country, and perchance, Johnny Chung made him the greatest of them all, a sports editor who checked everything.

Cooke also liked a humorous story, and he had just that in Johnny Chung, halfback, for, with a little sleuthing, Cooke discovered there was no Johnny Chung at all, and no Plainfield Teachers, either.

It was a total fabrication, and the Chung articles continued to fool those thousands of readers each weekend until well into the fall season, when my friend unmasked the hoax and announced to his stunned readership that Chung and Plainfield did not exist, that the person who called in the stories was a phony.

There might have been a lot of gnashing of teeth and some teardrops when readers learned that Johnny and the school did not exist, in fact, that the whole weekly exercise was scrolled in deceit, and please don't hammer the overworked sports staff.

Bob Cooke rode to fame on that editorial artistry, and his story of the incident was told in many top publications, including Sports Illustrated, Signature and Readers Digest magazines.

Bob and I became friends, and he turned out another story for me in the *New Hampshire Sunday News* which ran as a guest column and elicited a lot of positive response. I told Bob that I had pitched once upon a time for the Concord High Crimson against his St. Paul School nine, and that I had risked getting messed up by St. Paul's players when I decked one of the batters who was crowding the plate on me.
It all ended peacefully as our big first baseman, Jimmy Ceriello, wrapped his arms about the charging batter and forced him away from the mound, where I am sure I would have been decked in turn. That batter, by the way, went on to play for Harvard, and was a star of the team. The very next time he stepped up against me in the batter's box, I struck him out on three pitches. He was off the chalk line that time, and it did make a difference.

Those are some personal memories of Bob Cooke and of prestigious St. Paul School, perhaps the most highly rated prep school in America today.When a student graduates from there, he or she can pick just about any college he wishes to attend, usually in the Ivy League. Most of them, as I have said, wind up at one of the Big Three (Harvard, Yale or Princeton).

I kept up a correspondence with Bob Cooke, and at the last exchange, he had retired from his New York paper and was residing in Miami Shores in sunny Florida, just about a hundred miles or so from Marco Island ("O Paradiso") where my son Bobby Jr. and Shirley now reside in some luxury, and where I hang out for spring training with the Boston Red Sox at Fort Myers and their new camp, about 50 miles away.

Hey, that's an idea. I'll invite Cooke to accompany me there from Marco, and maybe together we can talk the Red Sox into a major league championship. It's been a long time since the Sox won one of those, back in 1918, in fact. Perhaps Cooke with his charm can lure a speedster like Johnny Chung to move on to Boston and to switch positions, from halfback to second base. The Sox need speed!

The Babe

THE BABE -- New York Yankee great Babe Ruth, in an original photo by Nickolas Muray, part of the National Portrait Gallery at the Smithsonian Institution in Washington, DC. The author met Babe once.

It was either 1928 or 1929 when I saw Babe Ruth in person for the first and only time.

Babe was the supreme slugger of his time. He set his famous record of 60 home runs in 1927 (154-game season).

I can remember only one thing clearly, watching Babe as he retrieved his light, calf-skin colored glove as the teams changed innings.

I remember hollering loudly every time he stepped to the plate: "Kiss one, Babe." But he never did that day at Fenway Park more than 70 years ago when my brother Harry, an avid baseball fan as well, and I had the opportunity to watch the most famous player in the history of the game.

I think Babe popped up once or twice; it's hard to remember. It was so long ago, and we were just kids.

At any rate, this was The Babe, the darling of the fans, the guy who revolutionized the game of baseball for all time. Babe may not have been the greatest player ever. He was probably content to leave that crown to his fellow competitor, Ty Cobb, "The Georgia Peach."

However, Ruth stood out as baseball's grand master. He hammered enormous home runs that seemed to go a mile high but had the distance to clear the fence. And, he was a stellar pitcher when he started his major league career with the Red Sox, playing only about once every four or so days.

Babe's stock in a trade with the Yankees is legendary folklore.

Babe could dress up any place with his flashy suits, sleek cars and warm smile. He spent his youthful days in a children's home in Baltimore and made the grade from there into the big time, first as a pitcher then as the slugger of all time after his prowess with the Louisville Slugger was discovered.

Some of my press box friends from Boston have told me that the Babe once clobbered a home run that went 3,000 miles. It bounced into an open-door freight car that happened to be passing the ballpark at the time, and someone on the West Coast discovered it. Longest Home

Run...that story made the rounds for several years, together with his gas-tronomical feat of downing 17 hot dogs before a game and getting a real tummyache.

Those stories seem somewhat fabricated.

I became acquanited with Babe Ruth's daughter in the days of Leo E. Cloutier's fabulous baseball dinners each winter, usually accompanied by some pretty nasty snowstorms. One day, Leo asked me, since he was tied up, if I could pick up Julia "Judy" Ruth Stevens at Logan Airport in Boston, since she was flying in from Flroida to join the celebrities at the dinner. The Arnolds, Billy and Bobbi, were happy to drive me to Boston, and we met Babe's beautiful daughter there; she was very appreciative and seemed quite happy to see us.

In the years that followed, we became good friends, and she would oftentimes talk of her famous daddy. She was only 12 when Babe married her mother, and Babe was the only father she ever knew. He gave in to her every wish, and she was the darling of his eye. She accompanied her parents to Japan in the celebrated postseason tours that they made in those days, and she remembers the great fun that she had. Babe was treated as a royal monarch by the Japanese fans, and Judy recalls "the fans followed us everywhere." As a young schoolgirl, that was delightful living.

Judy and her husband reside today in Conway, N.H., near where Babe used to come in the fall to play golf, and he was a good golfer. Cloutier told me that he could hit the ball "a mile, just as in baseball," although his short game left something to be desired. Judge Burnham B. Davis, a well-known attorney in the area, took me over to her home on two or three occasions, fun visits for me because of the vast collection of Babe Ruth memorabil-ia, which I hope someday Judy bequeaths to the Baseball Museum at Cooperstown. That is the ideal resting place for Judy's collection, and I hope someday they have a Babe Ruth Room there.

There are mementoes of his entire baseball career in Judy's collection, and I might add, lovingly cared for by his "little girl." They do belong in a museum...pictures, baseballs, every kind of artifact from a career unmatched even today.

The Babe started his career with the Boston Red Sox back before

World War I. He was a superb pitcher, lefthander of course. He was air-tight in the clutch occasions and threw a wicked curve with snapping speed, which made him extremely hard to hit. The fallacy grew that left-handers were wild, but Babe put that fallacy to rest; he had total control. I think if a baseball student were to check the record book, he'd discover that Ruth didn't issue many bases on balls.

His great hitting propensity was discovered shortly after he joined the Red Sox, who played their early games over on Huntington Avenue near where Northeastern University is situated today. The Red Sox moved into their new quarters at beautiful Fenway Park in April, 1912, the same day the liner Titanic sank in the iceberg-strewn waters of the turbulent North Atlantic; and there for all purposes did Babe's career begin.

In September of 1993, the Red Sox finally got around to honor their greats of World Series fame, circa 1918, with commemorative plaques, and there were no living members present, only families that received the honors for them posthumously. It is today a prized collection in the Stevens home in Conway. A visit there is like a prized moment to baseball of the past, to ancient Fenway, to Yankee Stadium and the celebrated "House That Ruth Built." We touch hands with the glorious past in Judy's house, to be sure, and it is a good feeling, for there you can imagine a smiling Babe Ruth greeting you at the door, with a jaunty "Come on in, Kid."

I've found in baseball, especially, memories and records are every-thing, the whole game, if you'll pardon. We remember all those great stars, The Babe, Ty Cobb, Rogers Hornsby, Honus Wagner (The Dutchman), and we bow reverently. I have said how Red Rolfe, a hometown boy, once introduced me to Hornsby and Grantland Rice, the famous writer, at the 1948 World Series at old Braves Field. I felt like I had met The Babe at Judy's house that day, really, with his daughter and all that memorabilia.

In my account, I don't like to put one individual over the other, Cobb over Ruth, Ruth over Cobb, for each was a standout in his own way. Ruth as the colorful home run basher with a total of 714, Cobb as the greatest hitter of all time.

So there you have it. They were the two imcomparable giants of the game, Ty the thinking man's player, scheming how to get a basehit or how to steal second or how to steal second AND third on the same play; and Babe swatting long-range homers like they were going out of style, signing autographs always for the kids, driving off in a classy car at Yankee Stadium while awed spectators gawked. Two different guys and two champions in their own individual ways.

I always enjoyed the story Leo Cloutier told of his first meeting with the Babe at Fenway Park in the late Twenties or early Thirties. Because of his youth, Cloutier had trouble convincing Red Sox authorities that he, indeed, was the sports editor of the *Berlin* (N.H.) *Reporter*.

"I was so young," he once told me, "that they didn't believe me, and I wanted to do that interview with the Babe so much. He was my hero, and I wondered how I would ever get on that field to see him after being rebuffed by the authorities on a press card bid.

"So, I had to do something fast. The Yanks were out there for their batting practice, and it would be all over in a half-hour or so. Babe was clouting them out. I never saw so many hit so far. I was standing near the railing near the Yankee dugout and just admiring the booming shots Babe was hitting. He finished and he started walking over to the dugout where I was. I looked around for a place where I might jump onto the field for my interview and then I got down on my knees to see if there was an opening there. I noticed a slat loose, and I started tugging on it. As Babe approached, he noticed the board wiggling.

"Always curious, he stopped and went over to the railing to see why that slat was shaking. He was like a big, curious kid. 'What the hell goes on here?' he said. He stooped down to see for himself, and I said, 'Hey, Babe, get me the... out of here, will ya, I gotta do a story on you for my paper.'

"The Babe bent to the task, pulling as I pushed and perspiring more than he had in the batting cage.

"Finally, the slat started to give and with a final mighty push by The King of Swat himself, and a giant push by me, the board came loose, and I crawled out. I stuck out my hand. 'Thanks, Babe,' I said, 'glad to meet you.'

"The Babe said, 'Nice to meetcha, kid. C'mon in the dugout.'"

"So we went into the dugout for a good 15-minute chat, and that is how I picked up my interview with Babe Ruth, the Sultan of Swat, the great Bambino himself. He treated me special, told me 'Don't hurry, kid, we got plenty of time.'"

As I have said, I saw the Babe play that one time, and since I had heard so much about him, I watched his every move. Funny, I remember the name of the catcher, Benny Bengough. That team is sometimes called the greatest in baseball history, with such greats as Tony Lazzeri, Bob Meusel, Lou Gehrig, Earle Combs and others. It was practically unstoppable.

It was the team for which Red Rolfe was to play a few years hence, fresh from Dartmouth College, the Newark Bears and White Park in Concord, N.H., and there are still Yankee rooters up there in the park who live and die with that team. Rolfe became the all-time New York Yankee third baseman after Joe McCarthy switched him from shortstop to that post.

Cobb and Ruth. The two greatest, positively; the movers, the shakers and, indeed, the makers of America's greatest pastime. And, from a bygone era when players had time for people other than themselves, when money didn't dictate their lives and when they felt blessed for their good fortunes in life, much unlike today's prevailing sentiment: "The world owes me millions to play this game because I'm that good."

Ruth and Cobb were the greatest, and they were grateful, and they are no doubt rolling over in their graves!

The Epic:
Game Six

BOSTON RED SOX catcher Carlton Fisk celebrates his 12th inning home run that won Game Six of the 1975 World Series. It was perhaps the greatest game of all time. (AP file photo)

October's supposed to be colorful in New England with the foliage season unfolding, but on this Indian summer day in 1975, all of the color seemed to be unfolding in historic Fenway Park, where the Boston Red Sox were hosting the Cincinnati Reds for Game 6 of the World Series.

The Reds led the Sox, three games to two, entering Game 6, and Sparky Anderson's legions needed only one more win to annex the world championship.

Off the form of their previous games in the Series, the Reds were made a slight favorite in Game 6, but they weren't a cocky bunch, and they knew the Red Sox could explode at any moment, whatever the odds.

This was to be a game to remember for all times, not just for Sox and Reds fans, but for baseball fans across the country. The dramatics were unmatched and haven't been matched since. New York Times sports writer Red Smith told me the next night that Game 6, in his mind, was "the greatest game of baseball" he'd ever seen, and Red had seen and covered thousands of them.

Game 6 was special, featuring every gem known to baseball, every imaginable heroic play. Fans were literally sitting on the edge of their seats; a cliffhanger in the truest of senses.

Red Smith and many others in the Fenway Park press box that night, and in the park itself (one of the prettiest in the Major Leagues, with its huge Green Monster in left field beckoning batters), sat in stunned disbelief at what was transpiring.

Early on, many in the overflow audience believed Freddy Lynn, lying crumpled at the foot of the wall, had been killed running into the fence head first, at top speed. He was motionless for several minutes, and fans expected to see an ambulance on the field any second. It was a crushing collision, but Freddy finally stirred and managed to get to his feet on two wobbly legs, "As Thousands Cheered," as the New York hit play of the late Twenties proclaimed. They did cheer, and thunderously so, as Fred stayed in the game, no doubt fighting off a giant headache.

I must admit I wasn't in the press box for Game 6. I wanted to sit downstairs to catch the fans' reaction to the game, and, therefore, I sat in the grandstand. Sitting in the stands, you get a far different reaction to sitting in the much too orderly press box, where it's advisable not to show favor one way or another... to be perfectly neutral and show no emotion.

And so it was, a writer who wanted to enjoy the game with some emotion, some passion if you will. What better place than the grandstand. It beats having to stifle your emotions in the press box.

I had a seat right behind third base on one of the most famous nights in baseball history, and that is where, I must confess, I became a real fan. Just before the game began, the umps made their appearance as The Holy Ones, their Blue Cloak of Sanctity, of Judgment and Honor.

I looked, and when the Holy Ones made their appearance, I singled out one that I thought Boston fans would be most interested in, Larry Barnett. Larry was a perfectly nice guy when he wasn't umpiring. Let's clarify that: When he wasn't umpiring a Red Sox-Cincinnati World Series game, and more precisely, from behind the plate.

The fans behind third base weren't exactly ready for me, and for what I had to say to them, but I said it anyway: "There he is, ladies and gentlemen," I shouted, "there he is, Barnett himself, and he is the one who cost us that game at Cincinnati. Let's hear it big for Barnett."

For a moment, there was deadly silence, and then it broke loose. A cascade of boos that thundered over quaint Fenway Park. The fans had heard my charge, and they responded in kind. "That's for you, Fat Boy, for the Armbrister decision against Fisk. We will not forget it, and neither should you." Barnett stood aloof, not pretending to hear all the calls from the Dear Inhabitants of Third Base, but I told myself he did hear all the calls, and in time he would think about them, and that would be quite a step in the right direction.

You fans must understand, the umpires are The Lords of the Earth, of all that moves and does not move, and we humble ones must abide by their decisions as sanctified and eternal; and so, the game must go on. They are not paid those princely salaries, but on the field of play, they alone are the gods of all they survey.

That was the introduction to Game 6, as Red Smith said, "The game of games."

In the early stages, as we mentioned, Lynn ran headlong into the fence in left center and took a resounding blow. He did not move for many seconds, and I actually thought he was dead with a broken neck or something. When he staggered to his feet, I breathed a sigh of relief that he was still alive. And what's more, he held the ball!

Earlier, there was Game 1, after a two-day rain delay. This was quite an occasion, for when the opening was postponed, a press conference was staged at The Park Plaza, at which Sparky Anderson, the Cincinnati manager, and Pete Rose were present. The news gatherers plied them with questions, and they dreaded the rain delay. Finally, the rain let up, and it was announced that Game 1 would be played.

Prior to the start of the game, I had to be on the field, interviewing the various players. I had two extra tickets behind the Red Sox dugout, and I gave them to my little granddaughter, Jennifer, then 13 and now a practicing attorney in Boston, and to Rev. Franklin Huntress, an Episcopal priest in our home church, with this admonition to the good father: Please keep an eye on Jennifer for me. I checked from time to time, and both were in their seats. Then, I looked about 10 minutes later and was somewhat mystified to see only Jennifer sitting there. I immediately went over to the boxes and yelled to my granddaughter: "Where's Father Huntress?"

She answered, "Oh, he's out in left field with the official party, with a blue towel about his neck. He's listening to all the ground rules."

I couldn't believe my ears and later asked Father Huntress about it.

"Oh, yes," he said, "I thought it would be fun, so I joined the fellows in their walk out to the Green Monster, and I had the grandest time."

"What," I asked Rev. Huntress, "were they talking about out there?"

"Oh," he said, "some of the most exotic things; I'm glad I went out there. One thing they discussed was that ladder on the Green Monster. Sparky Anderson asked what would be the ruling if a batted ball became stuck in the ladder, and Darrell Johnson (the Red Sox manager) replied: 'Hell, Sparky, if that happens, I'll give you a home run.' And that settled that dispute."

The other members must have thought Father Huntress was the offi-

cial representative from the clergy, and he did do a good job at that, pray-
ing for a Red Sox victory. The last I heard, Father Huntress was an
exchange rector somewhere in England, where I know he publicized the
great sport of baseball to all those British ears, who once knew the game
as Rounders, but gave up on its potential. Too bad, we might have had the
London Lancers playing in the American League. We ought to send
Sparky over to see what he can do about that.

The series in the meantime had bounded on and entering Game 6, the
Reds held a one-game lead, 3-2. It was a game the Red Sox had to win, for
the Reds could have closed it out that balmy evening with a fourth victory and a world championship.

After the Lynn collision, the Reds took the lead and, heading into the
eighth, were still up three runs. Then, Bernie Carbo stepped to the plate
with two runners aboard. He smacked a Lou Gehrig-type home run into
the seats in deep center field, a line drive that seemed to rise no higher
than 30 or 40 feet all the way. The roar that went up was deafening; the
Sox had finally tied it.

In the last of the ninth, the Sox loaded the bases with no one out, and
it looked like this might be the big moment. Denny Doyle was on third,
just waiting for a fly ball to center or to right, far enough so he could tag
and come home. I think the batter was Rico Petrocelli, and he lofted a fly
ball to short left.

In the confusion, Don Zimmer, the coach at third base, reportedly
said "Go," and Denny did just that after the catch. He was gunned down at
the plate, barely, stopping what would have been the winning run. Later,
Zimmer said he hollered to Doyle, "No, no," not "Go, go." In any regard,
the Sox went out of the inning, still tied.

In the late extra innings, as the clock in center field arched toward
midnight, the Reds struck again, and Joe Morgan blasted a long drive to
right, with Dwight Evans catching it in his sights and racing toward the
box seats. As Evans neared the short fence, he leaped high into the stands
to grab the ball, taking a certain homer from Morgan. That was a close call
for the Sox, but they sallied forth into the 12th, with the clock reading
midnight, and with Carlton Fisk, from New Hampshire, the batter due up.

Carlton seemed at perfect ease, and he picked out a good pitch and
swung with that graceful motion of his.

At that precise moment in the third base stands, the ball soared over my head, and I figured it had the distance if it stayed fair. Carlton hopped up and down on his way to first base, gesturing for the ball to stay fair (one of the most famous pictures in baseball history).

The ball did stay fair, and Fisk continued his leap and bounds around the bases for one of the most exciting and dramatic home runs in history, more famous now, almost than Paul Revere's ride, which had happened after midnight. Fisk's shot tied the Series at three and set the stage for a showdown the following evening on the Fenway greensward.

Fans stayed in their seats at Fenway that night, trying to piece together the amazing events of the night, lingering, too, on the streets outside Fenway and in Kenmore Square; it was pandemonium everywhere.

They were going wild in Boston, over a towering home run provided by a young man from neighboring New Hampshire. It was a glorious way to win it, and by most accounts, it was, indeed, the greatest game ever played.

What a story, and what a night. Never again will this drama be enacted in the same story form. It is almost one for Grand Opera, at that.

By the time this envoy had returned to New Hampshire, it was already past 3 o'clock, and Barbara couldn't sleep. My close friend, Frank Morono, was as wide awake as he might have been at 10 a.m. on a routine day. So, Barbara prepared a light lunch for us, and we talked of the evening we had just experienced and knew as we talked, nothing like it would ever happen again.

It was so monumental an evening that aides to President Ford in Washington awakened him to tell him what had happened in Boston, and he was overjoyed. He had retired about 11 that night after watching the game on television. He had a bad cold and didn't feel up to waiting for the outcome, but he was happy with the outcome.

The only thing on the horizon was Game 7, and that, too, was filled with heroics. As we entered Fenway Park for the deciding game, my friends in Section 28, behind third base, were there to greet me, telling all their friends how we had tackled Larry Barnett himself the evening before and made life miserable for him.

I felt good because someone should have reminded him how awful his decision was that evening in Cincinnati. I must confess, I was treated as something of a hero, but still in Game 7 we couldn't pick on Larry Barnett again as our fall guy because the series continued, and this was a whole new game, and why harp on Barnett at Cincinnati when this giant of a series was being concluded in Boston 800 miles away.

So, Barnett was left out of the script, and after shaking hands with all my revolutionaries of the night before, we made ready for the Big One, and, truly, all the drama was continued in this showdown as well.

I remember writing my game story and putting the blame for the loss on Denny Doyle, who stepped on second for a force on one runner and was so intimidated by the charging, snorting Pete Rose, that he threw wildly to first, with the ball sailing way over Carl YastrzemskI's head. Before the inning had ended, the Reds had three runs in and enough for the victory. Listen, with Rose charging into me, I would have been cowed, too, but I think I would have gotten that throw away to Yaz where he could have caught it for a double play and suffered the consequences with Rose later.

Anyway, that's how the 1975 World Series ended, with the Reds a winner, four games to three. We did come close, and we did put up a great battle, and as Sparky Anderson said later of the epoch: "No one won."

That was quite gallant of Anderson, and I loved the guy for it. He is still one of baseball's finest managers. Let us say, he knows baseball from every angle.

The next year at World Series time, Barbara had died. The rest of my family and I were heartbroken; she was my soulmate.

Barbara knew and loved baseball, and she was waiting up for us until 3 in the morning to hear our version of things in Boston. Every time I pass St. Paul Episcopal in Concord, right across from the State House, and look up and see her golden cross shining on the steeple, I think of that night, and thank my friend Frank for giving me the idea for a cross dedicated to Barbara's memory.

"Think of Barbara, Bob, when you look at that cross, and remember the night we barged in on her after Game 6."

I do still when I see her cross. Frankie died in 1986, 10 years later, with his ticket to Game 6 still among his treasured souvenirs.

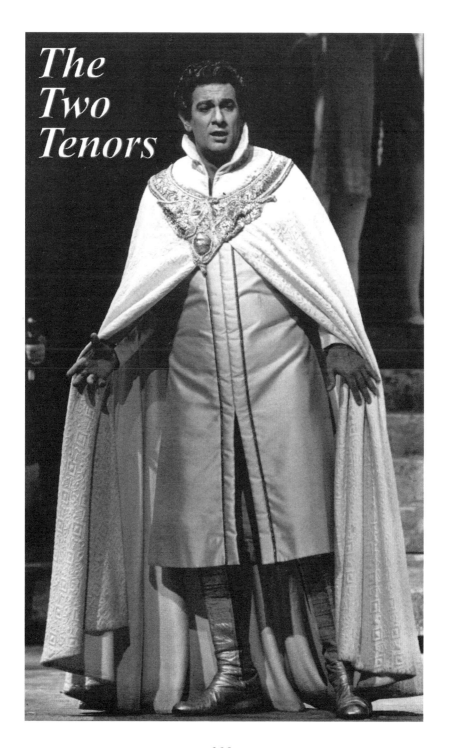

The Two Tenors

THE AUDIENCE heard some majestic singing from Placido Domingo in Act II, Scene 2 of Richard Wagner's stirring "Lohengrin" at the Metropolitan Opera in New York. Domingo, along with Luciano Pavarotti, are two of the greatest operatic tenors of all time. (Metropolitan Opera Photo by J. Heffernan)

All that separates them physically is about 100 pounds, give or take a few. Both are better than six feet, and both are strapping, commanding figures.

All that separates them artistically is that one is a lyrical giant, the other a dramatic tornado. And both are tenors of the opera stage.

We present: Luciano Pavarotti and Placido Domingo. Please let the arguments cease as to who grabs the top rung. Both are world-beaters, and they both extol the measurement of a tenor: a sweet, commanding voice. That is it, and that is as it should be. The world couldn't take two of the same brand; it wouldn't turn.

I've seen both perform many times, in concert and in opera, and it's a tie. Placido is perhaps better prepared for his roles musically, for he is also a conductor of note and anticipates what lies ahead. Luciano, on the other hand, knows his roles intimately, and he hates running over them every time he performs, as in the case of Renata Scotti, who wanted him bounced out of the house in San Francisco because of a lack of preparation, in which she claims, he put the onus on her for not helping him.

Oh, these opera stars, they do have their tantrums, but I love them all, and I know Miss Scotti is a most industrious singer who leaves no stone unturned in preparing for a performance. But alas, that Luciano, look at him!

When Renata conveyed her message to the House director, he replied: "That man," (meaning our haggard Lucie) "can do no wrong in this house."

In my book on sports, that meant he won by technical knockout, and please don't bother the man again, he's quite busy learning the role.

I can't recall what the precise opera was that evening in San Francisco, but I think the soprano was fit to be tied. I loved it all. What's an Italian Opera without a little fire?

The female impresario in Chicago is also a little fed up with Luciano for missing a few dates, like 16 or 17 or more, but this is not a condemnation of that heavenly voice. So, hearing this, I know he has arrived, probably the world's greatest, along with his pal from the Baths of Caracalla, Placido Domingo.

BRAVO -- Author Bob Hilliard, left, and Manchester neighbor Margo Trottier, congratulate opera star Luciano Pavarotti on another masterful performance. (*Union Leader* photo by Denis Paste)

Whenever either of these two artists is performing center-stage, they need absolutely no buildup. They are Grand Opera in their own distinctive way, and they've brought immeasurable joy to the many millions of viewers and listeners around the world.

They are here to stay until their time runs out. I can readily recall two operas I heard in person, Pavarotti in "Tosca," and Domingo in Wagner's "Lohengrin." Both were brilliant, and I began thinking how lucky we all were that "The Two Tenors" came to us in this generation, especially when television can bring it to countless millions who otherwise might never see such a spectacle.

Today, with the addition of Jose Carreras, they are The Three Tenors, sometimes performing together.

I remember one time asking Sir Rudolf Bing about the prospects of live television from the stage of the Metropolitan Opera House, and how enthused he was in his confident reply, "It is coming." Actually, the person quite responsible in those "Live From the Met" telecasts is a good friend of mine, Michael Bronson, who conceived the idea and became the executive producer.

THE METROPOLITAN OPERA's Pacido Domingo is happy and all smiles after singing in Wagner's monumental "Lohengrin," his first, and a stupendous triumph on the New York stage. Author Bob Hilliard shares in the big evening. (*Union Leader* photo by Denis Paiste)

If anybody spread the gospel of grand opera, it was Mr. Michael Bronson. It brought the stage, with the likes of Pavarotti and Domingo, right into the living rooms of America and of the world. What would Wagner and Verdi and Puccini and Mozart have said? Probably make mine money—and they would have been rolling in it. That might have blunted their desire, and we wouldn't have had those celebrated masterpieces after all, so I am just as happy that we won and those guys lost, even though they gave it to us. You win some, and you lose some, as they say.

Mario Del Monaco in the 1940s and '50s was perhaps the only tenor able to match the two of today, and I think in many cases he could actually surpass them. He could, I know, in his ringing high notes, unmatched even in Caruso's day. Mario was such a beloved figure, always gentlemanly, courteous and polite to a fault. I remember he would always hold the

GREAT WORK LUCIANO -- Bob Hilliard, standing with reporter's notebook in hand, salutes famed tenor Luciano Pavarotti on his concert appearance at the Wang Center in Boston. The concert attracted a sellout throng of 4,200. (*Union Leader* photo by Denis Paiste)

door for friends leaving the hotel. "After you," he would say with a smile.

There were other fine tenors in that era, including Jan Peerce, Richard Tucker and especially, Jussi Bjoerling, and they were a stripe above the rest, but not in the same class with Pavarotti and Domingo or Del Monaco. On three occasions, we had tickets for Bjoerling, but all three times he was indisposed and cancelled out. Thusly, I never did get a chance to hear him in person to make a valid comparison with the others. Only by radio and by his recordings was I afforded that opportunity.

I was fortunate enough in October 1991 to hear some elegant singing at Symphony Hall in Boston in a performance of Pique Dame, taped by BMG Classics for RCA Victor Red Seal. Officials there that evening called it the finest recording ever made, for tone of orchestra, caliber of singing and for overall acoustics, for which Symphony Hall is famous. It was the 100th anniversary year of the composer, Pyotr Ilyich Tchaikovsky, and it starred the shimmering voice of Mirella Freni, a long-time associate of Pavarotti, who would have been delighted to hear her that evening.

A few paragraphs tell the story of that evening:

"By BOB HILLIARD
Critic-at-Large
BOSTON -- With an inspired Seiji Ozawa imploring and pleading and pulling for every note, and a gallant cast cascading its vocal brilliancy over a packed Symphony Hall audience last week, Pyotr Ilyich Tchaikovsky's dazzling Pique-Dame observed its 100th birthday amidst one of its most epochal triumphs ever.

It was being taped for posterity by BMG Classics for RCA Victor Red Seal, the first such recording in the United States for that company in more than 25 years.

It was in every way a musical masterpiece, and it will no doubt be judged by operatic students of the future as one of the finest readings and presentations in all those long years.

It was, in short, a near-perfect production. A more appropriate cast could hardly have been selected, and it was entirely compatible with the beautifully toned Boston Symphony Orchestra, which by all reckonings is one of the greatest in the world. Indeed, the rich musical trappings may never again be served to the public in this quantity.

The reading was pinpoint and subtle, and it points to the fact that the composer did create something here far out of the ordinary.

Mirella Freni, who sang the role of Lisa, and who warmed to her task as the evening wore on with the most gorgeous tones, was ablaze with glory in the final act as she conquered all. Herman, sung powerfully and profoundly by Vladimir Atlantov, was a most tragic figure as he lay slumped over a card table, the loser in this highest-stake game of chance, which ends in the most tragic of circumstances, with Lisa throwing herself into the river; the Countess, sung by contralto Maureen Forrester, dying of fright when confronted by the mad Herman in search of the card combination that will bring him eternal wealth, and Herman himself succumbing in the end to the Countess' fatal spell.

It is a story of the greatest of intrigue and greed, and the winning combination of cards somehow manages to escape Herman's grasp. He comes close in his quest but loses his Lisa, and, yes, his very life at the hands of Prince Yeletsky, sung so brilliantly by Dimitri Hvorostovsky, and with so much style and full baritone and fervor.

It was certainly a night to cherish."

The Two Tenors have given us plenty of those evenings, to be sure. And they continue, even still.

Let's Ty One On

TY LEMLEY, who began his career with Guy Lombardo and the Royal Canadiens, performs later in his career with the Kinda Dixie Jazz Band. (Photo by Bill and Bobbi Arnold)

One of my closest friends in the Guy Lombardo Band of a former great day was Ty Lemley, the fantastic guitartist who made "Maria Elena" and so many other outstanding tunes. His handling of "Elena"—couched in the Lombardo manner and style—was superb, and it became a nation-wide hit, thanks in no small way to Ty's deft handling; purely a guitar special, and no strumming, please. That is not playing the guitar, strumming. Anybody can strum, but not play.

Anyway, I recently asked Ty to name a few highlights of his great career with Lombardos.

One of the most memorable, he replied, was meeting Sally Rand, the famous fan dancer, and telling what a wonderful woman she was. He said he had met many world famous people in his Lombardo days, not the least of which were a few Presidents of the United States, for Guy was always accorded the honor of first band at the Presidential Ball, and that gave the band members the opportunity of meeting American Royalty.

In fact, before Ty's fabulous career with the Royal Canadians, Guy played for Queen Elizabeth, and when Guy was introduced to her, he played some of her favorite tunes at her request. He asked if there was anything he could do for her, and she replied she would like a recording of some of her favorite songs. Guy made a special recording and sent it to Buckingham Palace. Just that recording was made, and only the Queen and the Lombardos know what it contained, for only one recording was made. "Berkeley Square," the World War II hit was doubtless one of the numbers, with its beautiful lyrics: "I may be right, I may be wrong, but I'm perfectly willing to swear, there were angels dining at the Ritz, and a nightingale sang in Berkeley Square." All the world knew that one, and it must have brought a lump to millions of British and American throats.

Before Ty Lemley, there was Don Rodney (Don Ragonese) whose brother, Carmen Ragonese, was one of the University of New Hampshire's greatest football players who starred professionally with the Baltimore Colts before a tenure in the Alumni Office at UNH. Before Don Rodney's great career with the Royal Canadians, there was Bill Flanagan. The original guitarist with Guy was Francis Henry, who married a steamship heiress and retired from the more rigorous life of a bandsman. Both Henry and Flanagan were outstanding musicians, probably the best in the country, proving, of course, that Guy knew how to pick music masters. Francis Henry wrote the big hit, "Little Girl."

Ty's experiences with the Lombardo Band were many and varied. Someone stole his electric guitar in Salem, Mass. In New Orleans one day, he devoured a crawfish that had him crawling before sundown and a concert before thousands... Once in Chapel Hill, N.C., a person in a flashy Cadillac flagged down Lombardo bus driver Don Byrnes, and out stepped band leader Kay Kyser ("The College of Musical Knowledge" host) and "We all proceeded to his house and took the time to eat, chit-chat and take pictures."

Ty remembers fondly The Battle of the Big Bands at Madison Square Garden: Guy Lombardo, Duke Ellington, Vaughan Munroe and Buddy DeFranco...At Carnegie Hall: "We played this "Palace" after concert tours of seven days a week, one of the days in your hometown of Concord, N.H., and when I came on stage, who is in the front row but Ethel Merman, Steve Lawrence and Edie Gorme, and anybody who was anybody in New York..."

The famed guitartist met three of the nation's presidents at Inaugural Balls—Carter, Nixon and Reagan...Ty was discovered by a famous musician, Larry Owen, at the Nevelle Country Club in New York's Catskills. Larry played saxaphone and sang in the trio from the band's very inception. "He asked if I'd like to be a Royal Canadian. I jumped at the chance, and met Mr. Lombardo at Jones Beach, N.Y., had an audition and signed a contract with a handshake..."

Ty still recalls the painful sprained back he had as the band arrived in Pittsburgh, his old hometown. "I had to play and sing sitting down." Again in the same city at a concert at Heinz Hall, Ty remembers a backup job he had with Eddy Arnold some years before, "and here I was, back with Guy as a featured perfomer."

Ty went over a lot of icy roads to Canada with Bobby Vinton to play an engagement he directed when he was just getting started. "He was driving an old rattletrap, but we made it." He worked with "Little Anthony and the Imperials" at Penn State, and with Danny Thomas at the Civic Arena in Pittsburgh, all before his Lombardo Days. In Las Vegas at a house party at Wayne Newton's, he looked over his Arabian horses on a break, and at Siegfried and Roy's mansion, he saw some beautiful white tigers.

Once, playing behind Robert Goulet, his string bass player dropped over dead drunk. Goulet appealed to Ty to take over—and he did, although he had never played a string bass before, but he made it work...Ty still has one of Sally Rand's feathers, "to prove I knew her."

Just before Ty's appearance with the new Lombardo Band a few years ago, he dropped me a line about the recording session, which was hailed by the critics for its clarity and sweet tones once the tape made its initial bow before the public at New Year's Time. Ty's note follows:

"Was in New York in early October filming a tribute to Guy. Was invited by PBS to participate. (I was the only original member of the orchestra there.) I just hope it came out all right 'cause I was one sick cat. I'll explain. I was feeling pretty lousy before leaving Las Vegas (where Ty still performs with his band.) So, I went to see a doctor to get some relief, and he prescribed the wrong medication (don't take any medicine with 'mycin' on the end of it). I took the pills for three days during rehearsal, but at 3 o'clock in the morning, it really hit me. Was staying at The Pennsylvanian, so I took a cab to St. Vincent's Hospital, waited four hours for treatment 'till 7, got back to the hotel around 8, and on the set at 10, and we filmed until around 10 that night. Whew. The show will air November 29th, and, of course, on New Year's Eve."

That was in 1994.

Poor Ty, and he still managed to give a brilliant performance vocalizing "When My Sugar Walks Down the Street" and others, plus some fancy work on his guitar. We would never have suspected he was so sick.

The treatment cost Ty $300 from the hospital, and $200 from the doctor, but it was money well spent if it gave the public that kind of a performance from Mr. Ty Lemley.

Some day, maybe Ty and Kenny Gardner, Guy's sensational vocalist, can team up on another New Year's performance that would match the 1994 production. As a critic, I would have to term it one of the most memorable in popular music annals. Ty says he still hopes to record one of the author's favorites, "The Girl With the Dreamy Eyes." Guy introduced the number many years ago. "Great song there," Ty told me recently.

Perhaps Ty's most famous, most revered, guitar rendition is of "Maria Elena." It is glorious and most memorable, and presented with Lebert Lombardo's moving trumpet solo, it demands the most orchestral and public attention. It is one of the finest numbers ever recorded by Mr. Guy Lombardo and His Royal Canadians, and Ty and Lebert really make it sing. If there is a heaven, it was there.

Vignettes in passing

HARD AT WORK -- Author Bob
Hilliard hammers out a column for
The Union Leader in this 1946 *Union
Leader* file photo.

Boston was agog.

The phenomenal teenager, Bobby Feller, was coming to town with his blazing fastball, which some baseball critics already were calling faster than Walter Johnson s best or Dazzy Vance at the top of his game.

That would be incredibly fast, to be sure; but this young man from the cornfields of Van Meter, Iowa could serve up bullets from the mound 60 feet, six inches away. That alone was enough to cause batters plenty of worry, especially when it was also known that the 17-year-old lacked control. Batters trembled at the thought of having to face Feller and his heralded cannonball.

He was designated to face the Boston Red Sox, and I hoped to get an interview with him that day, though I didn't know whether I'd be fortunate enough to talk with Feller because of his rapidly emerging prominence in the baseball world. Everyone was talking about him, especially after his recent feat in mowing down the heavy-hitting St. Louis Cardinals in an exhibition game. They couldn't even come close, swinging away at everything.

I was only 18 back in 1936, and there were many more experienced writers and sportscasters than me who were trying to get at the husky righthander for a chat session.

Feller was in the clubhouse getting dressed for the game when I approached him and asked whether I might be able to talk with him about his pitching feats, which had ignited the baseball world, becoming the topic on street corners across America.

"Sure," he said.

I told him I was only a year older than he and a little young for such an assignment, but he lightened up the moment with a big smile and said, "Put it there, pal," and we shook hands.

We talked for almost a half-hour, until we had to break it up for field practice. He answered all my questions openly and with patience, humbly brushing off his performance against the Cardinals as "a lot of luck." Then

CLEVELAND INDIANS fireballer Bob Feller made quite a splash when he came to the Major Leagues at the age of 17. Author Bob Hilliard interviewed the pitching ace when they still were both teens. (World War II Veterans Committee Photo)

he was fully dressed and ready for the assignment against the heavy-hitting Red Sox.

We shook hands again, and he said, "Good luck on that story," as he disappeared out the door, down the stairs through the tunnel and onto the emerald greem field at Fenway Park. There was some cheering as he appeared, but hey, the Red Sox are out to beat this guy, Feller, and let's not overdo it.

I can't remember the score, but I do recall the Red Sox player who took a toehold at the plate that day and bounced two of Feller's fastballs off the leftfield fence for extra bases: Billy Werber, a scrappy football and baseball hero from Duke University, who seemingly had no fear of Feller, hit that day as if he owned the fastball phenom.

Slugger Jimmy Foxx, the Double X of baseball repute, on the other hand, appeared worried and somewhat willing to strike at anything near the plate just to get out of there. That was the picture I have carried with me over the years, and while it isn't altogether flattering of Foxx, it does show a player's concern for getting one in the head and having to leave baseball forever, or even departing the world forever.

I think Foxx fanned three times that afternoon, and Feller counted several strikeouts. Had I been batting, I would have been three feet from the plate and looking for an escape route.

It's a remembrance of Feller that is lasting and several years later when he was an honored guest at another of Leo Cloutier's famed baseball dinners in Manchester, I had a chance to join Joe Barnea, the sports editor at the time, in getting a column on Feller.

Feller and I had a good laugh, recollecting his debut at Fenway Park. "I didn't know I was such an ogre," he said as he finished shaving and prepared to step into his tux, a real matinee idol for the huge crowd.

I think Barnea asked Feller about the possibility of the Russians taking up the sport of baseball, and he said something like, if they ever did, they'd probably beat our brains out.

That sunny day at Fenway I interviewed Feller and became one of the first in the New England area to do so; it was a most memorable occasion, for it afforded me the chance to see Bob Feller at his speed-ball best, when he was just wild enough to be a hazard, and with some of the batters swinging just to get out of his way. I had never seen a faster pitcher.

On another day at my favorite park, as a young writer just out of high school, I did an interview with Mickey Cochrane, then player-manager of the Detroit Tigers, his playing days with the Philadelphia Athletics under Connie Mack a vivid memory. We sat in the Detroit dugout, and Mickey proved the ideal host as I asked a veritable ton of questions. Cochrane was patient and answered everything. When I finished, he stood up and almost apoligized as he trotted toward the batting cage.

"Gotta get some work done with my hitters," he said over his shoulder. He had told me to watch the game from the dugout if I wanted, instead of from the press box on the roof, and I did for a few innings. I had many notes, and as I sat there contemplating them, a player slid over next to me, extended his hand and introduced himself as Hank Greenberg. We shook, and he displayed a winning smile.

Hank caught me a bit off guard. I had never planned on meeting Detroit's great slugging star, a towering batter who came within a hair of beating Babe Ruth's mark of 60 homers in one year, 154 games. I was a little flustered, I admit, in meeting Greenberg, and then he said: "You have a lot of notes, Bob. Did the boss say anything about me?"

"Yes he did," I said. "He said a whole lot about you, Hank. And pretty nice things, too."

"Can I see the notes, Bob," he asked. I turned them over, and Greenberg began reading.

"Wow," he said as a few of his teammates gathered around. "Listen to this. The best first baseman in the business. The greatest hitter in the game today & the ideal team-player."

Hank slapped his knee in exhultation and roared, "What a manager!"

When his spirits had simmered down, Greenberg said, "I think I'll hit him up for a raise tomorrow."

We all laughed. I always thought that whatever it was, it wasn't enough for the magnificent Greenberg. He deserved the best, and so, too, did Mickey Cochrane, college-educated at Boston University and, in my opinion, the greatest catcher-hitter ever.

Another day at nearby Braves Field was interesting. I had asked the great Dizzy Dean a few questions for the feature I planned, and he was most gracious in his loquacious manner. As we finished the interview and we walked under the stands toward the playing field, a wild thought crossing my mind.

"Dizzy," I asked, "do you mind if I take a few swings against you to test your fastball?"

Dizzy leaned over in laughter. "Hey, kid," he said, "if I should hit you, we'd both feel bad, you in a hospital bed and me in the dugout."

I'm glad the Dizzy One turned the proposition down. I had never thought of that hospital bed, being only 18. Later that day, I caught a good idea of Dean's speed as he mowed down the Boston Braves. It was late in the season, and both teams were out of pennant contention. Nothing really mattered on the outcome of the game, so late in the ninth inning, Rabbit Maranville, on behalf of the weak-hitting Braves, stepped to the plate. and like Babe Ruth on an earlier and historic date, he stopped the game and pointed toward the Jury Box in right field. That's where he would park a Dizzy Dean pitch. Dizzy laughed so hard he could barely stop, and he struck out the Rabbit on three straight pitches, some of the fastest this writer has ever seen. That ended the festivities for the afternoon.

"Leave 'em laughin,'" Dean must have muttered as he walked into the dugout. They were laughing, even the Rabbit, who, incidentally, was a good hitter in spite of his stature. He was about 5-5 or 5-6.

Clint Courtney played briefly in Manchester with the Giants, and the day that he arrived to play for manager Hal Gruber, I went over to greet him as the baseball writer for the Manchester Union. I was astonished to see that Courtney the Catcher wore glasses.

"A catcher with glasses?" I remarked. "What the hell are you wearing glasses for, Mr. Courtney?"

"To see with, stupid, what do you think?" Courtney said.

I lost that one, and Clint proved he could hit, and he did so later in the major leagues as the only bespectacled catcher in history that I know of. He was a fiery competitor, and opponents left the Louisiana star pretty much to himself. I knew that early on.

That was a fast league, the Class B New England League. The nearby Nashua Dodgers in the year I covered the Manchester Giants were managed by Walter Alston, who would go up to the majors a few years later with the parent Dodgers.

Don Newcomb was their star pitcher, and Roy Campanella their rugged, hard-hitting catcher. Those teams were Class B in name only. They could stay with anybody. Sal Yvars of the Manchester team graduated to the parent Giants of the National League, and one day he told off Leo Durocher, which was the wrong thing to do. He was a better catcher than Wes Westrum, who was No. 1 with the New York Giants, at that time.

Yvars, who was a better hitter, felt the job was his and told Durocher so. He left baseball shortly after and went home to Valhalla, N.Y. Yvars had a better arm than Westrum, too. In a throwing contest one evening in Manchester, I saw Sal throw the ball from the cinder track in center field into the last row of seats in the grandstand, nearly 400 feet. Infielders who took his throws on attempted steals developed severe bone sore. Maybe Yvars should have been a pitcher. I've thought of that often.

Bill Cunningham...
A 'Wah-Hoo-Wah'!

Back when football was still a two-way game, about a half century or so ago, there was an All-America-caliber player at Dartmouth College who got a mention for the honor but who deserves a bit more, so let me introduce you to Bill Cunningham...William Elijah Cunningham, to be more precise.

Cunningham's prowess on the field, however, was perhaps not as great as his power, or call it finesse, with the pen. After football, he put his talents to work as a sportswriter and then as a feature writer, first for the old *Boston Post* and later for the *Boston Herald*. He became syndicated and was read by millions.

In my early days as a writer, I covered a Dartmouth-Cornell game at Hanover one fall day and found myself sitting directly behind Cunningham. He had written that morning of how the Big Green were going to pull off the biggest upset of the season on Carl Snavaly's far superior Cornell team, which was the top-ranked team in the nation, and in doing so, Dartmouth would create havoc with the national standings.

Cunningham boldly laid out what he thought were sound reasonings as to how the Big Green could engineer such an incredible upset, and he did it with the kind of convincing rhetoric that sold many a reader, particularly those clad in green and white, on the idea that Dartmouth would, indeed, emerge victorious.

Dartmouth struck swiftly, perhaps on the extra adrenalin kick provided by Cunningham's column that morning. The Green scored, held Cornell on a succeeding series of downs and went on another march. The fans went berserk.

It appeared as though Cunningham was a prophet, foretelling of Dartmouth's victory in the sense that it was a team that could not be denied. The Big Green were striking on all cylinders—hitting, blocking and running.

Cunningham had at last called one for his old alma mater, or so it seemed.

Dartmouth, forever, was in his heart, and this time I believed Cunningham had written wisely, separating mind from heart.

Who was Cornell, anyway? Just a pumped-up array in red that had managed to win a few big games.

But as suddenly as it had appeared, the Dartmouth onslaught disappeared. Cornell had engineered a tie, then forged ahead to a lead that was never to be overcome. At the half, Cornell led by a couple of touchdowns, and the Big Green looked rather hapless.

Cunningham was working on his halftime story for the Post, and I thought it might be an appropriate time to question him on his morning game-day column.

"What is it, Bill, too much Cornell or not enough Dartmouth?" I asked. He answered, a bit dourly, "A little of both, I guess."

As I got up to return to my seat, I said to Bill, "Is it true you threw a guy downstairs when you were a student here and broke his collarbone?"

Bill looked surprised. "Who told you that story?" he asked.

I said I couldn't reveal the source, except to say he was a classmate, a distinguished classmate.

Bill grumbled for a second as I started to leave. "Hey," he said, "stick around. Where ya goin'?"

I said I was heading back up to my seat, but he pleaded, "No, no, wait a minute. I want to tell you what happened that day so you will know the rtue story."

So I sat down again beside Cunningham.

"I was starting to walk down the stairs when this senior ordered me to carry his books for him," Cunningham related. "I told him to carry them himself. I was not his servant. He said to "Carry 'em, or you'll be sorry...'

"That's when I picked the bastard up and threw him down the stairs, books and all. He landed in a heap, and the books went flying. All the time he's moaning about his collarbone. I went back to the frat house and forgot all about it.

It was about 7 or 7:30, and I was deep in studying. My roommate was Jess Neeley, the 'fightin' wonder from Texas, a guy with one arm. There was a knock on the door, and Neeley got up to answer it. He opened the door and about 10 seniors stormed in, knocking Neeley aside. They asked where Cunningham was, and he told them I was busy studying, and that they'd better leave.

"They didn't, and then a battle royal ensued, the likes of which Hanover had not seen in years, a real Pier 4 brawl, and since Neeley had only one arm, he was hitting the guys like a revolving door and not getting pinned down, either. I went to his side as soon as I heard the commotion, and I nailed a few of the guys myself, but eventually the 10 or 15 of them overpowered us, and lugged me down to the Connecticut River and threw me in with the admonition, 'Let that be a lesson to you,' and they took off with me struggling in the very cold water."

Cunningham laughed as he retold the story, and he had soon almost forgotten about the Cornell lead, and his column of that day predicting a Big Green upset victory.

Cunningham was a jovial figure and a born storyteller, hence his occupation as a columnist, a nationally known one. Several years later, on a vacation trip to New Orleans with my wife and son, we were shown through Antoine's, where we had just dined, and we came to a room with letters decorating the walls from world famous figures, and there was one from our friend, Bill Cunningham, himself. That guy could write.

"If there is a heaven, as surely there is, it certainly must have an Antoine's"or words to that effect. Cunningham was widely quoted, especially among the sporting gentry of America, and it was my pleasure to know him.

And, yes, I forgot to report this on the brawl recounted that lived in his memory, and in the college's. I interspersed the brawl story with the game story, such as: "And then I threw the guy downstairs, books and all...Oh, damn, there goes another Cornell touchdown. The day is doomed..."

And so on, so I managed to report both stories, Cunningham's account of the fist fight, and the football game, which Dartmouth ended up losing by a score too big to bother remembering.

About a week later, after it was published in my Aunt Addie E. Towne's *Franklin*, (N.H.) *Journal Transcript*, I had a letter from Bill: In part it read:

> "Dear Bob:
>   I have read your story over and over again. Several people have sent it to me, mostly members of my class at Dartmouth, and they thoroughly enjoyed it as well.
>   "It was very cleverly done, transporting one bit of action years ago into the present-day game account,and I hasten to compliment you on a wonderful article, which will make my own scrapbook."

Cunningham didn't say whether a copy of the article had been sent to that senior who triggered the fight. I can only assume some members of his class made sure he received a copy.

Cunningham treated each assignment as though it was the story of the decade, and strange to report, he made it sound just that way.

Once, the *Boston Post* ordered him to cover the Harvard-Yale crew race. Not knowing much about crew racing, he inquired of different people around the boathouse, which crewmen to watch in the race, past records and a rundown on what to expect from both crews in this heralded showdown that, at one time, was conducted on beautiful Lake Winnipesaukee in New Hampshire.

At any rate, Cunningham threw his writing skills into play and began his "major" story. After he had written several takes and considered his day's work done, The *Post* ordered him to write several more.

A slightly tired Bill Cunningham complained some years later:

"I thought I had written a pretty complete story, but Boston wanted more. They kept asking for more. At the end of the day, I had written about a full page. I dragged those crews up and down the river at least 10 times."

What Bill did not recognize, perhaps, was the lofty respect the editors and his thousands of readers held for his work. They couldn't get enough of it, so Bill's Harvard-Yale race that day became the feature story, outclassing politics and anything else in its way.

I think the greatest story about Bill Cunningham, the boy from Texas who made it big at Dartmouth College as a football player and then later as a syndicated writer, was the time the *Boston Post* sent him on another pilgrimmage, this time early in his journalistic career.

The *Post* suggested a personal interview with the noted Arctic explorer, Vilhjalmur Stefansson, and Bill, married only a few days earlier, took his bride along to meet the world famous explorer. She met Stefansson, and after a few minutes, she said she'd sit in the back of the room so the two could converse.

Stefansson told Cunningham that he was a busy man with a heavy work schedule, and that he would, as a consequence, narrate things only once, and for him to take his notes as fast as possible because in no way did he have time to repeat his words. Bill was rather taken aback by that broadside, and their interview started. About an hour later, it had concluded. "So nice meeting you, Mr. Cunningham, the explorer said stiffly, this interview is ended, and so nice, too, to meet the new bride."

Bill backed off as though hit by a crowbar and thanked his host for the story.

"I only caught parts of it, and I knew I had failed miserably. As I picked up my wife outside the room, she asked, 'How did it go, Dear?' I told her lousy, I had messed it all up. She replied: 'Don't worry, Dear, I took everything down in shorthand.'"

The following day, the *Post* printed everything. A startled Vilhjalmur Stefansson read the interview, word for word, paragraph after long paragraph, and said something that sounded like "My word."

He called Cunningham and heaped praise upon his diligence, and thanked him many times over for writing such a beautiful, accurate story. He also sent a letter covering the interview. For that one time, at least, Bill had to rely on his wife's intrepid work and not his own newspaper wiles, and it paid off. I think Bill told me that the *Post* came through with a raise as a reward for such an encompassing, word-for-word, brilliant interview.

Stefansson should have taken Cunningham with him on his voyages as a public relations man.

It is my understanding that the explorer never realized Bill Cunningham had a blissful assist that day, "With Love, Honey, All the Way."

Bill died many years ago, with all those magnificent stories behind him, and a career of football greatness at his beloved Dartmouth. He was a president of the Left-Handed Golfers Association and an accomplished pianist who often jazzed it up at alumni meetings and at golf tournaments. He was fun-loving and a rabblerouser at parties.

Once on a visit to Hanover, he was driving a Rolls (it was said) with a musical horn attached that played "Dartmouth's In Town Again" ("Run, Girls, Run," a student refrain adds), and all the kids near Bill's fraternity blocked his path so that he would sound his horn at them. They kept it going for several minutes, I was told.

Also, Cunningham created a legend of sorts at Dartmouth. He wrote in his column one day that when he was a student there, he and other students awoke one morning to find a cow in the belfry tower. Hundreds of students, professors and town officials gathered outside the tower to study the cow's plight and determine how best to get the poor animal down.

Many ways were suggested—block and pulley, widening the staircase, one team pushing, the other pulling, but none of them successful.Night fell with the cow still up there as the populace pondered. Morning broke, and the cow was gone with no traces. To this day, Bill wrote, no one knows how it was done, and no one confessed.

Bill referred to it as the Great Mystery of the Hanover Hills, and so it remains to this day.Any ideas, anybody?

His death left a great void in feature writing.He seemed to have a penchant for putting himself in the middle of events that were transpiring, and sadly, no one since has picked up the threat to follow.

It was adventurous writing of a kind that not only reports a crew race, or a cow in the belfry tower, or a Coconut Grove fire disaster, but the people surrounding the story, and that's where his greatness lay.

I think Bill should have been the craftsman behind Sports of the

Times in the *New York Times*, and I am surprised he was never named to this post. They did have some good ones.

Red Smith, to name one. At one time, I understand, overtures were made to Ruel Newton Colby, another Dartmouth Man with scholarly prose. He was the same individual who broke in this writer, at a time when I was headed for Boston University and its school of journalism. Under Ruel's guidance, I needed little else. He and Cunningham, by the way, were good friends.

Ty Cobb:
What a peach

BASEBALL's GREATEST -- Ty Cobb, the immortal Georgia Peach, held more than 90 records at one time, including what may never be surpassed, his hitting average for 24 years of play, a phenomenal .367. Some of his marks are only now being threatened. (George Naum/*Union Leader* photo)

Tyrus Raymond Cobb, in my mind, was the greatest baseball player ever, and I think I have the record book to back me up. He set practically every record known to baseball, and only now are some of his marks being broken.

His lifetime batting average, computed over 24 years of play, will, I'm sure, never be broken. It's an incredible .367, and I haven't seen anybody on the horizon good enough to better that. If a player hits .270 nowadays, he gets a contract for millions of dollars. Had Cobb played in this generation, he would, without a doubt, be baseball's wealthiest man.

Using Alez Rodriguez' $250 million, 10-year contract with the Texas Rangers as a barometer, you'd have to figure Cobb would command about $30-$35 million a year.

When Babe Ruth signed his famous $80,000-a-year contract, so, too, did Ty Cobb, although that's generally not known. In a radio interview with my friend, Leo E. Cloutier, one-time sports editor of *The Union Leader* and *N.H. Sunday News,* Ty confided that he made "the same money Babe did" during that year, and few knew about it.

And speaking of Ty and Babe, they led baseball into the 20th Century, no doubt of that for one moment, and they could have commanded stratospheric salaries.

At one time, Ty held about every major record in the book, and that included stolen bases. He had such keen reflexes, he could steal just about anytime he pleased.

I had the opportunity to interview Cobb at the old Carpenter Hotel in Manchester in the late 1950s when Cloutier brought him out of retirement and introduced him to the world of baseball banquets. I suggested that Leo do this because I believed Ty would just like being asked, and sure enough, he was delighted when Cloutier invited him.

Cobb didn't ask for any money, either, just that a contribution be made to the hospital he had donated to Royston, Ga. in his parents' name, and that, Cloutier did. It is a famous letter and still a part of Leo's

NUMBER ONE -- Ty Cobb, left, lifetime batting average 367; played 24 years and holds some 90 records.

immense collection. If I were a collector with oodles of money, I would give a million bucks for that letter, and the other treasures. Leo's widow, Laura, now resides in Stamford, Conn.

The afternoon I interviewed Cobb, I invited my son, Bob Jr., then a student at the University of New Hampshire, to accompany me so that he could say he'd met Cobb. With Bob Jr., came his roommate, Steve Knox, then of Medford, Mass., and a dyed-in-the-wool baseball fan. With us also was a close personal friend from the Boston bureau of the Associated Press, Bob Hoobing, more the football expert of the AP than baseball, but a disciple nonetheless of a man named Cobb.

I had heard so much of Cobb's feats on the diamond from my father and older brother, Harry, that I eagerly looked forward to the meeting, which Cloutier arranged. Before the interview actually began, the strangest thing happened. Cobb was stretched out on his bed, having a drink.

"When you get to be my age, boys," he told us, "you have to take care of yourself." He winked and laughed. The telephone rang, and Cobb answered it.

"Yes," he said, "this is he, Mr. Cobb. You what? You want to come up and shake my hand? How old are you, sir, by the way? You're 89 years old? My God. Where are you from? You're from St. Johnsbury, Vermont? How did you get here in this big snowstorm, by the way?"

Cobb paused a few seconds and arched his eyebrows as he heard something quite startling.

"You what? You hitchhiked more than a hundred miles in this weather just to see me? Look, my good friend, I want to see you, the heck with you wanting to see me! Hell, I'm nobody, but you, sir, you are, and I want to see you. Look, my friend, the room number is 4-- (I can't remember the number, although it was on the fourth floor), and I will have one of the young boys here let you in. OK?"

They hung up and a few minutes later, there came a knock and Bob and Steve went over to open the door. The elderly man was standing there, smiling broadly. He was attired in a lumberjack's Mackinaw, khaki pants tucked into woodsmen's boots, and he had a cap, which he doffed as he entered Mr. Cobb's presence. It was almost as though he were staring at God himself as he looked at the legendary star of the diamond.

Cobb bounded off the bed and rushed over and shook hands with him, then put his arm around him.

"How nice of you to come all the way down from Vermont just to see me," Cobb told him.

We all shook hands with the venerable visitor, and we congratulated him in making it in such indecent weather. Cobb and the visitor talked for a few minutes, and Ty gave him his autograph. Then Ty asked him if he had a ticket for the dinner in the evening at the huge State Armory.

"No, I don't," he said, "but I plan on getting one tonight at the door."

Cobb laughed. "That won't be necessary at all," Cobb said. "I will take care of it myself, and get you the best seat in the house."

When that 89-year-old left, he was walking on Cloud 9. The last I saw of him, he was putting on his cap again and walking down the hallway toward the elevators.

"That's what I call a real somebody," Ty remarked, "a real solid fan."

It was a good start for the interview, which lasted an hour or better, and we talked of many things. I asked Cobb a question about stealing bases, and he said, "You have to watch for everything: a pitcher making his move, the position of the infielder covering the base you intend to steal, the ability of the catcher to get off his throw. All have to be considered. Then, you go." Cobb smiled.

I had heard Cobb sometimes took two bases on a steal of second, and I questioned him about this. "Isn't that pretty difficult?" I asked.

"Naw," he answered, "but it has to be timed right and be executed in the proper manner. If you have an unwary third baseman and a shortstop who is dreaming out there," he said, "you are more than halfway to two stolen bases. By the time they wake up, you are on third base, and they're wondering what hit them."

Hoobing and I talked of Cobb's amazing style at the plate, and he had more than 4,100 basehits during his lifetime, broken only by Pete Rose in modern times. That's better than one hit in every three appearances at the plate, I noted.

"Yes, sure," Cobb replied. "Well, I will tell you fellows what worked for me." Demonstrating, he said, "It was just this, holding my two hands an inch or so apart on the bat, so I could place-hit the ball. That way I could drop one into left or pull one into right, wherever the outfielders were not playing. I tell baseball men that all the time, and they don't seem to listen. It's a form of place-hitting, of directing the ball where you want it to go. Most of the players today want to knock it over the fence, and they slug with the bat, and with both hands together at the very tip of the handle. It's a wonder they can hit it at all.

"I keep telling them that, but they are not placing their hands on the bat right. If they would grab the bat right, hands an inch or two apart, they would see their batting average climb, but I think most of them just want to hit home runs, not singles or doubles. One fan once told me I didn't know how to hit home runs, that's why I held my hands apart. 'Look,' I told him, 'just for you, I will hit a couple of home runs today,' and I did, but I had a little luck, too. The pitcher wasn't that good, and I nailed a couple of fast balls."

Cobb was a fiery competitor on the diamond, and he was embroiled in more than a few fisticuffs. He may not have won them all, but he never backed off. One of the Red Sox writers who covered the team in Cobb's years, told me that one day at Fenway Park when Detroit was visiting, the Tiger pitcher in the first game of a doubleheader lost a heartbreaker on a bad pitch and sat on the bench after the game rather than take a shower and risk the rage of a pent-up Cobb. When the squad came out for Game 2, the pitcher ducked into the dressing room for his shower, while Cobb barked out orders to his team from the dugout.

Ty was a ferocious runner on bases and would tear into an infielder spikes first. In fact, he often would sit in the dugout before a game, sharpening the spikes. Once in Havana in an exhibition game, a groundskeeper moved second base 10 feet toward center field, making it that much longer to reach.

The crowd came out to see Cobb perform that day at the plate and to see him steal second base a few times. Each time he rapped out a single, he tried to steal second. He was tagged out easily. Finally, Ty called time and had them measure the base paths. They found second was 10 feet out of the way. It was no wonder Cobb was being thrown out. He still stole second later that day, and the Cuban fans got a good look at his speed and skill running bases when the bag was put in its proper place.

A professor at Plymouth State College in Plymouth, N.H., whose father ran the old Havana Red Sox that toured up in New England each summer, told me that story about Cobb and the wayward second base. Cobb could have tried all day and never made it. His sharp perception picked it up finally, and the base was moved back where it belonged.

During his sensational career, Cobb was credited with 892 stolen bases and for 12 out of 13 years, he led the American League in hitting, three times batting above .400. He had 4,191 base hits in all, and the third time his average soared above the .400 mark, he was 37 years old.

One year, Cobb beat out the famed Shoeless Joe Jackson in a wild race for the American League batting title. The final: Cobb .420, Jackson .408.

Jackson, who played for Cleveland and the Chicago White Sox, went hitless in three games of a season-ending, six-game series with Ty's Tigers, and that turned the trick. Ty made sure that it would: When Jackson, a good-natured, gullible guy passed Ty on the field before the opening game, Joe greeted him sincerely: "Hi, Brother Ty." Both were from the South.

Cobb snarled coldly at him: "Get away from me, you creep," and the rejoinder completely upset Jackson so much that he went hitless for three games in a row.

That information came from an article in *This Week* magazine in 1966, and it told the story of Ty's burning desire to come out on top. He never liked finishing second.

Grantland Rice, then a young writer for a New York daily, B.C. (Before Cobb), started receiving penny post cards from Georgia: "Watch this guy Cobb; four hits today, three stolen bases."

"Keep your eye on Cobb; five hits today, one stolen base."

"I think Cobb slumped today: Only three hits, no stolen bases."

It kept up for a couple of weeks, and finally Rice, a grand person, went to the sports editor and told him of his collection of penny post cards from some fan in Georgia.

"Better get down there, Granny, and see if he is real." Shortly after, Rice was on his way to look over this guy, Cobb.

On the first day of Rice's visit, Cobb collected five hits and totally amazed Rice with about three stolen bases to add to the carnage of the day. Granny wrote about his find of the year in the New York paper, with several follows, and shortly, America was Cobb-conscious; every baseball fan was awaiting news from Georgia on what the young player was doing each day, and it wasn't long after that Cobb moved up to the Majors.

Many years later, when Cobb and Rice got together out in California for a little golf, Cobb, according to Rice, asked the latter if he had ever received some penny postcards from Georgia about the young sensation, Ty Cobb. "Yeah, I did," Granny responded. "How'd you know about them?"

"I sent them," Ty laughed, and Rice joined in, although he had been suckered on the play.

Rice, incidentally, called Ty Cobb the world's worst driver. "He is so bad a driver," the writer once pointed out, "that he almost hit a plane taking off at Los Angeles Airport."

Cobb died in 1961 at the age of 75. On a postcard to Heaven, where Ty no doubt has improved his average, I wish to send him a message: "Your batting mark is still intact, Ty—.367."

Yogi Berra: Grin and Berra It

LEGENDS -- NEW YORK YANKEE legend Yogi Berra, left, poses with teammate Mickey Mantle at Yankee Stadium in 1956, Mantle's Triple Crown year. (AP file photo)

Like a Roman general of yore, Yogi Berra commanded the respect of his young baseball warriors. Though small in stature, Berra was huge among his troops.

I remember him vividly one beautiful spring day at Al Lang Field in St. Petersburg, Fla., arms folded across his chest, scowling a bit as he supervised practice before a Red Sox-Yankees exhibition game.

Berra was unquestionably the best catcher of his time and one of the best hitting catchers of all time. His approach to the game was masterful, built on a foundation of intense desire and tremendous skills, which ultimately culminated in his enshrinement into baseball's Hall of Fame. His approach to managing was built on much the same, with the added bonus of years of experience playing the game at the highest level.

Berra had a keen eye for the ball behind the plate, and his hitting prowess was no doubt the product of the same. So, too, was he a watchful manager with a keen eye trained on unwary players not accustomed to his workout and practice regimen. He saw everything, and he barked, "Run it out; move faster on that play; be sure to cover the bag."

As a manager, Berra no doubt had to put up with all those celebrated quotes of another day, and this may have stunted somewhat his effectiveness as a field marshal, but I hardly think so. Berra was a master of the game of baseball, and his players knew that, and they worked hard for him.

As a player-hitter, Berra never waited around for the perfect pitch or the perfect game of catching. He just went out and did his job, whether behind the plate or up to bat.

Leo Durocher told me he'd seen Yogi hit balls off the fence that had skimmed the ground from the pitcher. "You could see the dirt fly up," Durocher once said, "as the pitcher threw it, and Yogi would hit it a mile."

Unlike Ted Williams, who always waited for the perfect pitch, Yogi swung when he felt like it, or when the pitch was reasonably decent, and he broke open many a game doing just that. Can you imagine Berra and

Casey Stengel in a close game, and the latter exhorting Yogi to "pick one out, baby." It might be over his head, but Yogi, in that curious swing of his, would swat it, and oftentimes it would fall in for a double.

I find myself agreeing with Yogi Berra in that there is seldom a perfect pitch. No pitcher in his right mind is going to serve up that kind of a pitch, especially to a guy like Ted Williams or Stan Musial. He might do it with Berra by mistake, but then the victim would be himself when he tries to toss-away pitch to Yogi, hoping he goes for it, and learns, to his dismay, that Yogi can hit it even further.

Yogi has an exceptionally keen mind that translates to things on the playing field, and more often than not, he is correct. In that regard, I would call him as good a manager as he was a player, and a very sincere manager as well. If I were a major leaguer, I would love to play under Berra, knowing that he, too, plays percentages, but his own intuitions, too.

Berra came from St. Louis, "from the Hill," he once told me, the same area that also gave Joe Garagiola to big league baseball. He was a rugged, tough kid playing sandlot baseball, and he learned to shift for himself early on, to fight for everything. He became the most celebrated graduate of "The Hill," and went on to fame with an outside team, the New York Yankees.

Then came a time when St. Louis fans, among the very best in baseball, awoke to the fact that they had never honored their hometown player, and they decided to give him a night.

Announcer Curt Gowdy told me one night at the annual Baseball Dinner in Manchester, N.H., all about Yogi's big evening and how hilarious it was. Berra was always one of Gowdy's favorite characters, and his performance that night in St. Louis more than fulfilled Curt's expectations.

"When Yogi learned there was to be a night for him," recalled Gowdy, "he came to me and asked whether he would have to make a speech that night, and I told him I was sure it would be expected, with 50,000 people there ready and waiting to hear him. So, he asked me if I would type out a little speech for him, and I said I would be happy to do it.

"I typed out a few short paragraphs for him, and that night I gave him the piece of paper with the speech on it. The game was about ready to start, and they had scheduled the ceremonies just before game time, when I passed the sheet of paper to him at home plate. As luck would have it, a gust of wind blew up at the precise time I handed Yogi the speech, and it blew out of his hand.

"Yogi was frantic as he tried to retrieve it. He was on his hands and knees clutching for the paper, and I was yelling at him, 'Yogi, just say something, they're waiting for you.'

"The paper kept blowing farther and farther away from him, and finally he gave up. He got to his feet and went over to the mike, while thousands awaited his words, and in the growly voice, Yogi delivered a speech even shorter than mine, and three times as effective. He said: 'Ladies and gentlemen, I want to thank you for making this night necessary. Thank you very much.'"

It was Berra's answer to Lincoln's Gettysburg Address: short and succinct and to the point.

After that, Yogi got up and swatted everything in sight.

Curt had another Berra story that I hadn't heard, and it bears retelling.

It seems Yogi had gone to Italy to direct a baseball clinic for youngsters there. A friend in New York wanted to contact him and asked for his number in Italy. It was given to him, and the friend went over to the phone and called. It was about 9 in the evening when he placed the call.

The phone kept ringing and ringing, and finally a sleepy, gravely voice answered, "Hullo."

The friend in New York said: "Hello, this you Yogi?"

"Yes, sir, this is Yogi Berra speaking."

"Gee," said the friend, "you sound half-asleep, Yogi."

Berra responded, "Yeah, well I am. It's about half-past three in the morning."

His friend, somewhat flabbergasted, replied: "Oh, geez, Yogi, I'm sorry I woke you up. I forgot all about the time zone. It's only a little after 9 here in New York."

Ever mindful of his friend's solicitousness, Yogi made him feel a little better: "Oh, that's OK, I had to get up to answer the phone anyway."

Yogi made the dinner in Manchester one winter's night and got into his tux for the dressy affair. Or I should say he was busy getting into his tux, when Leo Durocher came over to me and said: "Hey, Bob, let's rough up Yogi. Tell him he's making the main speech tonight. After you tell him, I'll walk over and congratulate him on being the main speaker of the evening."

I thought that might be a new twist, so I did what Leo suggested, and told Berra: "As you know, Yogi, you're giving the main speech tonight, and good wishes to you. I know you will do a great job with all your anecdotes." Durocher congratulated him, too.

Yogi turned pale. He was in the process of putting on his trousers, and he stopped at once. "Whadda ya mean, I'm giving the main speech," he stammered. "If I am supposed to give the main speech tonight, there ain't gonna be no main speech given. When do the planes leave for New York?"

He was already removing his tux and was ready to leave the hotel at that moment, regardless of the dinner.

Durocher and I had to convince Berra we were only kidding, before he would resume dressing, and it did take a few minutes of convincing Yogi, and of course, he gave a short talk and received a big ovation from the 2,000-plus fans in attendance.

If memory serves correctly, former Dodger skipper Walter Alston was also a guest that night. He heard the entire conversation. "That one almost misfired on you guys," he told us afterward.

I used to cover Wally Alston's games with the Manchester Giants of the Class B New England League when he was player-coach of the Nashua Dodgers, his first real step toward stardom. That was in 1946, I believe, and I think Alston went on to win the Governor's Cup that season, emblematic of the league championship.

We were lucky, Leo and I, that Yogi didn't take a swing at us, but he recognized it as just a little joke, and I was glad that he did.

Yogi Berra was a superstar, whose tremendous asset to the game went far beyond the field of play. But then again, Yogi was from a simpler time, a bygone era.

With enough stars like Yogi, baseball will never perish. But without more of his kind, baseball's future will always be tenuous.

Nackey and William Loeb served as owners and publishers of *The Union Leader* and *New Hampshire Sunday News* during the author's career. The paper's were purchased and made famous by William Loeb, whose scathing frontpage editorials frequently made national news. Nackey Loeb took over the operation upon her husband's death.

I must make a confession.

All that I achieved in my writing career I owe to the late William and Nackey Loeb, for it was they who provided the opportunities, the encouragement and the advice. When I joined the Board of Overseers of The Boston Opera Association many years ago at the invitation of Judge Lawrence T. Perera, it was a warm note from Nackey that gave me the confidence.

William Loeb at all times was a man who looked to the future in running his newspaper. I remember once telling him that I thought it appropriate to make an excursion to Ancient Persia (Iran) to learn how our Oriental Rugs were made, and to pick up a few other notes on how the Shah was doing in his efforts to move the country into the 20th Century.

He liked the idea, and said, "We can arrange some interviews for you, also, while you are there. Just let me know."

Instead, Bobby Jr. and I went to Egypt to view the Pyramids and Sphinx, still considered among the Seven Wonders of the Ancient World.

At the outset, as I mentioned, I was helped immeasurably by Ruel Newton Colby, then sports editor of the *Concord Monitor*. He instructed me in sentence structure and a few hundred other things, like how to spot a story and how to make it appealing so the reader wants to read on. It was a big lift without which I could not have made it. His lessons continued intact as I moved to *The Union Leader*.

About the same time I was submitting stories to Ruel, I was also turning in interviews to Aunt Addie's *Franklin*, (N.H.) *Journal Transcript*, a weekly publication, and my contributions came under close editorial scrutiny, for Addie was a scholar of the first class, being a Mount Holyoke graduate and a professor of German at that school.

Thus, I had some pretty good training as I looked to The Union Leader for a continuation of my writing career.

It was a profound moment for me as I joined the Manchester paper in July of 1943. My son, Bobby, was five, and Barbara was kept busy each day seeing that he had a healthy beginning. He had come down with pneumonia at the age of three, and we almost lost him. That weighed heavily on us, and Barbara's wonderful care pulled him through. She was tremendous, and her spirit inspired us all.

Managing Editor Robert M. Blood, another Dartmouth man, hired me that day upon learning that I had been tutored by Colby, who was well-known in the state, and he told me to report Monday for work. He discovered the next day that Monday was a Newspaper Guild paid holiday, and he dispatched a note at once informing me to come to work the following day, Tuesday, and not on Monday.

While a double-time day would have been nice, I hadn't earned it in any way, and I didn't want it, so I started on a Tuesday. I was soon swept up in a multitude of stories, city and state, and it was all so exciting. Blood was a fascinating teacher and editor. Many a time he crooked his finger and said to me in his gruff voice, "Robert, may I see you in my office?"

If you could not learn by that method of education, you were lost for sure. Once he took me to task for writing that a Navy man had reported to his ship as a "boat." I looked at my notes, and they confirmed my belief that he had, in fact, said "boat," but I learned something valuable. A boat is a rowboat, as Mr. Blood made clear, while a ship is a stely thing, a woman of beauty, and is to be reported as such, using the pronoun "she" to describe the vessel.

When I learned in my interview with Mr. Blood that I had been hired, I decided it was cause for celebration, so I treated myself to a vanilla milk shake at a nearby counter, and took the next train home to Concord to spread the tidings. It was a grand feeling, and Barbara joined in the happiness of the moment, as did her family. The work would follow, but it was a program that I had wanted.

I covered court for a brief period, took pictures and gradually inched toward sports, in which I felt right at home. The war was still on, however, and that is where I ultimately landed, as military editor, or service editor, doing interviews galore with returning veterans. Reg Abbott, an outstanding writer and editor, turned it all over to me one day, saying, "Robert, it is all yours, and good luck."

After World War II, I swung toward the sports desk, becoming night sports editor. Just prior to that assignment, I was on sports, and covered the Class B Manchester Giants under Hal Gruber, the manager. I saw a lot of baseball that year, and it should have rightly been Class AA, what with all the stars-to-be on the member teams: Don Newcombe and Roy Campanella at Nashua, N.H., and Bobby Cain, Sal Yvars and others in Manchester. It was close to major league baseball.

One night, I covered a game between the Nashua Dodgers and Manchester Giants in which Campanella walloped one of the longest home runs I have ever seen. Mo Mozzalli, Giants outfielder, said afterwards, "I lost it in the lights, honest." It looked playable, but it really wasn't. I don't think any outfielder, minors or majors, could have caught it.

After that assignment, I moved to the night sports desk, and I stayed there for many years until I was named sports editor of the *New Hampshire Sunday News*, under the direction of the talented late Bernard J. McQuaid, whose son, Joe, I broke in and who is today the paper's energetic publisher.

You'll often see Joe being interviewed in connection with the the New Hampshire presidential primary. Because of his position running the politically powerful newspapers—*The Union Leader* and *New Hampshire Sunday News*—in the first-in-the-nation primary state, Joe McQuaid is the one person in New Hampshire that the regional and national media most wants to talk politics with to get his insight on the race.

B.J. McQuaid was a renowned war-time journalist who worked for a Chicago paper on the far-flung war front. He once had an interview with Field Marshal Montgomery of the British Army. Montgomery gave him time for one question only, and B.J. zinged it: "Will the Germans break through at Bastogne?"

Monty's answer, typically, was succinct and four words in length: "Not in this war," he told a bemused McQuaid. Monty added four more words: "That concludes this interview."

When B.J. returned from wartime duties, he was of immeasurable help in cutting and strengthening stories. Once when I was handling a 7-foot-long report from one of our veteran correspondents, I complained about having trouble boiling it down to readable length.

B.J. said, "Give it to me, and I'll show you how."

With that, he picked up the oversized shears and cut it completely in half, handing me both halves.

"There," he said, "does that take care of it?"

The only trouble with that story was that it came back to me two days later. The second half that hadn't been used had a brand new lead affixed, and the total loss was about three feet in all, with an irate correspondent looking on quite offended. I still back B.J. on that one; most stories should be shortened.

When I first started in Manchester, Col. Frank Knox, the former vice presidential candidate, was the owner and publisher. He was away often during the war years, serving in President Roosevelt's cabinet as Secretary of the Navy, a most important post during the struggle with Hitler and Tojo.

One late afternoon, the switchboard buzzed, and no one was around to answer it, the operator having taken a coffee break or something.

The Colonel, home for a few days, asked, "Bob, do you know how to answer this thing?"

I said I didn't.

"Well," he said, "let's give it a try." He plugged it in and jogged a few levers, and suddenly he had a caller.

"Is this *The Union Leader*?" a woman asked.

"Yes, it is," the Colonel answered, "what is your problem, Mam?"

"It is just this, sir," she replied. "I have not received my paper yet, and it is already past 3 o'clock."

The Colonel replied that he was terribly sorry, and that it should have been delivered two hours ago. "But I will have one hand-delivered to you within the hour, and I hope that that meets with your approval."

The caller was happy; the Colonel had pleased another reader.

Little did she know she had been talking with the Secretary of the Navy himself, who was in the habit of having people run for him in Washington, and who now was racing to help a distressed woman on Manchester's West Side. It isn't everyone who has the Secretary of the Navy jumping for them.

There were few dull moments from the time I started work at *The Union Leader* until I retired one summer's day in 1985. As I have said, a lot is owed to the many people who helped me from time to time. Early on, I knew I had made a smart choice in picking journalism for a career, and I made the choice at the age of 12, which rather baffles me now. One needs a lot of luck, and I had it.

Along the way, I received tremendous help from the editors and from the numerous deskmen and copy-readers who operate those very important posts. They are numerous, but they are vital cogs in the machinery which moves the newspaper through mostly hectic times, since deadlines are a constant presence.

Reg Abbott was a constant help, especially during World War II, while I handled the service editor's post on the military page. Ralph Robinson and Walter Mullen were sports editors with solid advice, and editors Jim Mahony, Eddie Garner, Jim Mooney, Walter Emerson and Walt Healy were invaluable.

Healy was perhaps the quickest man on the desk this side of Dodge City. His headlines rolled off as if on an assembly line. From time to time, he had a few heads that bounced (we called them "rubber heads"), but he was constantly under pressure, and he had a quickness that was totally becoming. I think he wrote heads as he was running up the stairs to a busy composing room. At least it appeared that way. He was always in a rush. I called him "Hurry-Up Healy."

This is all to show that everyone needs help in an active City Room to get the paper out on the streets, and it is little wonder that many more mistakes do not slip through.

Mr. Blood himself, a talented editor, caught a few from my desk that taught me lessons, and I still shudder when I see him crooking his finger at me to come into his office for a little chat. He had sort of a hoarse voice, and he wore an orange sweater, out at the elbows, and an eye shade, and you knew once you stepped into his office you were about to get pilloried. It was truly a learning experience, not the kind you liked, but learning, so that you wouldn't make the same mistake again.

When I was 76, motorsports columnist Kevin Provencher and the late columnist Jack Ratta invited me to Loudon, N.H. one morning for trials for Big Car (Indy) racing at New Hampshire International Speedway, the then-new track that today seats about 100,000 spectators.

I did an article on race driver Teo Fabi from Milan, Italy, and it was a lot of fun. I knew little about the sport, and I just imagined that anyone from Milano must know their opera, and must sing it, as well.

My lead mentioned that Fabi, as "he hurtled down the track at 185 mph, was probably singing 'Pagliacci,' for that is one of his favorites."

He got a big kick out of that lead and as we departed for Manchester and the newsroom, Teo and his team were waving goodbye to us.

I plan to see them all—and maybe Paul Newman, whom I interviewed in 1975—at the same track another summer season when they return. The young driver Herta, who graduated from Ohio State, also caught my eye for a possible story. Fabi finished seventh at Indy that year, 1994, with Herta ninth, I believe. Two torrid drivers, believe me.

So, in my later years, I have added another hat to my repertory: car racing. Joe Sullivan did a story from the pits, on the phone to the driver, and Ratta and Provencher turned out some exciting stories.

It's never too late to learn, so they say.